P9-ELR-283

D0014942

HYMNS
OF THE
SPIRIT

SHAPE NOTE EDITION

Editor / Connor B. Hall

Assistant Editor / Jimi Hall

PATHWAY MUSIC
A DIVISION OF PATHWAY PRESS
P.O. Box 2250, Cleveland, TN 37320-2250

PREFACE

From the Hebrew psalm to the hymns, spirituals, and new songs of the New Testament, singing has been a distinctive feature of the Christian faith. It is believed that present and succeeding generations ought to add to this sincere outpouring of man, because of the continuing presence of God in the hearts of His people.

Responding to a general demand as well as a widespread need, the Editorial and Publications Board of Pathway Press authorized a Hymnal Commission to prepare a hymnal for both individual and corporate worship. From the beginning it was determined that a flexible hymnbook suited to various types of services and worship experiences would be necessary. Such a hymnal would draw from the rich heritage of the past, search for the soul of the present, and project its musical and spiritual influence into the future. It would contain the basic truths of the gospel and make it possible for all ages to sing of a common faith in Christ as Lord and Savior.

The title "Hymns of the Spirit" was chosen to symbolize the work of the Holy Spirit in the early church and especially in the twentieth century. The early church was exhorted to be filled with the Spirit which would enable them to speak to one another in psalms, hymns, and spiritual songs, singing amd making melody in their hearts unto the Lord (Ephesians 5:18, 19). Paul explains ". . . I will sing with the spirit, and I will sing with the understanding also" (I Corinthians 14:15). Jesus predicted that ". . . the true worshipers shall worship the Father in spirit, and in truth: for the Father seeketh such to worship him. God is a Spirit: and they that worship him must worship him in spirit and in truth" (John 4:23, 24).

The logical grouping of songs by dominant thought should facilitate the finding of suitable selections for most services. Where a special topic is required the detailed topical index is invaluable in quickly locating an appropriate hymn. In addition, there are complete indexes of titles, topics, and responsive readings. An additional distinctive of "Hymns of the Spirit" is its high percentage of familiar and meaningful gospel songs and gospel hymns.

A special section includes responses suitable for use at the opening of a service, before and after prayers, either spoken, silent, or concert; and at the close of the service. The scriptures in the responsive reading section have been carefully selected and each is capable of multiple uses and appropriate for different topics. All scripture, patriotic pledges and statements of faith are arranged for use as either responsive or unison readings.

Careful attention has been given to the functions of the church whether worshiping, proclaiming, evangelizing, educating or ministering. It is hoped that this treasury of traditional, scriptural and gospel hymnody might find a broad use, serving the musical needs of all departments of Christian service such as church, school, home, college, club, class, community and interrelated agencies.

Sincere appreciation is expressed to all who have contributed to the compilation of "Hymns of the Spirit." Special gratitude is extended to the many pastors, ministers of music, laymen, writers and church executives who through surveys, questionnaries, counsel and personal conferences have assisted in this achievement. Pathway Press deeply appreciates and is greatly indebted to the members of the Hymnal Commission and its subcommittees who have given of their time and tireless energies working together with a sense of devotion, purpose, and ministry.

We therefore commend these materials to you for both private and public use, to the end that God may be exalted and praised, that the lost may be saved, and the believer be strengthened in both faith and belief. May this book become a sacred trust that expresses your spiritual heritage. May you sing its messages, melodies and harmonies with a glad heart, a fervent spirit, and a prayer that it may gender an unceasing harmonious relationship between God and man.

The Publishers

Pathway Press acknowledges grateful appreciation to the following who assisted in the creation of this work.

THE HYMNAL COMMISSION

Delton L. Alford	Connor B. Hall, Editor
W. C. Byrd	Bennie S. Triplett
C. S. Grogan	Ralph E. Williams

E. C. Thomas, Chairman

EDITORIAL ASSISTANCE

Jimi Hall, Charles Towler, Lewis J. Willis

TABLE OF CONTENTS

Introductions _____ I-VIII

Worship _____ 1- 30

Trinity _____ 31-109

The Word _____ 110-114

The Church _____ 115-120

The Christian Life _____ 121-318

Choir Arrangements _____ 319-320

Choruses _____ 321-326

Special Days And Occasions _____ 327-361

Call To Worship And Response _____ 362-376

Responsive Readings _____ 456-495

Indexes _____ 496-512

Make a joyful noise unto the Lord, all ye lands.

Serve the Lord with gladness: come before his presence with singing.

Know ye that the Lord he is God: it is he that hath made us, and not we ourselves; we are his people, and the sheep of his pasture.

Enter into his gates with thanksgiving, and into his courts with praise: be thankful unto him, and bless his name.

For the Lord is good; his mercy is everlasting; and his truth endureth to all generations.—Psalm 100

HYMNS of the SPIRIT

1   Praise To The Lord, The Almighty

Joachim Neander
Tr. by Catherine Winkworth

From "Praxis Pietatis Melica," 1668

1. Praise to the Lord, the Al - might - y, the King of cre - a - tion!
2. Praise to the Lord, who o'er all things so won - drous - ly reign - eth,
3. Praise to the Lord, who doth pros - per thy work and de - fend thee;
4. Praise to the Lord, O let all that is in me a - dore Him!

O my soul, praise Him, for He is thy health and sal - va - tion!
Shel - ters thee un - der His wings, yea, so gen - tly sus - tain - eth!
Sure - ly His good - ness and mer - cy here dai - ly at - tend thee.
All that hath life and breath, come now with prais - es be - fore Him.

All ye who hear, Now to His tem - ple draw near;
Hast thou not seen How thy de - sires e'er have been
Pon - der a - new What the Al - might - y can do,
Let the A - men Sound from His peo - ple a - gain,

Join me in glad ad - o - ra - tion!
Grant - ed in what He or - dain - eth?
If with His love He be - friend thee.
Glad - ly for aye we a - dore Him.

All Hail The Power Of Jesus' Name

Edward Perronet

Oliver Holden

1. All hail the pow'r of Je - sus' name, Let an - gels pros-trate fall;
2. Ye cho - sen seed of Is - rael's race, Ye ran - somed from the fall;
3. Let ev - 'ry kin - dred, ev - 'ry tribe, On this ter - res - trial ball;
4. Oh, that with yon - der sa - cred throng, We at His feet may fall;

Bring forth the roy - al di - a - dem, And
Hail Him Who saves you by His grace, And
To Him all maj - es - ty as - cribe, And
We'll join the ev - er - last - ing song, And

crown Him Lord of all; Bring forth the roy - al
crown Him Lord of all; Hail Him Who saves you
crown Him Lord of all; To Him all maj - es -
crown Him Lord of all; We'll join the ev - er -

di - a - dem, And crown Him Lord of all.
by His grace, And crown Him Lord of all.
ty as - cribe, And crown Him Lord of all.
last - ing song, And crown Him Lord of all.

All Hail The Power Of Jesus' Name

Edward Perronet
Alt. by John Rippon

James Ellor

1. All hail the power of Je - sus' name! Let an-gels pros-trate
2. Ye cho - sen seed of Is - rael's race, Ye ran-somed from the
3. Let ev - ery kin - dred, ev - ery tribe, On this ter - res-trial
4. O that with yon - der sa - cred throng We at His feet may

fall, Let an - gels pros - trate fall; Bring forth the roy - al
fall, Ye ran - somed from the fall; Hail Him who saves you
ball, On this ter - res - trial ball; To Him all maj - es -
fall, We at His feet may fall! We'll join the ev - er -

di - a - dem, And crown - - - - - - - - - - - - - Him,
by His grace, And crown Him, crown Him, crown Him, crown Him,
ty as - cribe, And crown Him, crown Him,
last - ing song, crown - - - - - -

crown Him, crown Him, crown Him, And crown Him Lord of all.
- - - - - - - - - - - - - - - - Him,

4 All Hail The Power Of Jesus' Name

Edward Perronet
Alt. by John Rippon

William Shrubsole

1. All hail the power of Je - sus' name! Let an - gels
2. Ye cho - sen seed of Is - rael's race, Ye ran - somed
3. Let ev - 'ry kin - dred, ev - 'ry tribe, On this ter -
4. O that with yon - der sa - cred throng We at His

pros - trate fall; Bring forth the roy - al di - a - dem, And
from the fall, Hail Him who saves you by His grace, And
res - trial ball, To Him all maj - es - ty as - cribe, And
feet may fall! We'll join the ev - er - last - ing song, And

crown Him, crown Him, crown   Him, crown Him Lord of   all.
crown Him, crown Him, crown   Him, crown Him Lord of   all.
crown Him, crown Him, crown   Him, crown Him Lord of   all.
crown Him, crown Him, crown   Him, crown Him Lord of   all.

5 O Love That Wilt Not Let Me Go

George Matheson

Albert L. Peace

1. O Love that wilt not let me go,   I rest my
2. O Light that fol - lowest all my way,   I yield my
3. O Joy that seek - est me through pain,   I can - not
4. O Cross that lift - est up my head,   I dare not

weary soul in thee; I give thee back the life I owe
flick-'ring torch to thee; My heart re-stores its bor-rowed ray,
close my heart to thee; I trace the rain-bow thro' the rain,
ask to hide from thee; I lay in dust life's glo-ry dead,

That in thine o-cean depths its flow May rich-er, full-er be.
That in thy sun-shine's glow its day May bright-er, fair-er be.
And feel the prom-ise is not vain That morn shall tear-less be.
And from the ground there blos=soms red Life that shall end-less be.

6 O Worship The King

Robert Grant

Johann M. Haydn

1. O wor-ship the King, all glo-rious a-bove, And grate-ful-ly sing
2. O tell of His might, O sing of His grace, Whose robe is the light,
3. Thy boun-ti-ful care what tongue can re-cite? It breathes in the air,
4. Frail chil-dren of dust, and fee-ble as frail, In Thee do we trust,

His won-der-ful love; Our shield and De-fend-er, the An-cient of
whose can-o-py space! His char-iots of wrath the deep thun-der-clouds
it shines in the light, It streams from the hills, it de-scends to the
nor find Thee to fail: Thy mer-cies how ten-der, how firm to the

Days, Pa-vil-ioned in splen-dor, and gird-ed with praise.
form, And dark is His path on the wings of the storm.
plain, And sweet-ly dis-tills in the dew and the rain.
end, Our Mak-er, De-fend-er, Re-deem-er, and Friend.

7 All Creatures Of Our God And King

Francis of Assisi
Tr. by William H. Draper

Melody from "Geistliche Kirchengesang", 1623

In unison

1. All crea-tures of our God and King, Lift up your voice and with us sing Al-le-lu-ia!
2. Thou rush-ing wind that art so strong, Ye clouds that sail in heaven a-long, O praise Him!
3. Dear moth-er earth, who day by day Un-fold-est bless-ings on our way, O praise Him!
4. Let all things their Cre-a-tor bless, And wor-ship Him in hum-ble-ness, O praise Him!

Al-le-lu-ia!

Thou burn-ing sun with gold-en beam, Thou sil-ver moon with soft-er gleam! O
Thou ris-ing morn, in praise re-joice, Ye lights of eve-ning, find a voice! O
The flowers and fruits that in thee grow, Let them His glo-ry al-so show! O
Praise, praise the Fa-ther, praise the Son, And praise the Spir-it, Three in One! O

praise Him, O praise Him! Al - le - lu - ia!

Al - le - lu - ia! Al - le - lu - ia! A - men.

8   My Faith Looks Up To Thee

Ray Palmer   Lowell Mason

1. My faith looks up   to Thee, Thou Lamb of Cal - va - ry,
2. May Thy rich grace im - part Strength to   my faint - ing heart,
3. While life's dark maze I tread, And griefs a - round me spread,
4. When ends life's tran - sient dream, When death's cold, sul - len stream

Sav - iour di - vine! Now hear me while I pray, Take all my
My zeal in - spire; As Thou hast died for me, O   may my
Be Thou my guide; Bid dark - ness turn to day, Wipe sor - row's
Shall o'er me roll, Blest Sav - iour, then, in love, Fear and dis -

guilt a - way, O let   me   from this day Be whol - ly Thine!
love to Thee Pure, warm, and change - less be A liv - ing fire!
tears a - way, Nor let   me   ev - er stray From Thee a - side.
trust re - move; O bear me safe a - bove, A ran - somed soul!

9 Rock Of Ages

Augustus M. Toplady

Thomas Hastings

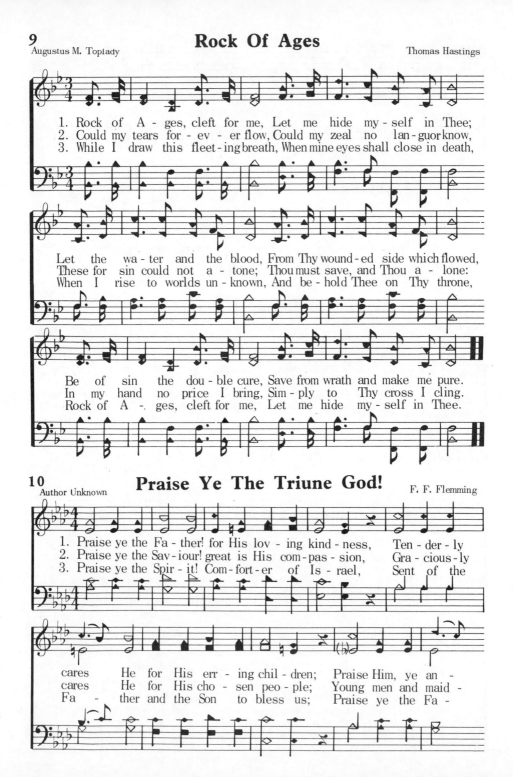

1. Rock of A - ges, cleft for me, Let me hide my - self in Thee;
2. Could my tears for - ev - er flow, Could my zeal no lan - guor know,
3. While I draw this fleet - ing breath, When mine eyes shall close in death,

Let the wa - ter and the blood, From Thy wound - ed side which flowed,
These for sin could not a - tone; Thou must save, and Thou a - lone:
When I rise to worlds un - known, And be - hold Thee on Thy throne,

Be of sin the dou - ble cure, Save from wrath and make me pure.
In my hand no price I bring, Sim - ply to Thy cross I cling.
Rock of A - ges, cleft for me, Let me hide my - self in Thee.

10 Praise Ye The Triune God!

Author Unknown

F. F. Flemming

1. Praise ye the Fa - ther! for His lov - ing kind - ness, Ten - der - ly
2. Praise ye the Sav - iour! great is His com - pas - sion, Gra - cious - ly
3. Praise ye the Spir - it! Com - fort - er of Is - rael, Sent of the

cares He for His err - ing chil - dren; Praise Him, ye an -
cares He for His cho - sen peo - ple; Young men and maid -
Fa - ther and the Son to bless us; Praise ye the Fa -

gels, praise Him in the heav - ens, Praise ye Je - ho - vah!
ens, ye old men and chil - dren, Praise ye the Sav - iour!
ther, Son and Ho - ly Spir - it, Praise ye the Tri - une God!

11   Come, Thou Almighty King

Anonymous   Felice de Giardini

1. Come, Thou Al - might - y King, Help us Thy name to sing,
2. Come, Thou In - car - nate Word, Gird on Thy might - y sword,
3. Come, Ho - ly Com - fort - er, Thy sa - cred wit - ness bear,
4. To Thee, great One in Three, The high - est prais - es be,

Help us to praise: Fa - ther! all glo - ri - ous, O'er all vic -
Our prayer at - tend! Come, and Thy peo - ple bless, And give Thy
In this glad hour! Thou, who al - might - y art, Now rule in
Hence ev - er - more; His sov'reign maj - es - ty May we in

to - ri - ous, Come, and reign o - ver us, An - cient of Days.
word suc - cess: Spir - it of ho - li - ness, On us de - scend.
ev - 'ry heart, And ne'er from us de - part, Spir - it of pow'r.
glo - ry see, And to e - ter - ni - ty Love and a - dore.

Holy, Holy, Holy

Reginald Heber

John B. Dykes

1. Ho - ly, ho - ly, ho - ly! Lord God Al - might - y!
2. Ho - ly, ho - ly, ho - ly! all the saints a - dore Thee,
3. Ho - ly, ho - ly, ho - ly! tho' the dark - ness hide Thee,
4. Ho - ly, ho - ly, ho - ly! Lord God Al - might - y!

Ear - ly in the morn - ing our song shall rise to Thee;
Cast - ing down their gold - en crowns a - round the glass - y sea;
Tho' the eye of sin - ful man Thy glo - ry may not see;
All Thy works shall praise Thy name, in earth, and sky, and sea;

Ho - ly, ho - ly, ho - ly, mer - ci - ful and might - y!
Cher - u - bim and ser - a - phim, fall - ing down be - fore Thee,
On - ly Thou art ho - ly; there is none be - side Thee,
Ho - ly, ho - ly, ho - ly; mer - ci - ful and might - y!

God in three Per - sons, bless - ed Trin - i - ty!
Who wert, and art, and ev - er - more shalt be.
Per - fect in power, in love, and pur - i - ty.
God in three Per - sons, bless - ed Trin - i - ty!

Lead On, O King Eternal

Ernest W. Shurtleff

Henry Smart

1. Lead on, O King E-ter-nal, The day of march has come;
2. Lead on, O King E-ter-nal, Till sin's fierce war shall cease;
3. Lead on, O King E-ter-nal, We fol-low, not with fears;

Hence-forth in fields of con-quest, Thy tents shall be our home:
And ho-li-ness shall whis-per, The sweet a-men of peace;
For glad-ness breaks like morn-ing, Wher-e'er Thy face ap-pears;

Through days of prep-a-ra-tion, Thy grace has made us strong,
For not with swords' loud clashing, Or roll of stir-ring drums;
Thy cross is lift-ed o'er us, We jour-ney in its light:

And now, O King E-ter-nal, We lift our bat-tle song.
With deeds of love and mer-cy, The heav'n-ly king-dom comes.
The crown a-waits the con-quest, Lead on, O God of might.

For The Beauty Of The Earth

F. S. Pierpoint

Conrad Kocher

14

1. For the beau-ty of the earth, For the glo-ry
2. For the won-der of each hour, Of the day and
3. For the joy of hu-man love, Bro-ther, sis-ter,
4. For Thy church that ev-er-more Lift-eth ho-ly

of the skies, For the love which from our birth
of the night, Hill and vale, and tree and flow'r,
par-ent, child, Friends on earth, and friends a-bove,
hands a-bove, Of-f'ring up on ev-'ry shore,

O - ver and a-round us lies; Christ our God, to
Sun and moon and stars of light; Christ our God, to
For all gen-tle thoughts and mild; Christ our God, to
Her pure sac-ri-fice of love; Christ our God, to

Thee we raise This our hymn of grate-ful praise.
Thee we raise This our hymn of grate-ful praise.
Thee we raise This our hymn of grate-ful praise.
Thee we raise This our hymn of grate-ful praise.

This Is My Father's World

Maltbie D. Babcock

Franklin L. Sheppard

1. This is my Fa-ther's world, And to my lis-t'ning ears, All
2. This is my Fa-ther's world, The birds their car-ols raise; The
3. This is my Fa-ther's world, O let me ne'er for-get That

na - ture sings, and round me rings The mus - ic of the spheres.
morn - ing light, the lil - y white De - clare their Mak - er's praise.
though the wrong seems oft so strong, God is the Rul - er yet.

This is my Fa-ther's world, I rest me in the thought Of
This is my Fa-ther's world, He shines in all that's fair; In the
This is my Fa-ther's world, The bat - tle is not done; Je -

rocks and trees, of skies and seas; His hand the won-ders wrought.
rust - ling grass I hear Him pass, He speaks to me ev - 'ry-where.
sus who died shall be sat - is - fied, And earth and heav-en be one.

Come, Thou Fount

Robert Robinson

John Wyeth

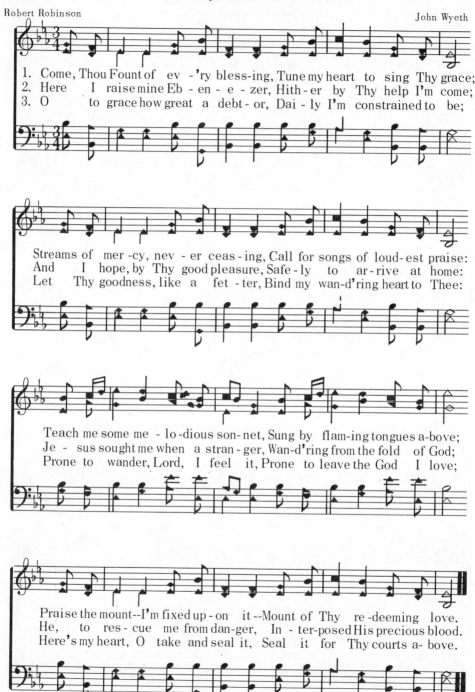

1. Come, Thou Fount of ev-'ry bless-ing, Tune my heart to sing Thy grace;
2. Here I raise mine Eb-en-e-zer, Hith-er by Thy help I'm come;
3. O to grace how great a debt-or, Dai-ly I'm constrained to be;

Streams of mer-cy, nev-er ceas-ing, Call for songs of loud-est praise:
And I hope, by Thy good pleasure, Safe-ly to ar-rive at home:
Let Thy goodness, like a fet-ter, Bind my wan-d'ring heart to Thee:

Teach me some me-lo-dious son-net, Sung by flam-ing tongues a-bove;
Je-sus sought me when a stran-ger, Wan-d'ring from the fold of God;
Prone to wander, Lord, I feel it, Prone to leave the God I love;

Praise the mount--I'm fixed up-on it--Mount of Thy re-deeming love.
He, to res-cue me from dan-ger, In-ter-posed His precious blood.
Here's my heart, O take and seal it, Seal it for Thy courts a-bove.

17 Glory To His Name

Elisha A. Hoffman

John H. Stockton

1. Down at the cross where my Sav-iour died, Down where for
2. I am so won-drous-ly saved from sin, Je-sus so
3. Oh, pre-cious foun-tain that saves from sin, I am so
4. Come to this foun-tain so rich and sweet; Cast thy poor

cleans-ing from sin I cried, There to my heart
sweet-ly a-bides with-in; There at the cross
glad I have en-tered in; There Je-sus saves
soul at the Sav-iour's feet; Plunge in to-day,

was the blood ap-plied; Glo-ry to His name.
where He took me in; Glo-ry to His name.
me and keeps me clean; Glo-ry to His name.
and be made com-plete; Glo-ry to His name.

REFRAIN

Glo-ry to His name, Glo-ry to His name:

There to my heart was the blood ap-plied; Glo-ry to His name.

18 Praise Him! Praise Him!

Fanny J. Crosby

Chester G. Allen

1. Praise Him! praise Him! Je - sus, our bless - ed Re - deem - er!
2. Praise Him! praise Him! Je - sus, our bless - ed Re - deem - er!
3. Praise Him! praise Him! Je - sus, our bless - ed Re - deem - er!

Sing, O Earth, His won - der - ful love pro - claim!
For our sins He suff - ered and bled and died;
Heav - 'nly por - tals loud with ho - san - nas ring!

Hail Him! hail Him! high - est arch - an - gels in glo - ry;
He our Rock, our hope of e - ter - nal sal - va - tion,
Je - sus, Sav - iour, reign - eth for - ev - er and ev - er;

Strength and hon - or give to His ho - ly name!
Hail Him! hail Him! Je - sus the cru - ci - fied:
Crown Him! crown Him! proph - et and priest and king!

Like a shep - herd, Je - sus will guard His child - ren,
Sound His prais - es! Je - sus Who bore our sor - rows,
Christ is com - ing, o - ver the world vic - to - rious,

In His arms He car-ries them all day long:
Love un-bound-ed, won-der-ful, deep, and strong:
Pow'r and glo-ry un-to the Lord be-long:

REFRAIN

Praise Him! praise Him! tell of His ex-cel-lent great-ness;

Praise Him! praise Him! ev-er in joy-ful song!

19   O For A Thousand Tongues To Sing

Charles Wesley

Carl G. Glaser
Arr. by Lowell Mason

1. O for a thou-sand tongues to sing, My great Re-deem-er's praise;
2. My gra-cious Mas-ter and my God, As-sist me to pro-claim;
3. Je-sus, the name that calms my fears, That bids my sor-rows cease;
4. He breaks the pow'r of can-celed sin, He sets the pris-'ner free;

The glo-ries of my God and King, The tri-umphs of His grace!
To spread through all the earth a-broad, The hon-ors of His name.
'Tis mu-sic in the sin-ner's ears, 'Tis life and health and peace.
His blood can make the foul-est clean, His blood a-vailed for me.

20 To God Be The Glory

Fanny J. Crosby

William H. Doane

1. To God be the glory, great things He hath done;
2. O per - fect re - demp - tion, the pur - chase of blood,
3. Great things He hath taught us, great things He hath done,

So loved He the world that He gave us His Son,
To ev - 'ry be - liev - er the prom - ise of God;
And great our re - joic - ing thro' Je - sus the Son;

Who yield - ed His life an a - tone - ment for sin,
The vil - est of - fend - er who tru - ly be - lieves,
But pur - er, and high - er, and great - er will be

And o - pened the life - gate that all may go in.
That mo - ment from Je - sus a par - don re - ceives.
Our won - der, our trans - port, when Je - sus we see.

REFRAIN

Praise the Lord, praise the Lord, Let the earth hear His voice!

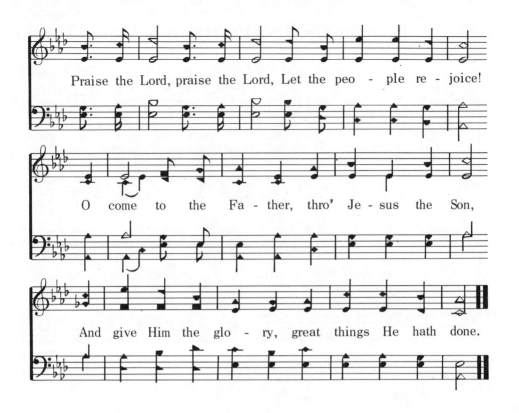

Praise the Lord, praise the Lord, Let the peo - ple re - joice!

O come to the Fa - ther, thro' Je - sus the Son,

And give Him the glo - ry, great things He hath done.

21 Praise God, From Whom All Blessings Flow

Thomas Ken

From the "Genevan Psalter," 1551

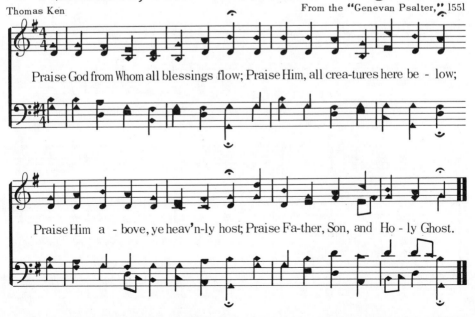

Praise God from Whom all blessings flow; Praise Him, all crea-tures here be - low;

Praise Him a - bove, ye heav'n-ly host; Praise Fa-ther, Son, and Ho - ly Ghost.

Leaning On The Everlasting Arms

Elisha A. Hoffman   Anthony J. Showalter

1. What a fel - low - ship, what a joy di - vine, Lean-ing on the ev - er -
2. Oh, how sweet to walk in this pil - grim way, Lean-ing on the ev - er -
3. What have I to dread, what have I to fear, Lean-ing on the ev - er -

last - ing arms; What a bless - ed - ness, what a peace is mine,
last - ing arms; Oh, how bright the path grows from day to day,
last - ing arms? I have bless - ed peace with my Lord so near,

REFRAIN

Lean - ing on the ev - er - last - ing arms. Lean - ing,
Lean-ing on Je - sus,

lean - ing, Safe and se - cure from all a - larms; Lean -
lean-ing on Je - sus,   Lean-ing on

ing, lean - ing, Lean-ing on the ev - er - last - ing arms.
Je - sus, lean-ing on Je - sus,

Near To The Heart Of God

Cleland B. McAfee   Cleland B. McAfee

1. There is a place of qui - et rest, Near to the heart of God,
2. There is a place of com - fort sweet, Near to the heart of God,
3. There is a place of full re - lease, Near to the heart of God,

A place where sin can - not mo - lest, Near to the heart of God.
A place where we our Sav - iour meet, Near to the heart of God.
A place where all is joy and 'peace, Near to the heart of God.

REFRAIN

O Je - sus, blest Re - deem - er, Sent from the heart of God,

Hold us who wait be - fore Thee Near to the heart of   God.

Love Divine

Charles Wesley

John Zundel

1. Love di - vine, all love ex - cell - ing, Joy of heav'n, to earth come down;
2. Breathe, Oh! breathe Thy loving Spir - it In - to ev - 'ry trou - bled breast;
3. Come, Al - might - y to de - liv - er, Let us all Thy life re - ceive;
4. Fin - ish, then, Thy new cre - a - tion; Pure and spot - less let us be;

Fix in us Thy hum - ble dwell - ing, All Thy faith - ful mer - cies crown.
Let us all in Thee in - her - it, Let us find the prom - ised rest;
Sud - den - ly re - turn, and nev - er, Nev - er - more Thy tem - ples leave:
Let us see Thy great sal - va - tion Per - fect - ly re - stored in Thee;

Je - sus, Thou art all com - pas - sion, Pure, un - bound - ed love Thou art;
Take a - way the love of sin - ning, Al - pha and O - me - ga be;
Thee we would be al - ways bless - ing, Serve Thee as Thy hosts a - bove,
Changed from glory in - to glo - ry Till in heav'n we take our place,

Vis - it us with Thy sal - va - tion, En - ter ev - 'ry trem - bling heart.
End of faith, as its be - gin - ning, Set our hearts at lib - er - ty.
Pray, and praise Thee with - out ceas - ing, Glo - ry in Thy per - fect love.
Till we cast our crowns be - fore Thee, Lost in won - der, love, and praise.

My Saviour's Love

25

Charles H. Gabriel

Charles H. Gabriel

1. I stand a-mazed in the pres-ence Of Je-sus the Naz-a-rene,
2. For me it was in the gar-den He prayed, "Not my will, but Thine,"
3. In pit-y, an-gels be-held Him, And came from the world of light,
4. When with the ran-somed in glo-ry His face I at last shall see,

And won-der how He could love me, A sin-ner, con-demned, un-clean.
He had no tears for His own griefs, But sweat drops of blood for mine.
To com-fort Him in the sor-rows He bore for my soul that night.
'Twill be my joy thro' the a-ges To sing of His love for me.

REFRAIN

How mar-vel-ous! how won-der-ful! And my
Oh, how mar-vel-ous! oh, how won-der-ful!

song shall ev-er be; How mar-vel-ous! how
Oh, how mar-vel-ous! oh, how

won-der-ful! Is my Sav-iour's love for me!

Worship The Triune God

Edward L. Williams   Edward L. Williams

1. Praise to the Fa - ther, hal - lowed be Thy name, All of earth and
2. Praise to the Sav - iour, res - ur - rect - ed Lord, Gave Him-self a
3. Praise to the Spir - it, bless - ed com - fort - er, Come, O, Ho - ly

heav - en doth Thy works pro - claim; God, the cre - a - tor, God of
ran - som, fal - len were re - stored; He's ev - er reign - ing, bless-ed
Spir - it, as in days of yore; Spir - it of God a - bid - ing

REFRAIN

right - eous-ness, Praise Him for - ev - er-more.
Prince of Peace, Prais - es to Him we bring. Praise the Fa - ther, let His
ev - er - more, Wor - ship the tri - une God.

will be done, praise the Sav - iour, Je - sus Christ, the Son; Praise the

Spir - it, He's the Ho - ly One, Wor - ship the tri - une God.

27 Worship The King

Bennie S. Triplett

Bennie S. Triplett

1. Wor - thy is the Lamb that's slain, Sin - less, blame - less, One who came;
2. Loft - y One up - on a throne, An - gels wor - ship Him with song;
3. Ris - en Con - quer - or of death, Liv - eth e - ven as He saith;

Bear - ing all the world's dis-dain, Mag - ni - fy His name.
Con - de - scend-ed to a - tone, For my sins a - lone.
Com - ing for the saved and blest, Glo - rious day of rest.

REFRAIN

Prais - es to the Prince of Peace, Hon -
Prais - es, prais - es to the Prince of Peace Hon - or,

or Him who came to die; Bless - ings
hon - or Him who came to die; Bless - ings, bless - ings

nev - er let them cease, Wor - ship the King on high.
nev - er let them cease,

Glory To His Name

Joe E. Parks

Joe E. Parks

1. Hail the Son of Right-eous-ness, Cre-a-tor, Lord and King,
2. Come be-fore His pres-ence, let His prais-es loud-ly ring,
3. Bow in hum-ble ad-o-ra-tion, on your fac-es fall,

Glo-ry to His name, glo-ry to His name;

Let the na-tions of the earth, His prais-es loud-ly sing,
With a shout of ex-ul-ta-tion, let His peo-ple sing,
Then be quick to an-swer when you hear the Sav-iour call,

Glo-ry to His match-less name.

Fair - est of ten thou - sand, He's the bright and morn - ing star,

Glo - ry to His name, glo - ry to His name;

Lil - y of the Val - ley, He's the lov - li - est by far,

Glo - ry to His match - less name, match - less name.

Let Us Sing

J. R. Baxter, Jr.

Dwight Brock

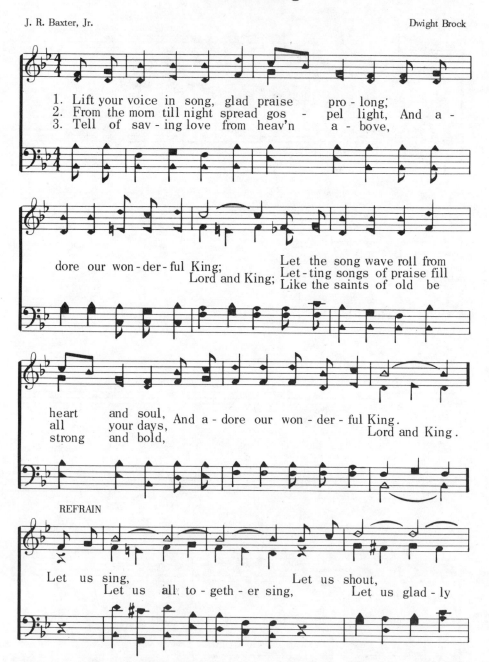

1. Lift your voice in song, glad praise pro - long;
2. From the morn till night spread gos - pel light, And a -
3. Tell of sav - ing love from heav'n a - bove,

dore our won - der - ful King;
Lord and King;
Let the song wave roll from
Let - ting songs of praise fill
Like the saints of old be

heart and soul, And a - dore our won - der - ful King.
all your days, Lord and King.
strong and bold,

REFRAIN

Let us sing, Let us shout,
Let us all to - geth - er sing, Let us glad - ly

Let us praise, And a - dore our
sing and shout, Let us sing a song of praise,

won - der - ful King; Let us sing,
Lord and King; Let us all to - geth - er sing,

Let us shout, Let us praise,
Let us glad - ly sing and shout, Let us sing a

And a - dore our won - der - ful King.
song of praise, Lord and King.

Sing Unto The Lord

Mrs. P. H. McSwain   Mrs. P. H. McSwain

1. Sing un - to the Lord   all ye lands, and make His prais - es ring,
2. Mag - ni - fy the Lord throughout the world, this might - y King di - vine,

Joy - ful - ly pro - claim His won - drous love, oh, come and let us sing;
Tell of His great love and sav - ing pow'r, His gift to all man - kind;

His glo - ry and His maj - es - ty, shall reign for - ev - er - more,
Shout glad ho - san - nas clear and strong, let hal - le - lu - jahs swell,

He's on the throne in ev - 'ry heart, who will His name a - dore.
Stand up and sing for Christ our Lord, our King E - man - u - el.

REFRAIN

We'll sing   of His re - deem - ing grace, we'll strive   to
We'll sing   we'll strive

see His bless - ed face, We'll work and try to fill the place,
We'll work

where - in the Lord has called; Come ye who would be
Come ye

free from sin, He'll par - - don, give you peace with - in, You'll
He'll par - don,

sing and shout His prais - es then, He reigns for - ev - er - more.
You'll sing

Last time only

Sing un - to the Lord, Oh, sing un - to the Lord, Praise His name.

A Mighty Fortress Is Our God

Martin Luther
Tr. by Frederick H. Hedge

Martin Luther

1. A might-y for - tress is our God, A bul - wark nev-er
2. Did we in our own strength con - fide, Our striv-ing would be
3. And tho' this world, with dev - vils filled, Should threaten to un -
4. That word a - bove all earth - ly powers, No thanks to them, a -

fail - ing; Our help-er He, a - mid the flood
los - ing; Were not the right Man on our side,
do us, We will not fear, for God hath willed
bid - eth; The Spir-it and the gifts are ours

Of mor-tal ills pre-vail - ing: For still our an - cient foe
The Man of God's own choos - ing: Dost ask who that may be?
His truth to tri-umph through us: The Prince of Dark - ness grim -
Thro' Him who with us sid - eth: Let goods and kin - dred go,

Doth seek to work us woe; His craft and power are great, And,
Christ Je - sus, it is He; Lord Sa - ba - oth, His name, From
We trem - ble not for him; His rage we can en - dure, For
This mor - tal life, al - so; The bod - y they may kill: God's

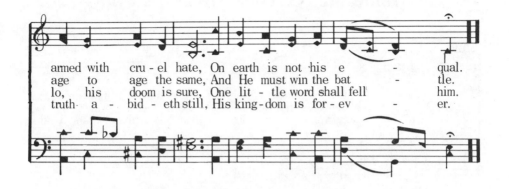

armed with cru - el hate, On earth is not his e - qual.
age to age the same, And He must win the bat - tle.
lo, his doom is sure, One lit - tle word shall fell him.
truth a - bid - eth still, His king-dom is for - ev - er.

32   O God, Our Help In Ages Past

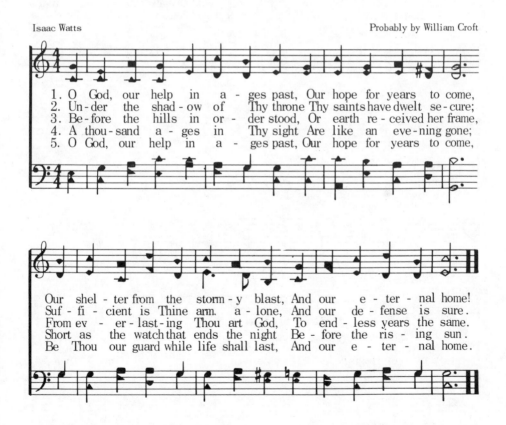

Isaac Watts   Probably by William Croft

1. O God, our help in a - ges past, Our hope for years to come,
2. Un - der the shad - ow of Thy throne Thy saints have dwelt se - cure;
3. Be - fore the hills in or - der stood, Or earth re - ceived her frame,
4. A thou - sand a - ges in Thy sight Are like an eve - ning gone;
5. O God, our help in a - ges past, Our hope for years to come,

Our shel - ter from the storm - y blast, And our e - ter - nal home!
Suf - fi - cient is Thine arm. a - lone, And our de - fense is sure.
From ev - er - last - ing Thou art God, To end - less years the same.
Short as the watch that ends the night Be - fore the ris - ing sun.
Be Thou our guard while life shall last, And our e - ter - nal home.

Guide Me, O Thou Great Jehovah

William Williams

Thomas Hastings

1. Guide me, O Thou great Je - ho - vah, Pil - grim thru this bar - ren land;
2. O - pen now the crys - tal foun - tain, Whence the heal-ing wa - ters flow;
3. When I tread the verge of Jor - dan, Bid my anx - ious fears sub-side;

I am weak, but Thou art might - y; Hold me with Thy pow'r-ful hand;
Let the fi - ery, cloud-y pil - lar Lead me all my jour - ney thru:
Bear me thru the swell-ing cur - rent, Land me safe on Ca - naan's side.

Bread of heav - en, Feed me till I want no more;
Strong De - liv - 'rer, Be Thou still my strength and shield;
Songs of prais - es I will ev - er give to Thee;

Bread of heav - en, Feed me till I want no more.
Strong De - liv - 'rer, Be Thou still my strength and shield.
Songs of prais - es I will ev - er give to Thee.

God Of Our Fathers

Daniel C. Roberts

George W. Warren

Trumpets

1. God of our fa - thers, whose al - might - y
2. Thy love di - vine hath led us in the
3. From war's a - larms, from dead - ly pes - ti -
4. Re - fresh Thy peo - ple on their toil - some

hand   Leads forth in beau - ty all the star - ry band,
past,   In this free land by Thee our lot is cast;
lence,   Be Thy strong arm our ev - er sure de - fense;
way,   Lead us from night to nev - er - end - ing day;

Of shin - ing worlds in splen - dor through the skies,
Be Thou our rul - er, guard - ian, guide, and stay,
Thy true re - li - gion in our hearts in - crease,
Fill all our lives with love and grace di - vine,

Our grate - ful songs be - fore Thy throne a - rise.
Thy Word our law, Thy paths our cho - sen way.
Thy boun - teous good - ness nour - ish us in peace.
And glo - ry, laud, and praise be ev - er Thine.

The Love Of God

F. M. Lehman   F. M. Lehman

1. The love of God is great-er far   than tongue or pen
2. When hoar-y time shall pass a-way,   and earth-ly thrones
3. Could we with ink the o-cean fill,   and were the skies

can ev-er tell, It goes be-yond the high-est star
and king-doms fall, When men who here re-fuse to pray
of parch-ment made, Were ev-'ry stalk on earth a quill,

and reach-es to the low-est hell; The guilt-y pair,
on rocks and hills and moun-tains call; God's love, so sure,
and ev-'ry man a scribe by trade; To write the love

bowed down with care, God gave His Son to win,
shall still en-dure, all meas-ure-less and strong,
of God a-bove, would drain the o-cean dry,

His err - ing child He rec - on - ciled   and par - doned
Re - deem - ing grace to Ad - am's race,   the saints' and
Nor could the scroll con - tain the whole,   though stretched from

from   his sin. O love of God, how rich   and pure!
an - gels'song.
sky   to sky.

REFRAIN

How meas - ure - less   and strong! It shall for - ev -

er - more en - dure, The saints' and an - gels' song.

God Will Take Care Of You

C. D. Martin

W. Stillman Martin

1. Be not dis - mayed what-e'er be - tide, God will take care of you;
2. Thro' days of toil when heart doth fail, God will take care of you;
3. All you may need He will pro-vide, God will take care of you;
4. No mat-ter what may be the test, God will take care of you;

Be - neath His wings of love a-bide, God will take care of you.
When dan-gers fierce your path as-sail, God will take care of you.
Noth-ing you ask will be de-nied, God will take care of you.
Lean, wear-y one, up-on His breast, God will take care of you.

REFRAIN

God will take care of you, Thro' ev-'ry day, o'er all the way;

He will take care of you, God will take care of you.

Blessed Be The Name

Charles Wesley

Ralph E. Hudson

1. O for a thou-sand tongues to sing, Bless-ed be the name of the
2. Je-sus, the name that calms my fears, Bless-ed be the name of the
3. He breaks the power of can - celed sin, Bless-ed be the name of the

Lord! The glo-ries of my God and King, Bless-ed be the name
Lord! 'Tis mu-sic in the sin – ner's ears, Bless-ed be the name
Lord! His blood can make the foul - est clean, Bless-ed be the name

REFRAIN

of the Lord! Bless-ed be the name, Bless-ed be the name,

Bless-ed be the name of the Lord! Bless-ed be the name,

Bless-ed be the name, Bless-ed be the name of the Lord.

I Will Sing Of My Redeemer

Philip P. Bliss

James McGranahan

1. I will sing of my Re-deem-er And His won-drous love to me;
2. I will tell the won-drous sto-ry, How my lost es-tate to save,
3. I will praise my dear Re-deem-er, His tri-um-phant power I'll tell,
4. I will sing of my Re-deem-er, And His heaven-ly love to me;

On the cru-el cross He suf-fered From the curse to set me free.
In His bound-less love and mer-cy, He the ran-som free-ly gave.
How the vic-to-ry He giv-eth O-ver sin and death and hell.
He from death to life hath brought me, Son of God, with Him to be.

REFRAIN

Sing, oh, sing of my Re-deem-er,
Sing, oh, sing of my Re-deem-er, Sing, oh, sing of my Re-deem-er,

With His blood He pur-chased me;
With His blood He purchased me, with His blood He purchased me,

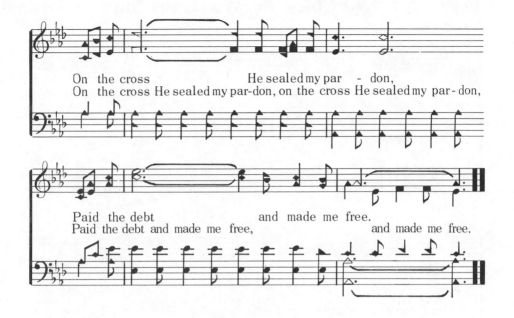

On the cross   He sealed my par - don,
On the cross He sealed my par-don, on the cross He sealed my par - don,

Paid the debt   and made me free.
Paid the debt and made me free,   and made me free.

39

Hallelujah, What A Saviour!

P. P. Bliss   P. P. Bliss

Moderato   mf

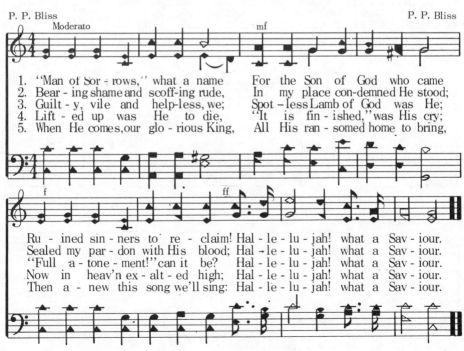

1. "Man of Sor - rows," what a name   For the Son of God who came
2. Bear - ing shame and scoff-ing rude,   In my place con-demned He stood;
3. Guilt - y, vile and help-less, we;   Spot - less Lamb of God was He;
4. Lift - ed up was He to die,   "It is fin - ished," was His cry;
5. When He comes, our glo - rious King,   All His ran - somed home to bring,

Ru - ined sin - ners to re - claim! Hal - le - lu - jah! what a Sav - iour.
Sealed my par - don with His blood; Hal - le - lu - jah! what a Sav - iour.
"Full a - tone - ment!" can it be? Hal - le - lu - jah! what a Sav - iour.
Now in heav'n ex - alt - ed high; Hal - le - lu - jah! what a Sav - iour.
Then a - new this song we'll sing: Hal - le - lu - jah! what a Sav - iour.

I Will Sing The Wondrous Story

Francis H. Rowley

Peter P. Bilhorn

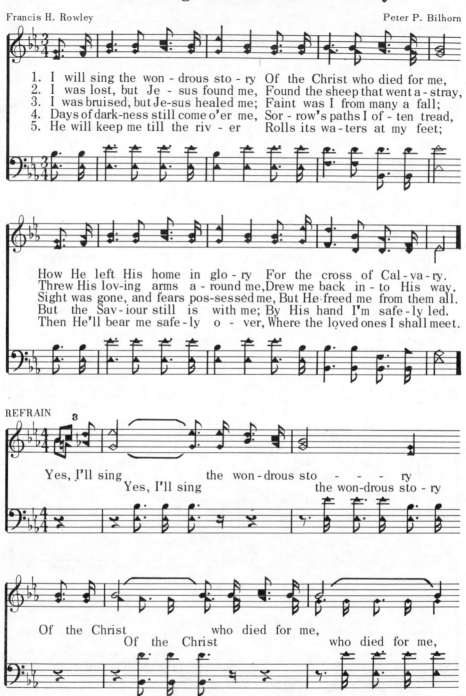

1. I will sing the won-drous sto-ry Of the Christ who died for me,
2. I was lost, but Je-sus found me, Found the sheep that went a-stray,
3. I was bruised, but Je-sus healed me; Faint was I from many a fall;
4. Days of dark-ness still come o'er me, Sor-row's paths I of-ten tread,
5. He will keep me till the riv-er Rolls its wa-ters at my feet;

How He left His home in glo-ry For the cross of Cal-va-ry.
Threw His lov-ing arms a-round me, Drew me back in-to His way.
Sight was gone, and fears pos-sessed me, But He freed me from them all.
But the Sav-iour still is with me; By His hand I'm safe-ly led.
Then He'll bear me safe-ly o - ver, Where the loved ones I shall meet.

REFRAIN

Yes, I'll sing the won-drous sto - - - - ry
Yes, I'll sing the won-drous sto-ry

Of the Christ who died for me,
Of the Christ who died for me,

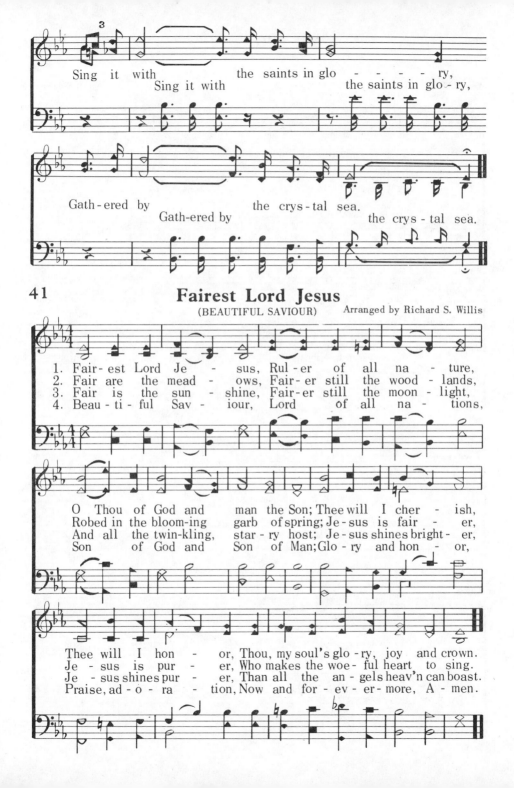

Sing it with the saints in glo - - - - ry,
Sing it with the saints in glo - ry,

Gath - ered by the crys - tal sea.
Gath - ered by the crys - tal sea.

41

Fairest Lord Jesus

(BEAUTIFUL SAVIOUR)

Arranged by Richard S. Willis

1. Fair - est Lord Je - sus, Rul - er of all na - ture,
2. Fair are the mead - ows, Fair - er still the wood - lands,
3. Fair is the sun - shine, Fair - er still the moon - light,
4. Beau - ti - ful Sav - iour, Lord of all na - tions,

O Thou of God and man the Son; Thee will I cher - ish,
Robed in the bloom-ing garb of spring; Je - sus is fair - er,
And all the twin-kling, star - ry host; Je - sus shines bright - er,
Son of God and Son of Man; Glo - ry and hon - or,

Thee will I hon - or, Thou, my soul's glo - ry, joy and crown.
Je - sus is pur - er, Who makes the woe - ful heart to sing.
Je - sus shines pur - er, Than all the an - gels heav'n can boast.
Praise, ad - o - ra - tion, Now and for - ev - er-more, A - men.

Jesus Loves Me

Anna B. Warner

William B. Bradbury

1. Je - sus loves me! this I know, For the Bi - ble tells me so;
2. Je - sus loves me! He who died Heav-en's gates to o - pen wide!
3. Je - sus loves me! loves me still, Tho' I'm ver - y weak and ill;
4. Je - sus loves me! He will stay Close be - side me all the way;

Lit - tle ones to Him be - long; They are weak, but He is strong.
He will wash a - way my sin, Let His lit - tle child come in.
From His shin - ing throne on high, Comes to watch me where I lie.
If I love Him, when I die He will take me home on high.

REFRAIN

Yes, Je - sus loves me, Yes, Je - sus loves me,

Yes, Je - sus loves me, The Bi - ble tells me so.

Jesus Loves Even Me

Philip P. Bliss   Philip P. Bliss

1. I am so glad that our Fa - ther in heav'n Tells of His love in the
2. Tho' I for - get Him and wan - der a - way, Kind - ly He fol - lows wher-
3. Oh, if there's on - ly one song I can sing, When in His beau - ty I

Book He has giv'n; Won - der - ful things in the Bi - ble I see;
ev - er I stray; Back to His dear lov - ing arms would I flee
see the great King, This shall my song in e - ter - ni - ty be,

REFRAIN

This is the dear - est, that Je - sus loves me.
When I re - mem - ber that Je - sus loves me. I am so glad that
Oh, what a won - der that Je - sus loves me.

Je - sus loves me, Je - sus loves me, Je - sus loves me; I am so

glad that Je - sus loves me, Je - sus loves e - ven me.

Tell Me More About Jesus

C. S. Grogan

C. S. Grogan

1. I love that grand old sto-ry of Je-sus, my King,
2. Oh, tell a-bout the man-ger where first He was laid,
3. Now tell how He as-cend-ed to heav-en that day,

How He came down from glo-ry, sal-va-tion to bring;
And tell a-bout the gar-den where of-ten He prayed;
How He blessed His dis-ci-ples as He went a-way;

There is no sweet-er name by mor-tal ev-er heard,
Tell how at Cal-va-ry He died for sin-ful men,
Tell how, as they looked up, they heard an an-gel say,

Oh, tell me more a-bout Him, I thrill with ev-'ry word!
Then tell how He was bur-ied, and how He rose a-gain.
"Just as you saw Him leav-ing, He'll come a-gain some day."

Tell me more, tell me more, tell me more a-bout Je-sus,

Nev-er has a sweet-er sto-ry been told, been told;

Tell me more, tell me more, tell me more a-bout Je-sus,

Ev-er new, this sto-ry nev-er grows old, grows old.

More About Jesus

Eliza E. Hewitt

John R. Sweney

1. More a - bout Je - sus would I know, More of His grace to oth - ers show;
2. More a - bout Je - sus let me learn, More of His ho - ly will dis - cern;
3. More a - bout Je - sus, in His Word, Hold - ing com-mun - ion with my Lord;
4. More a - bout Je - sus on His throne, Rich - es in glo - ry all His own;

More of His' sav - ing full - ness see, More of His love who died for me.
Spir - it of God, my teach-er be, Show - ing the things of Christ to me.
Hear - ing His voice in ev - 'ry line, Mak - ing each faith-ful say - ing mine.
More of His king - dom's sure in - crease; More of His com - ing Prince of peace.

REFRAIN

More, more a - bout Je - sus, More, more a - bout Je - sus; More of His

sav - ing full - ness see, More of His love who died for me.

46 Jesus Is All The World To Me

Will L. Thompson

Will L. Thompson

1. Je - sus is all the world to me, My life, my joy, my all;
2. Je - sus is all the world to me, My friend in tri - als sore;
3. Je - sus is all the world to me, And true to Him I'll be;
4. Je - sus is all the world to me, I want no bet - ter friend;

He is my strength from day to day, With - out Him I would fall:
I go to Him for bless - ings, and He gives them o'er and o'er:
Oh, how could I this friend de - ny, When He's so true to me?
I trust Him now, I'll trust Him when Life's fleet - ing days shall end:

When I am sad, to Him I go, No oth - er one can cheer me so;
He sends the sun - shine and the rain, He sends the har - vest's gold - en grain;
Fol - low - ing Him I know I'm right, He watch - es o'er me day and night;
Beau - ti - ful life, with such a friend, Beau - ti - ful life that has no end;

When I am sad, He makes me glad, He's my friend.
Sun - shine and rain, har - vest of grain, He's my friend.
Fol - low - ing Him by day and night, He's my friend.
E - ter - nal life, e - ter - nal joy, He's my friend.

47 A Shelter In The Time Of Storm

Vernon J. Charlesworth

Ira D. Sankey

1. The Lord's our rock in Him we hide, A shel-ter in the time of storm;
2. A shade by day, de-fense by night, A shel-ter in the time of storm;
3. The rag-ing storms may round us beat, A shel-ter in the time of storm;
4. O rock di-vine, O ref-uge dear, A shel-ter in the time of storm;

Se-cure what-ev-er ill be-tide, A shel-ter in the time of storm.
No fears a-larm, no foes af-fright, A shel-ter in the time of storm.
We'll nev-er leave our safe re-treat, A shel-ter in the time of storm.
Be Thou our help-er, ev-er near, A shel-ter in the time of storm.

REFRAIN

Oh, Je-sus is a rock in a wea-ry land, A wea-ry land,

a wea-ry land; Oh, Je-sus is a rock in a

wea-ry land, A shel-ter in the time of storm.

What A Friend We Have In Jesus

Joseph Scriven

Charles C. Converse

1. What a friend we have in Je - sus, All our sins and griefs to bear!
2. Have we tri - als and temp-ta-tions? Is there trou - ble an - y-where?
3. Are we weak and heav-y lad - en, Cum-bered with a load of care?

What a priv - i - lege to car - ry Ev - 'ry-thing to God in prayer!
We should nev-er be dis-cour-aged, Take it to the Lord in prayer:
Pre - cious Sav-iour still our ref - uge; Take it to the Lord in prayer:

Oh, what peace we of - ten for - feit, Oh, what need-less pain we bear,
Can we find a friend so faith - ful Who will all our sor-rows share?
Do thy friends de-spise, for-sake thee? Take it to the Lord in prayer;

All be-cause we do not car - ry Ev - 'ry-thing to God in prayer!
Je - sus knows our ev - 'ry weak - ness, Take it to the Lord in prayer.
In His arms He'll take and shield thee; Thou wilt find a sol - ace there .

What A Saviour

Marvin P. Dalton   Marvin P. Dalton

1. Once I was stray - ing in sin's dark val - ley, No hope with-
2. He left the Fa - ther, with all His rich - es, With calm - ness
3. Death's chilly wa - ters I'll soon be cross - ing, His hand will

in could I see; They searched thru heav - en and found a
sweet and se - rene, Came down from heav - en and gave His
lead me safe o'er; I'll join the cho - rus in that great

REFRAIN

Sav - iour To save a poor lost soul like me.
life - blood, To make the vil - est sin - ner clean. O what a
cit - y, And sing up there for - ev - er - more.

Sav - iour, O hal - le - lu - jah, His heart was bro - ken

on Cal - va - ry; His hands were nail - scarred, His side was

riv-en, He gave His life-blood for e-ven me.

50 Footprints Of Jesus

Mary B. C. Slade

Asa B. Everett

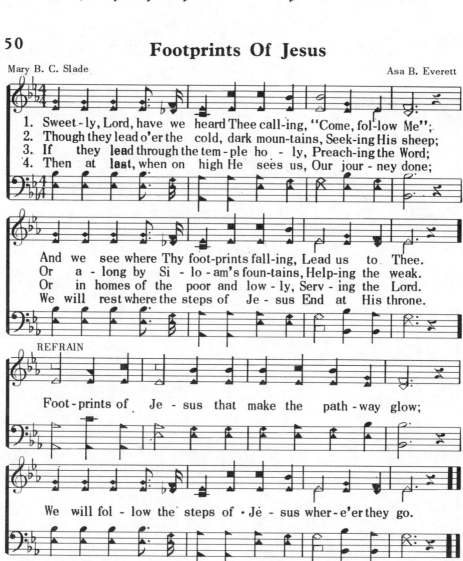

1. Sweet-ly, Lord, have we heard Thee call-ing, "Come, fol-low Me";
2. Though they lead o'er the cold, dark moun-tains, Seek-ing His sheep;
3. If they lead through the tem-ple ho - ly, Preach-ing the Word;
4. Then at last, when on high He sees us, Our jour-ney done;

And we see where Thy foot-prints fall-ing, Lead us to Thee.
Or a - long by Si - lo-am's foun-tains, Help-ing the weak.
Or in homes of the poor and low - ly, Serv-ing the Lord.
We will rest where the steps of Je - sus End at His throne.

REFRAIN

Foot-prints of Je - sus that make the path-way glow;

We will fol - low the steps of Je - sus wher-e'er they go.

Jesus, Lover Of My Soul

Charles Wesley

Simeon B. Marsh

1. Je - sus, lov - er of my soul, Let me to Thy bos - om fly,
2. Oth - er ref - uge have I none, Hangs my help-less soul on Thee,
3. Thou, O Christ, art all I want, More than all in Thee I find,
4. Plenteous grace with Thee is found, Grace to cov - er all my sin,

While the near - er wa - ters roll, While the tem-pest still is high:
Leave, O leave me not a - lone, Still sup-port and com-fort me:
Raise the fall - en, cheer the faint, Heal the sick and lead the blind:
Let the heal-ing streams abound, Make and keep me pure with-in:

Hide me, O my Sav-iour, hide, Till the storm of life is past;
All my trust on Thee is stayed, All my help from Thee I bring;
Just and ho - ly is Thy name, I am all un-righteousness;
Thou of life the foun-tain art, Free - ly let me take of Thee;

Safe in - to the ha - ven guide, O re-ceive my soul at last.
Cov - er my de-fenseless head, With the shad-ow of Thy wing.
False and full of sin I am, Thou art full of truth and grace.
Spring Thou up with - in my heart, Rise to all e - ter - ni - ty.

My Jesus, I Love Thee

William R. Featherston

Adoniram J. Gordon

1. My Je - sus, I love Thee, I know Thou art mine,
2. I love Thee be - cause Thou hast first lov - ed me,
3. I'll love Thee in life, I will love Thee in death,
3. In man - sions of glo - ry and end - less de - light,

For Thee all the fol - lies of sin I re - sign;
And pur - chased my par - don on Cal - va - ry's tree;
And praise Thee as long as Thou lend - est me breath;
I'll ev - er a - dore Thee in heav - en so bright;

My gra - cious Re - deem - er, my Sav - iour art Thou,
I love Thee for wear - ing the thorns on Thy brow,
And say when the death dew lies cold on my brow,
I'll sing with the glit - ter - ing crown on my brow,

If ev - er I loved Thee, my Je - sus 'tis now.
If ev - er I loved Thee, my Je - sus 'tis now.
If ev - er I loved Thee, my Je - sus 'tis now.
If ev - er I loved Thee, my Je - sus 'tis now.

The Lily Of The Valley

Charles W. Fry

Arr. from William S. Hays

1. I have found a friend in Je - sus, He's ev - ery - thing to me,
2. He all my griefs has ta - ken, and all my sor - rows borne;
3. He will nev - er, nev - er leave me, nor yet for - sake me here,

He's the fair - est of ten thou - sand to my soul;
In temp - ta - tion He's my strong and might - y tower;
While I live by faith and do His bless - ed will;

The Lil - y of the Val - ley, in Him a - lone I see
I have all for Him for - sak - en, and all my i - dols torn
A wall of fire a - bout me, I've noth - ing now to fear,

All I need to cleanse and make me ful - ly whole.
From my heart, and now He keeps me by His power.
With His man - na He my hun - gry soul shall fill.

In sor - row He's my com - fort, in trou - ble He's my stay;
Though all the world for - sake me, and Sa - tan tempt me sore,
Then sweep - ing up to glo - ry to see His bless - ed face,

He tells me ev - ery care on Him to roll:
Through Je - sus I shall safe - ly reach the goal:
Where riv - ers of de - light shall ev - er roll:

He's the Lil - y of the Val - ley, the Bright and Morn - ing Star,

He's the fair - est of ten thou - sand to my soul.

'Tis So Sweet To Trust In Jesus

Louisa M. R. Stead

Wm. J. Kirkpatrick

1. 'Tis so sweet to trust in Je - sus, Just to take Him at His Word;
2. O how sweet to trust in Je - sus, Just to trust His cleans-ing blood;
3. Yes, 'tis sweet to trust in Je - sus, Just from sin and self to cease;
4. I'm so glad I learned to trust Thee, Pre-cious Je-sus, Sav-iour, Friend;

Just to rest up - on His prom-ise; Just to know, "Thus saith the Lord,"
Just in sim - ple faith to plunge me 'Neath the heal - ing, cleans-ing flood!
Just from Je - sus sim-ply tak - ing Life and rest and joy and peace.
And I know that Thou art with me, Wilt be with me to the end.

REFRAIN

Je - sus, Je - sus, how I trust Him! How I've proved Him o'er and o'er!

Je - sus, Je - sus, pre - cious Je - sus! O for grace to trust Him more!

The Great Physician

William Hunter

John H. Stockton

55

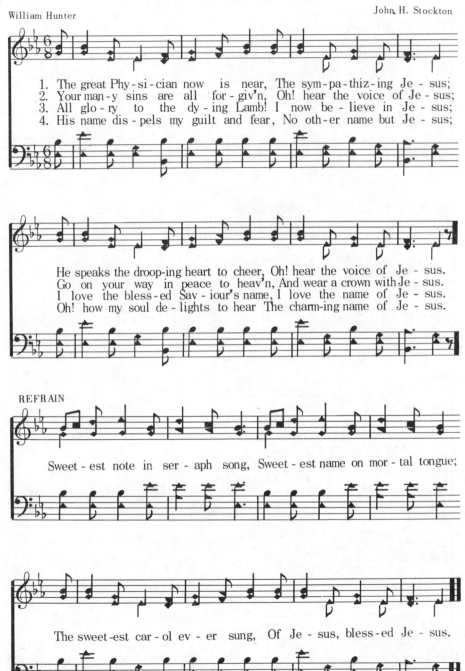

1. The great Phy-si-cian now is near, The sym-pa-thiz-ing Je - sus;
2. Your man-y sins are all for-giv'n, Oh! hear the voice of Je - sus;
3. All glo-ry to the dy-ing Lamb! I now be-lieve in Je - sus;
4. His name dis-pels my guilt and fear, No oth-er name but Je - sus;

He speaks the droop-ing heart to cheer, Oh! hear the voice of Je - sus.
Go on your way in peace to heav'n, And wear a crown with Je - sus.
I love the bless-ed Sav-iour's name, I love the name of Je - sus.
Oh! how my soul de-lights to hear The charm-ing name of Je - sus.

REFRAIN

Sweet-est note in ser-aph song, Sweet-est name on mor-tal tongue;

The sweet-est car-ol ev-er sung, Of Je - sus, bless-ed Je - sus.

What A Lovely Name

Charles B. Wycuff   Not too fast   Charles B. Wycuff

1. There's a name a - bove all oth - ers, Won - der - ful to
2. Thru His name there's won - drous pow - er, Pow - er to re -
3. He'll re - turn in clouds of glo - ry, Saints of ev - 'ry

hear, won-der-ful to hear, bring-ing hope and cheer, yes, hope and cheer;
deem, pow - er to re - deem, mak-ing sin-ners clean, the sin-ners clean;
race, saints of ev-'ry race, shall be-hold His face, His lov - ing face;

It's the love - ly name of Je - sus, Ev - er - more the
By His pow'r He cleansed the lep - er, O - pened blind - ed
With Him en - ter heav - en's cit - y, Ev - er to ac -

same, ev - er - more the same, what a love - ly name, a love - ly name.
eyes, o-pened blind-ed eyes, caused the dead to rise, the dead to rise.
claim, ev - er to ac-claim, what a love - ly name, a love - ly name.

REFRAIN

What   a love - ly name, the name of Je - sus,   Reach-ing high-er
What   a   name, the name of Je - sus,

far   than the bright-est star;
Reach-ing high-er far,   than the bright-est star;

Sweet - er than the songs they sing in heav - en, Let the world pro -
Sweet - er   songs they sing in heav - en,

claim   what a love - ly name, a love - ly name!
Let the world pro - claim,

The Old Rugged Cross

George Bennard

George Bennard

1. On a hill far a - way stood an old rug - ged cross,
2. Oh, that old rug - ged cross so de - spised by the world,
3. In the old rug - ged cross, stained with blood so di - vine,
4. To the old rug - ged cross I will ev - er be true,

The em - blem of suf - f'ring and shame;
Has a won - drous at - trac - tion for me;
A won - drous beau - ty I see;
Its shame and re - proach glad - ly bear;

And I love that old cross where the dear - est and best,
For the dear Lamb of God left His glo - ry a - bove,
For 'twas on that old cross Je - sus suf - fered and died,
Then He'll call me some day to my home far a - way,

For a world of lost sin - ners was slain.
To bear it to dark Cal - va - ry.
To par - don and sanc - ti - fy me.
Where His glo - ry for - ev - er I'll share.

REFRAIN

So I'll cher-ish the old rug-ged cross,
Cross, the old rug-ged cross,
Till my tro-phies at last I lay down;
I will cling to the old rug-ged cross,
Cross, the old rug-ged cross,
And ex-change it some day for a crown.

At The Cross

Issac Watts

Ralph E. Hudson

1. A - las! and did my Sav - ior bleed? And did my Sov'reign die?
2. Was it for crimes that I had done, He groaned up - on the tree?
3. Well might the sun in dark - ness hide, And shut his glo - ries in,
4. But drops of grief can ne'er re - pay The debt of love I owe,

Would He de - vote that sa - cred head For sin - ners such as I?
A - maz - ing pit - y! grace unknown! And love be - yond de - gree!
When Christ, the mighty Mak - er, died For man the crea - ture's sin.
Here, Lord, I give my - self a - way, 'Tis all that I can do.

REFRAIN

At the cross, at the cross where I first saw the light, And the

bur - den of my heart rolled a - way, It was there by
rolled a - way,

faith I re - ceived my sight, and now I am hap - py all the day.

Jesus Paid It All

Elvina M. Hall

John T. Grape

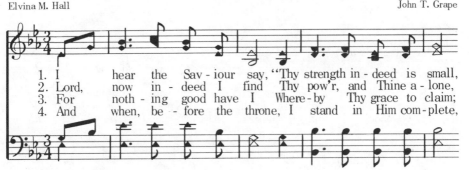

1. I hear the Sav - iour say, "Thy strength in - deed is small,
2. Lord, now in - deed I find Thy pow'r, and Thine a - lone,
3. For noth - ing good have I Where - by Thy grace to claim;
4. And when, be - fore the throne, I stand in Him com - plete,

Child of weak - ness, watch and pray, Find in Me Thine all in all."
Can change the lep - er's spots, And melt the heart of stone.
I'll wash my gar - ments white In the blood of Cal - v'ry's Lamb.
"Je - sus died my soul to save," My lips shall still re - peat.

REFRAIN

Je - sus paid it all, All to Him I owe;

Sin had left a crim - son stain, He wash'd it white as snow.

60　Blessed Redeemer

Avis Burgeson Christiansen　　　　　　　　Harry Dixon Loes

1. Up Cal - v'ry's moun - tain one dread - ful morn, Walked Christ my
2. "Fa - ther, for - give them!" thus did He pray, E'en while His
3. O how I love Him, Sav - iour and friend, How can my

Sav - iour wea - ry and worn; Fac - ing for sin - ners death on the
life - blood flowed fast a - way; Pray - ing for sin - ners while in such
prais - es ev - er find end! Thro' years un - num - bered on heav - en's

REFRAIN

cross, That He might save them from end - less loss.
woe—— No one but Je - sus ev - er loved so. Bless - ed Re -
shore, My tongue shall praise Him for - ev - er more.

deem - er! pre - cious Re - deem - er! Seems now I see Him on

Cal - va - ry's tree; Wound - ed and bleed - ing, for sin - ners

plead - ing - Blind and un - heed - ing, dy - ing for me!

61 Must Jesus Bear The Cross Alone?

Thomas Shepherd

George N. Allen

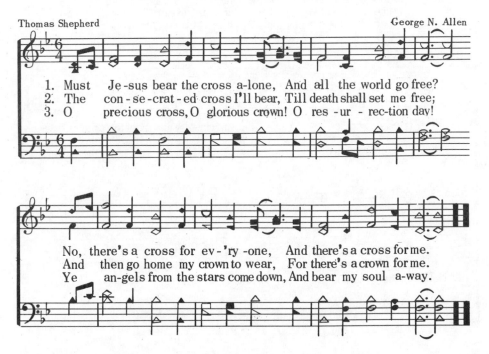

1. Must Je -sus bear the cross a -lone, And all the world go free?
2. The con - se -crat - ed cross I'll bear, Till death shall set me free;
3. O precious cross, O glorious crown! O res -ur - rec-tion day!

No, there's a cross for ev -'ry -one, And there's a cross for me.
And then go home my crown to wear, For there's a crown for me.
Ye an-gels from the stars come down, And bear my soul a -way.

62 Hallelujah For The Cross

Horatius Bonar   James McGranahan

1. The cross it stand - eth fast, Hal - le - lu - jah! Hal - le - lu - jah!
2. It is the old cross still, Hal - le - lu - jah! Hal - le - lu - jah!
3. 'Twas here the debt was paid, Hal - le - lu - jah! Hal - le - lu - jah!

De - fy - ing ev - 'ry blast, Hal - le - lu - jah! Hal - le - lu - jah!
Its tri - umph let us tell, Hal - le - lu - jah! Hal - le - lu - jah!
Our sins on Je - sus laid, Hal - le - lu - jah! Hal - le - lu - jah!

The winds of hell have blown, The world its hate hath shown,
The grace of God here shone Through Christ the bless-ed Son,
So round the cross we sing Of Christ, our of - fer - ing,

Yet it is not o - ver - thrown, Hal-le-lu-jah for the Cross!
Who did for sin a - tone, Hal-le-lu-jah for the Cross!
Of Christ, our liv - ing King, Hal-le-lu-jah for the Cross!

REFRAIN

Hal - le - lu - jah, hal - le - lu - jah, hal - le - lu - jah for the cross;

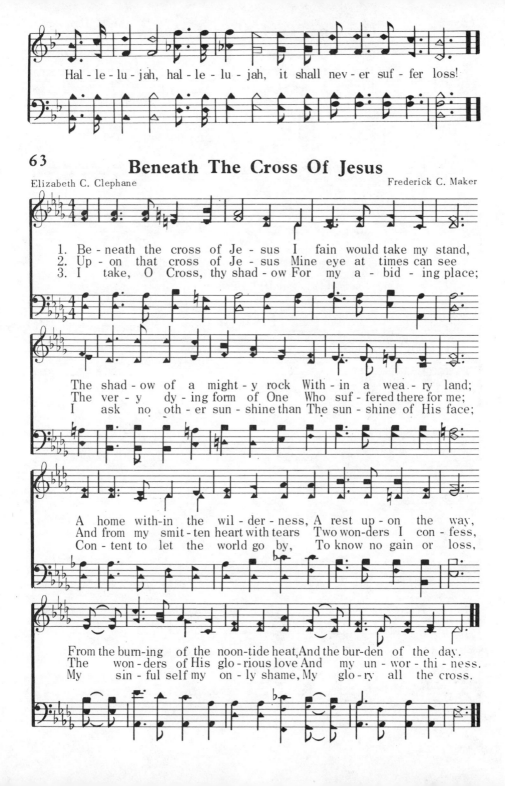

Hal - le - lu - jah, hal - le - lu - jah, it shall nev - er suf - fer loss!

63

Beneath The Cross Of Jesus

Elizabeth C. Clephane

Frederick C. Maker

1. Be - neath the cross of Je - sus I fain would take my stand,
2. Up - on that cross of Je - sus Mine eye at times can see
3. I take, O Cross, thy shad - ow For my a - bid - ing place;

The shad - ow of a might - y rock With - in a wea - ry land;
The ver - y dy - ing form of One Who suf - fered there for me;
I ask no oth - er sun - shine than The sun - shine of His face;

A home with-in the wil - der - ness, A rest up - on the way,
And from my smit - ten heart with tears Two won-ders I con - fess,
Con - tent to let the world go by, To know no gain or loss,

From the burn-ing of the noon-tide heat,And the bur-den of the day.
The won - ders of His glo - rious love And my un - wor - thi - ness.
My sin - ful self my on - ly shame, My glo - ry all the cross.

64 He Had To Go To Calvary

Charles E. Moody

Charles E. Moody

1. Christ had to go to Cal-va-ry, Bear-ing the cross of shame;
2. Christ had to go to Cal-va-ry, With thorns upon His brow;
3. Christ had to go to Cal-va-ry, Seem-eth the sun went down;

To save the world from mis-er-y, Meek-ly He took the blame.
That all the world might ransomed be, And in His presence bow.
"Now it is finished," murmured He, His face bore not a frown.

REFRAIN

He had to go, He had to go
to Cal - v'ry, and suf - fer,

His life He had to pay; He went a - lone,
and suf - fer,

sin to a - tone, There was no oth - er way.

65 Back Of The Cross

Lacy Maynor

Margaret Maynor

1. Je - sus a won - der - ful Friend to me, Je - sus who made the blind to see; Won - der - ful Sav - iour, Heal - er di - vine, Sav - ing the lost, oh, glo - ry He's mine.

2. Je - sus is seek - ing those who be - lieve, Read - y our bur - dens to re - lieve; Christ our Re - deem - er, soon com - ing King, Prais - es for - ev - er to Him we sing. Back of the cross

3. Je - sus is com - ing some day for me, Je - sus who set the cap - tive free; Guilt of our sins up - on Him was laid, Free-dom from guilt then Cal - v'ry was made.

REFRAIN

of Cal - va - ry, More of His pow - er is re - vealed; This is the mes - sage bro't to me, By His stripes we're healed.

66   He Was Nailed To The Cross For Me

F. A. Graves   F. A. Graves

1. What a won-der-ful, won-der-ful Sav-iour, Who would die on the cross for me! Free-ly shed-ding His pre-cious life-blood, That the sin-ner might be made free.

2. Thus He left His heav-en-ly glo-ry To ac-com-plish His Fa-ther's plan; He was born of the Vir-gin Ma-ry, Took up-on Him the form of man.

3. He was wound-ed for our trans-gres-sions, And He car-ried our sor-rows, too; He's the Heal-er of ev-'ry sick-ness, This He came to the world to do.

4. So He gave His life for oth-ers In re-deem-ing this world from sin, And He's gone to pre-pare a man-sion, That at last we may en-ter in.

REFRAIN

He was nailed to the cross for me,
He was nailed to the cross,
He was nailed

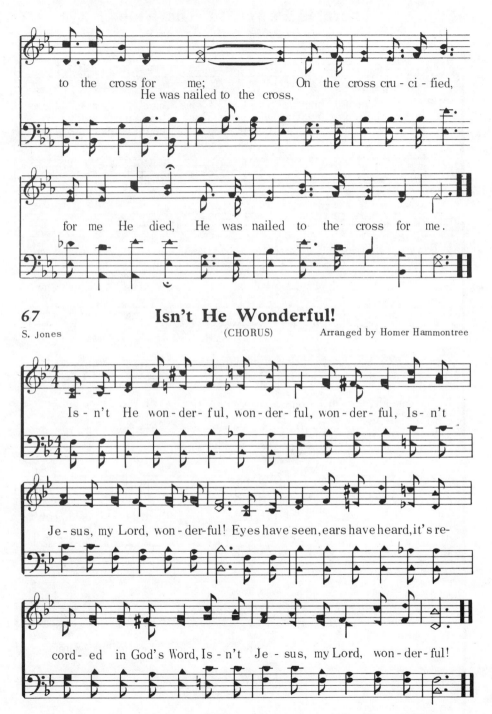

to the cross for me; On the cross cru-ci-fied,
He was nailed to the cross,

for me He died, He was nailed to the cross for me.

67
S. Jones

Isn't He Wonderful!

(CHORUS)

Arranged by Homer Hammontree

Is-n't He won-der-ful, won-der-ful, won-der-ful, Is-n't

Je-sus, my Lord, won-der-ful! Eyes have seen, ears have heard, it's re-

cord-ed in God's Word, Is-n't Je-sus, my Lord, won-der-ful!

68 There Is Power In The Blood

Lewis E. Jones

Lewis E. Jones

1. Would you be free from the bur - den of sin? There's pow'r in the blood,
2. Would you be free from your pas - sion and pride? There's pow'r in the blood,
3. Would you be whit - er, much whit-er than snow? There's pow'r in the blood,
4. Would you do ser - vice for Je - sus your King? There's pow'r in the blood,

pow'r in the blood; Would you o'er e - vil a vic - to - ry win? There's
pow'r in the blood; Come for a cleans-ing to Cal - va - ry's tide; There's
pow'r in the blood; Sin stains are lost in its life - giv - ing flow; There's
pow'r in the blood; Would you live dai - ly His prais - es to sing? There's

REFRAIN

won - der - ful pow'r in the blood. There is pow'r, pow'r, Won-der-work-ing pow'r
There is

in the blood of the Lamb; There is pow'r, pow'r,
In the blood of the Lamb; There is

Won - der - work - ing pow'r In the pre - cious blood of the Lamb.

Nothing But The Blood

Robert Lowry

Robert Lowry

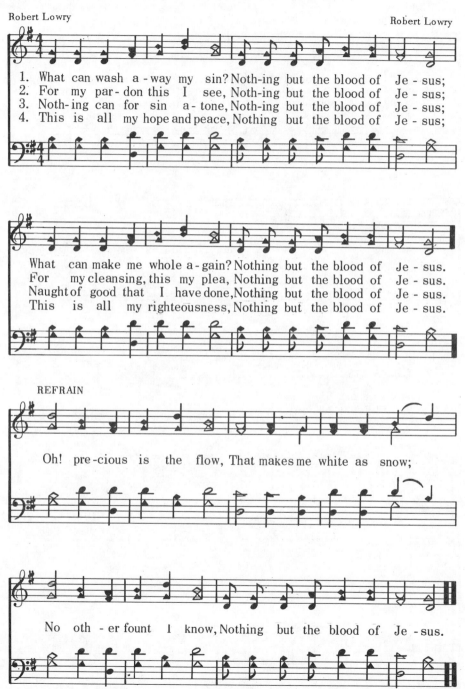

1. What can wash a-way my sin? Noth-ing but the blood of Je-sus;
2. For my par-don this I see, Noth-ing but the blood of Je-sus;
3. Noth-ing can for sin a-tone, Noth-ing but the blood of Je-sus;
4. This is all my hope and peace, Nothing but the blood of Je-sus;

What can make me whole a-gain? Nothing but the blood of Je-sus.
For my cleansing, this my plea, Nothing but the blood of Je-sus.
Naught of good that I have done, Nothing but the blood of Je-sus.
This is all my righteousness, Nothing but the blood of Je-sus.

REFRAIN

Oh! pre-cious is the flow, That makes me white as snow;

No oth-er fount I know, Nothing but the blood of Je-sus.

Saved By The Blood

S. J. Henderson

D. B. Towner

1. Saved by the blood of the Cru - ci - fied One! - Ran - somed from
2. Saved by the blood of the Cru - ci - fied One! The an - gels re -
3. Saved by the blood of the Cru - ci - fied One! The Fa - ther He
4. Saved by the blood of the Cru - ci - fied One! All hail to the

sin and a new work be - gun; Sing praise to the Fa - ther and
joic - ing be - cause it is done; A child of the Fa - ther, joint -
spake and His will it was done; Great price of my par - don, His
Fa - ther, all hail to the Son; All hail to the Spir - it, the

praise to the Son,
heir with the Son,
own pre - cious Son, Saved by the blood of the Cru - ci - fied One!
great Three in One!

REFRAIN

Saved!   Saved!   My sins are all
Glo - ry, I'm saved! glo - ry, I'm saved!

par - doned my guilt is all gone! Saved! Saved!

Glo - ry, I'm saved! glo - ry I'm saved!

I'm saved by the blood of the Cru - ci - fied One!

71

Thank You, Lord

Mr. and Mrs. Seth Sykes
(CHORUS)
Mr. and Mrs. Seth Sykes

Thank you, Lord, for sav - ing my soul, Thank you, Lord, for

mak - ing me whole; Thank you, Lord, for giv - ing to

me, Thy great sal - va - tion so rich and free.

Wonderful Power In The Blood

R. E. Winsett

R. E. Winsett

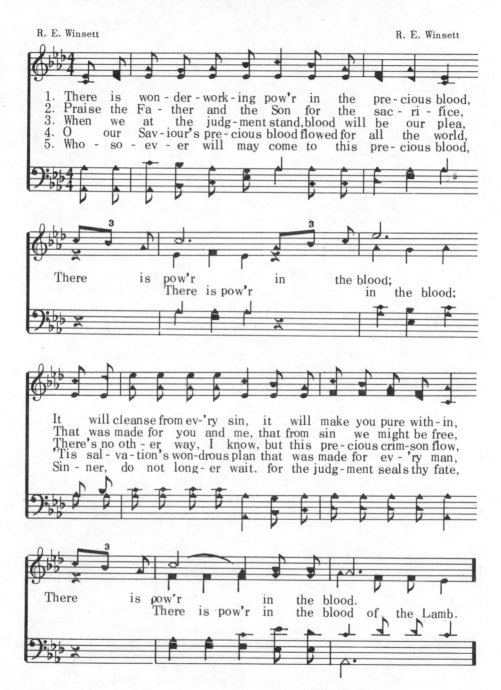

1. There is won - der - work - ing pow'r in the pre - cious blood,
2. Praise the Fa - ther and the Son for the sac - ri - fice,
3. When we at the judg - ment stand, blood will be our plea,
4. O our Sav - iour's pre - cious blood flowed for all the world,
5. Who - so - ev - er will may come to this pre - cious blood,

There is pow'r in the blood;
There is pow'r in the blood;

It will cleanse from ev - 'ry sin, it will make you pure with - in,
That was made for you and me, that from sin we might be free,
There's no oth - er way, I know, but this pre - cious crim - son flow,
'Tis sal - va - tion's won - drous plan that was made for ev - 'ry man,
Sin - ner, do not long - er wait, for the judg - ment seals thy fate,

There is pow'r in the blood.
There is pow'r in the blood of the Lamb.

REFRAIN

Won-der-ful pow'r in the blood, pow'r in the precious blood, in the blood, wonderful power in the blood of the Lamb.

Won-der-ful pow'r in the blood of the Lamb, O the blood has wonderful pow'r, There is per-fect cleans-ing pow'r in the precious blood, Won-der-ful pow'r in the blood of the Lamb, O the blood has won-der-ful pow'r, There is won-der-work-ing pow'r in the blood, of the Lamb.

When I See The Blood

J. G. Foote   J. G. Foote

1. Christ our Re-deem-er died on the cross, Died for the
2. Chief-est of sin-ners, Je-sus can save, As He has
3. Judg-ment is com-ing, all will be there, Who have re-
4. O what com-pas-sion, O bound-less love! Je-sus hath

sin-ner, paid all his due; All who re-ceive Him
prom-ised, so will He do; O sin-ner, hear Him
ject-ed, who have re-fused? O sin-ner, has-ten,
pow-er, Je-sus is true; All who be-lieve are

need nev-er fear, For He will pass, will pass o-ver you.
trust in His word, Then He will pass, will pass o-ver you.
let Je-sus in, Then God will pass, will pass o-ver you.
safe from the storm, O He will pass, will pass o-ver you.

REFRAIN

When I see the blood, When I
When I see the blood, When I

see the blood, When I see the blood;
see the blood, When I see the blood;

I will pass, I will pass o-ver you, o-ver you.

74 Wonderful

Haldor Lillenas (CHORUS) Haldor Lillenas

Won-der-ful, won-der-ful, Je-sus is to me! Coun-sel-or,

Prince of Peace, Might-y God is He! Sav-ing me, keep-ing me

from all sin and shame, Won-der-ful is my Re-deem-er, praise His name!

Whiter Than Snow

Delma Day

T. W. Day

1. I was sin stained with-in by the wa-ges of sin,
2. Oh, the price that He paid when His own life He gave,
3. By His blood so di-vine, I am His, He is mine,

With no com-fort or peace for my soul;
As He hung on the cross there for me;
And He keeps me each hour of the day;

Then I met Christ the Lord and be-lieved on His Word,
There He made us a way if we trust and o-bey,
Just to know He is near, drives a-way doubt and fear,

Je-sus' blood washed me whit-er than snow.
By His blood we can have vic-to-ry.
He is with me each step of the way.

REFRAIN

Whit - er than snow, yes, whit - er than snow,
Oh,

Je - sus' blood wash - es whit - er than snow;

He for - gives ev - 'ry sin makes my heart pure with - in,

Yes, His blood wash - es whit - er than snow.

There Is A Fountain

William Cowper

Lowell Mason

1. There is a foun - tain filled with blood Drawn from Im-man-uel's veins;
2. The dy - ing thief re - joiced to see That foun - tain in his day;
3. Dear dy - ing Lamb, Thy pre - cious blood Shall nev - er lose its pow'r,
4. E'er since, by faith, I saw the stream Thy flow - ing wounds sup - ply,
5. Then in a no - bler, sweet-er song, I'll sing Thy pow'r to save,

And sin - ners, plunged be -neath that flood, Lose all their guilt - y stains:
And there may I, though vile as he, Wash all my sins a - way:
Till all the ran - somed church of God Be saved, to sin no more:
Re - deem - ing love has been my theme, And shall be till I die:
When this poor lisp - ing, stamm-'ring tongue Lies si - lent in the grave:

Lose all their guilt - y stains,   Lose all their guilt - y stains;
Wash all my sins a - way,   Wash all my sins a - way;
Be saved, to sin no more,   Be saved to sin no more;
And shall be till I die,   And shall be till I die;
Lies si - lent in the grave,   Lies si - lent in the grave;

And sin - ners, plunged be -neath that flood, Lose all their guilt - y stains.
And there may I, though vile as he, Wash all my sins a - way.
Till all the ran - somed church of God Be saved, to sin no more.
Re - deem - ing love has been my theme, And shall be till I die.
When this poor lisp - ing, stamm'ring tongue Lies si - lent in the grave.

The Great Physician

C. S. Grogan   C. S. Grogan

1. Are you af - flict - ed in bod - y, Are you dis - tressed in your
2. Reach out by faith now and touch Him, Cast ev - 'ry doubt to the
3. Bow at the cross and con - fess Him, Pray 'till your fears are all

soul; Then come to the Great Phy - si - cian, He's
wind; Trust all to the Great Phy - si - cian, He'll
gone; Hold on to the hand that was riv - en, He'll

a - ble to make you whole.
make all your sor - rows end. The Great Phy - si - cian can
nev - er for - sake His own.

REFRAIN

heal you, Be - lieve Him, He's pass - ing this way; The Great

Phy - si - cian can save you, Re - ceive Him, He'll help you to - day.

The Healing Waters

H. H. Heimar

L. L. Pickett

1. Oh, the joy of sins for-giv'n, Oh, the bliss the blood-wash'd know;
2. Now with Je - sus cru - ci - fied, At His feet I'm rest - ing low;
3. Oh, this pre - cious per - fect love! How it keeps the heart a - glow,
4. Oh, to lean on Je - sus breast, While the tem - pests come and go!
5. Cleans'd from ev - 'ry sin and stain, Whit - er than the driv - en snow,

Oh, the peace a - kin to heav'n, Where the heal - ing wa - ters flow.
Let me ev - er - more a - bide, Where the heal - ing wa - ters flow.
Stream-ing from the fount a - bove, Where the heal - ing wa - ters flow.
Here is bless - ed peace and rest, Where the heal - ing wa - ters flow.
Now I sing my sweet re-frain, Where the heal - ing wa - ters flow.

REFRAIN

Where the heal - ing wa - ters flow,
Where the heal - ing wa - ters flow, where the heal-ing wa - ters flow,

Where the joys ce - les - tial glow,
Where the joys ce - les - tial glow, where the joys ce - les - tial glow,

Oh, there's peace and rest and love,
Oh, there's peace and rest and love, Oh, there's peace and rest and love,

Where the heal - - - - ing wa - ters flow!
Where the heal - ing wa - ters flow, where the heal - ing wa - ters flow!

79

Paul Rader

Only Believe

(CHORUS)

Paul Rader

On - ly be - lieve, on - ly be - lieve, All things are

pos - si - ble, on - ly be - lieve; On - ly be - lieve,

on - ly be - lieve, All things are pos - si - ble, on - ly be - lieve.

Christ Arose!

Robert Lowry   Robert Lowry

1. Low in the grave He lay, Je - sus my Sav - iour! Wait - ing the
2. Vain - ly they watch His bed, Je - sus my Sav - iour! Vain - ly they
3. Death can - not keep his prey, Je - sus my Sav - iour! He tore the

REFRAIN

com - ing day,
seal the dead, Je - sus my Lord! Up from the grave He a -
bars a - way,

rose,   With a might - y tri - umph 'o'er His foes;
    He a - rose,   He a - rose!

He a - rose a vic - tor from the dark do - main, And He

lives for - ev - er with His saints to reign, He a - rose!
                                        He a - rose!

He a - rose! ..... He a - rose! ..... Hal - le - lu - jah! Christ a - rose!

81

My God Can Do Anything

Vep Ellis

(CHORUS)

Vep Ellis

My God can do an - y - thing, an - y - thing, yes, an - y - thing, My God can do an - y - thing; He made the earth with all its full - ness and all that time shall bring, My God can do an - y - thing, an - y - thing.

Christ The Lord Is Risen Today

Charles Wesley

From "Lyra Davidica," 1708

1. Christ the Lord is risen to - day, Al - - - - - le - lu - ia!
2. Lives a - gain our glo - rious King, Al - - - - - le - lu - ia!
3. Love's re - deem - ing work is done, Al - - - - - le - lu - ia!
4. Soar we now where Christ has led, Al - - - - - le - lu - ia!

Sons of men and an - gels say, Al - - - - - le - lu - ia!
Where, O Death, is now thy sting? Al - - - - - le - lu - ia!
Fought the fight, the bat - tle won, Al - - - - - le - lu - ia!
Fol - lowing our ex - alt - ed Head, Al - - - - - le - lu - ia!

Raise your joys and tri - umphs high, Al - - - - - le - lu - ia!
Dy - ing once He all doth save, Al - - - - - le - lu - ia!
Death in vain for - bids Him rise, Al - - - - - le - lu - ia!
Made like Him, like Him we rise, Al - - - - - le - lu - ia!

Sing, ye heav'ns, and earth, re - ply, Al - - - - - le - lu - ia!
Where thy vic - to - ry, O Grave? Al - - - - - le - lu - ia!
Christ hath o - pened Par - a - dise, Al - - - - - le - lu - ia!
Ours the cross, the grave, the skies, Al - - - - - le - lu - ia!

Crown Him With Many Crowns

Matthew Bridges
Godfrey Thring

George J. Elvey

1. Crown Him with man - y crowns, The Lamb up - on His throne;
2. Crown Him the Lord of life, Who tri - umphed o'er the grave,
3. Crown Him the Lord of peace, Whose pow'r a scep - ter sways
4. Crown Him the Lord of love, Be - hold His hands and side,

Hark! how the heav'n - ly an - them drowns All mu - sic but its own:
And rose vic - to - rious in the strife For those He came to save;
From pole to pole, that wars may cease And all be prayer and praise:
Those wounds, yet vis - i - ble a - bove, In beau - ty glo - ri - fied:

A - wake, my soul, and sing Of Him who died for thee,
His glo - ries now we sing Who died, and rose on high,
His reign shall know no end, And round His pierc - ed feet.
All hail, Re - deem - er, hail! For Thou hast died for me:

And hail Him as thy match - less King Through all e - ter - ni - ty.
Who died e - ter - nal life to bring, And lives that death may die.
Fair flowers of par - a - dise ex - tend Their fra - grance ev - er sweet.
Thy praise and glo - ry shall not fail Throughout e - ter - ni - ty.

He Rose Triumphantly

Oswald J. Smith

B. D. Ackley

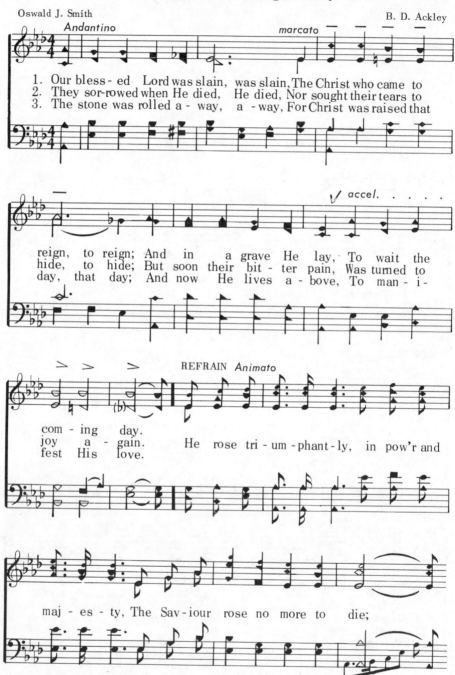

1. Our bless - ed Lord was slain, was slain, The Christ who came to
2. They sor-rowed when He died, He died, Nor sought their tears to
3. The stone was rolled a - way, a - way, For Christ was raised that

reign, to reign; And in a grave He lay, To wait the
hide, to hide; But soon their bit - ter pain, Was turned to
day, that day; And now He lives a - bove, To man - i-

com - ing day.
joy a - gain. He rose tri - um - phant - ly, in pow'r and
fest His love.

maj - es - ty, The Sav - iour rose no more to die;

O let us now pro-claim the glo-ry of His name,

And tell to all, He lives to - day.

85   Jesus Breaks Every Fetter

(CHORUS)

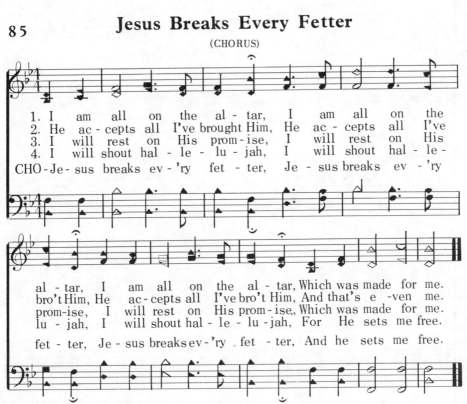

1. I am all on the al-tar, I am all on the
2. He ac-cepts all I've brought Him, He ac-cepts all I've
3. I will rest on His prom-ise, I will rest on His
4. I will shout hal-le-lu-jah, I will shout hal-le-

CHO-Je-sus breaks ev-'ry fet-ter, Je-sus breaks ev-'ry

al-tar, I am all on the al-tar, Which was made for me.
bro't Him, He ac-cepts all I've bro't Him, And that's e-ven me.
prom-ise, I will rest on His prom-ise, Which was made for me.
lu-jah, I will shout hal-le-lu-jah, For He sets me free.

fet-ter, Je-sus breaks ev-'ry fet-ter, And he sets me free.

He Lives

Alfred H. Ackley

Alfred H. Ackley

1. I serve a ris - en Sav -iour, He's in the world to - day,
2. In all the world a - round me I see His lov - ing care,
3. Re-joice, re-joice, O Chris-tian, lift up your voice and sing,

I know that He is liv - ing, what-ev - er men may say;
And tho my heart grows wea-ry, I nev - er will de-spair;
E - ter - nal hal - le - lu - jahs to Je - sus Christ the King!

I see His hand of mer - cy, I hear His voice of cheer,
I know that He is lead-ing through all the storm - y blast,
The hope of all who seek Him, the help of all who find,

And just the time I need Him, He's al - ways near.
The day of His ap - pear - ing will come at last.
None oth - er is so lov - ing, so good and kind.

He lives, He lives, Christ Je-sus lives to-day!
He lives, He lives,

He walks with me and talks with me a - long life's nar - row way;

He lives, He lives, sal - va-tion to im-part,
He lives, He lives,

rit.

You ask me how I know He lives, He lives with-in my heart.

He Is Alive

Glen Thomas

Delton L. Alford

Legato (smooth)

1. There is a sto - ry of the sweet Son of God,
2. My Lord was placed in the hill - side that day,
3. That glo - r'ous morn - ing, He came from the grave,

It tells us of Cal - v'ry and the path He did trod;
And man - y no doubt thought, there He would stay;
For death could not hold Him, the great price He paid;

He was nailed to the cross de - spised of all men,
A huge stone was placed in front of the grave,
Now He is a - live my Sav - iour and King,

Heart bro - ken with sor - row, He died for our sins.
The third day He rose, and rolled it a - way.
And an - gels de - clared He is com - ing a - gain.

REFRAIN

Now He's a - live, a - live, He a - rose a - gain,

He came from the grave, a vic - tor o - ver sin;

He is my Lord, my Sav - iour King, He died,

a - rose, He's com - ing a - gain.

Our Lord's Return To Earth

James M. Kirk

James M. Kirk

1. I am watch-ing for the com-ing of the glad mil-len-nial day,
2. Je - sus' com - ing back will be the an - swer to earth's sorrowing cry,
3. Yes, the ran - som'd of the Lord shall come to Zi - on then with joy,
4. Then the sin and sor-row, pain and death of this dark world shall cease,

When our bless-ed Lord shall come and catch His wait-ing Bride a - way;
For the knowl-edge of the Lord shall fill the earth and sea and sky;
And in all His ho - ly moun-tain noth - ing hurts or shall de - stroy;
In a glo - rious reign with Je - sus of a thou-sand years of peace;

Oh! my heart is filled with rap - ture as I la - bor, watch and pray,
God shall take a - way all sick - ness and the suff'rer's tears will dry,
Per - fect peace shall reign in ev - 'ry heart, and love with-out al - loy,
All the earth is groan-ing, cry - ing for that day of sweet re-lease,

For our Lord is com - ing back to earth a - gain.
When our bless - ed Je - sus shall come back a - gain.
Af - ter Je - sus shall come back to earth a - gain.
For our Je - sus to come back to earth a - gain.

Oh! our Lord is com - ing back to earth a - gain,
is com - ing back to earth a - gain,

Yes, our Lord is com - ing back to earth a - gain,
is com - ing back to earth a - gain,

Sa - tan will be bound a thou - sand years, we'll have no tempt-er then,

Af - ter Je - sus shall come back to earth a - gain.

Hallelujah! We Shall Rise

J. E. Thomas
4v. R. E. Winsett

J. E. Thomas

1. In the res - ur - rec - tion morn - ing, When the trump of
2. In the res - ur - rec - tion morn - ing, What a meet - ing
3. In the res - ur - rec - tion morn - ing, Bless-ed tho't it
4. In the res - ur - rec - tion morn - ing, We shall meet Him

God shall sound,
it will be, We shall rise, Hal - le - lu - jah! we shall rise!
is to me,
in the air,

Then the saints will come re - joic - ing, And no tears will
When our fa - thers and our moth - ers, And our loved ones
I shall see my bless-ed Sav - iour, Who so free - ly
And be car - ried up to glo - ry, To our home so

e'er be found,
we shall see, We shall rise, Hal - le - lu - jah! we shall
died for me,
bright and fair,

I Shall Be Changed

W. L. (Bill) Hopper   W. L. (Bill) Hopper

1. If the Lord could speak this world in - to ex - is - tence,
2. When the trump of God shall sound on that great morn - ing,

And could hang the moon and stars up in the sky, up in the sky;
And the Sav - iour shall de - scend from heav-en fair, from heav - en fair;

Then I know that He can change this mor - tal bod - y, praise His name,
When the graves of sleep-ing saints are burst-ing o - pen, o - pen wide,

I'll be changed in the twin - kling of an eye, of an eye.
I'll be changed and shall meet them in the air, in the air.

I shall be changed - - - oh, hal - le - lu - jah, praise the Lord!

I shall be changed - - - some by and by, some by and by;

When the dead in Christ shall rise to meet Je - sus in the skies,

I'll be changed in the twin - kling of an eye, of an eye.

Old-Time Power

Charlie D. Tillman

Charlie D. Tillman

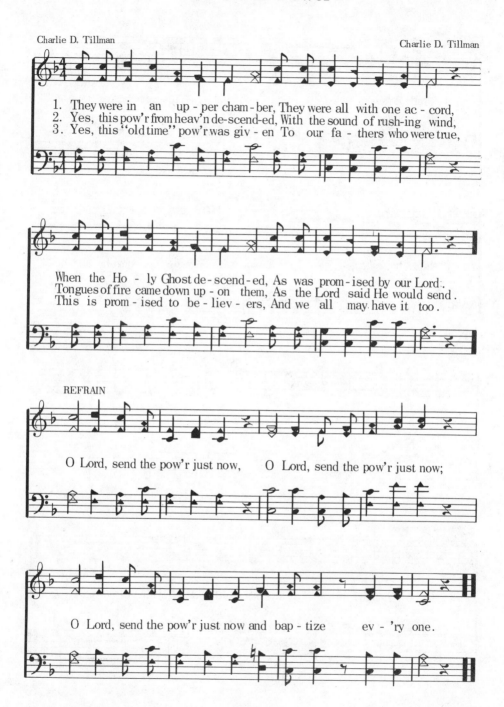

1. They were in an up-per cham-ber, They were all with one ac-cord,
2. Yes, this pow'r from heav'n de-scend-ed, With the sound of rush-ing wind,
3. Yes, this "old time" pow'r was giv-en To our fa-thers who were true,

When the Ho-ly Ghost de-scend-ed, As was prom-ised by our Lord.
Tongues of fire came down up-on them, As the Lord said He would send.
This is prom-ised to be-liev-ers, And we all may have it too.

REFRAIN

O Lord, send the pow'r just now, O Lord, send the pow'r just now;

O Lord, send the pow'r just now and bap-tize ev-'ry one.

Fill Me Now

E. R. Stokes

Jno. R. Sweney

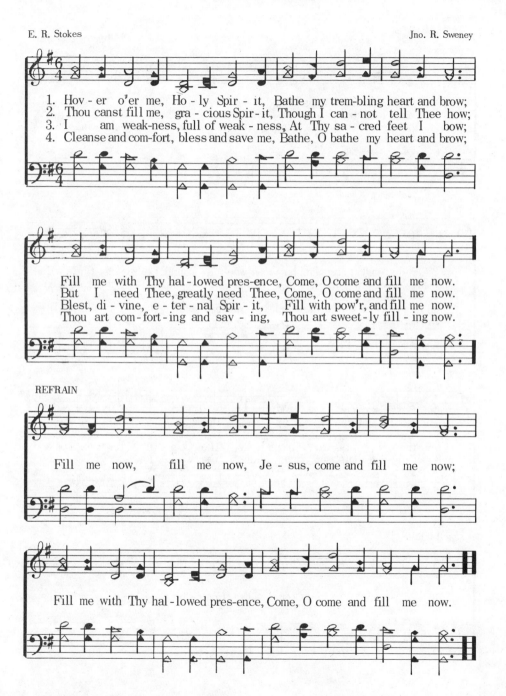

1. Hov-er o'er me, Ho-ly Spir-it, Bathe my trem-bling heart and brow;
2. Thou canst fill me, gra-cious Spir-it, Though I can-not tell Thee how;
3. I am weak-ness, full of weak-ness, At Thy sa-cred feet I bow;
4. Cleanse and com-fort, bless and save me, Bathe, O bathe my heart and brow;

Fill me with Thy hal-lowed pres-ence, Come, O come and fill me now.
But I need Thee, greatly need Thee, Come, O come and fill me now.
Blest, di-vine, e-ter-nal Spir-it, Fill with pow'r, and fill me now.
Thou art com-fort-ing and sav-ing, Thou art sweet-ly fill-ing now.

REFRAIN

Fill me now, fill me now, Je-sus, come and fill me now;

Fill me with Thy hal-lowed pres-ence, Come, O come and fill me now.

The Comforter Has Come

F. Bottome

William J. Kirkpatrick

1. Oh, spread the ti - dings 'round, wher - ev - er man is found, Wher -
2. The long, long night is past, the morn - ing breaks at last, And
3. Lo, the great King of kings, with heal - ing in His wings, To
4. Oh, bound-less love di - vine! how shall this tongue of mine To

ev - er hu - man hearts and hu - man woes a - bound; Let ev - 'ry Chris - tian
hushed the dread-ful wail and fu - ry of the blast, As o'er the gold - en
ev - 'ry cap - tive soul a full de - liv'rance brings; And thro' the va - cant
wond'ring mor - tals tell the match-less grace di - vine - That I a child of

tongue pro - claim the joy - ful sound: The Com - fort - er has come!
hills the day ad - vanc - es fast! The Com - fort - er has come!
cells the song of tri - umph rings; The Com - fort - er has come!
hell, should in His im - age shine! The Com - fort - er has come!

REFRAIN

The Com - fort - er has come, The Com - fort - er has come! The

Ho - ly Ghost from Heav'n, The Fa-ther's prom-ise giv'n; Oh, spread the ti - dings

'round, wher - ev - er man is found - The Com - fort - er has come!

94   **Spirit Of God, Descend**

George Croly   Frederick C. Atkinson

1. Spir - it of God, de - scend up - on my heart, Wean it from
2. Hast Thou not bid us love Thee, God and King? All, all Thine
3. Teach me to feel that Thou art al - ways nigh, Teach me the
4. Teach me to love Thee as Thine an - gels love, One ho - ly

earth, through all its puls - es move; Stoop to my weak-ness, might - y
own, soul, heart and strength and mind; I see Thy cross there teach my
strug - gles of the soul to bear; To check the ris - ing doubt, the
pas - sion fill - ing all my frame; The bap-tism of the heav'n-de -

as Thou art, And make me love Thee as I ought to love.
heart to cling, O let me seek Thee, and O let me find.
reb - el sigh, Teach me the pa - tience of un - an - swered prayer.
scend - ed Dove, My heart an al - tar; and Thy love the flame.

Pentecostal Fire Is Falling

George Bennard

George Bennard

1. In the Book of God so pre-cious we are told of
2. Pen - te -cost can be re - peat -ed, for the Lord is
3. When the Church of Je - sus tar -ries, Pen-te - cost-al

Pen - te - cost, How the bless- ed Lord's dis-
just the same, Yes - ter - day, to - day, for-
fire will fall, Sin and wrong will be de-

ci - ples tar - ried for the Ho - ly Ghost;
ev - er, glo - ry to His pre-cious name!
feat - ed, sin - ners on the Lord will call;

Pen - te - cost - al fire fell on them, burn-ing up their
Saints of God can be vic - to - r'ous, o - ver sin and
She will march to glo - r'ous vic - t'ry o - ver ev - 'ry

sin and dross, Fill - ing them with pow'r for
death and hell, Have a full and free sal -
land and sea, Lift - ing high the blood-stained

serv - ice, mak - ing them a might - y host.
va - tion, and the bless - ed sto - ry tell.
ban - ner, hol - li - ness her mot - to be.

REFRAIN

Pen - te - cost-al fire is fall-ing, praise the Lord, it fell on me,

Pen - te - cost-al fire is fall- ing, broth-er, let it fall on thee!

Pentecostal Power

Charles H. Gabriel

Charles H. Gabriel

1. Lord, as of old at Pen - te - cost Thou didst Thy pow'r display;
2. For might - y works for Thee, pre-pare And strengthen ev - 'ry heart;
3. All self con-sume, all sin de - stroy! With ear-nest zeal en - due;
4. Speak, Lord! be-fore Thy throne we wait, Thy prom - ise we be - lieve;

With cleans-ing, pu - ri - fy - ing flame, De-scend on us to - day.
Come, take pos- ses - sion of Thine own, And nev - er - more de-part.
Each wait-ing heart to work for Thee, O Lord, our faith re - new!
And will not let Thee go un - til The bless-ing we re-ceive.

REFRAIN

Lord, send the old - time pow'r, the Pen - te - cost - al pow'r!

Thy flood - gates of bless - ing on us throw o - pen wide!

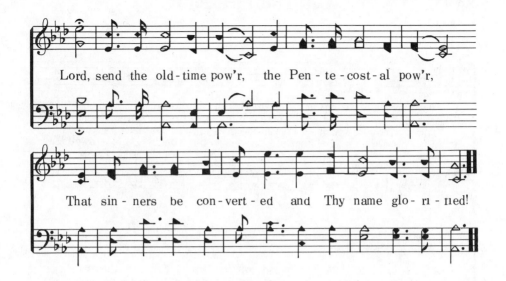

Lord, send the old-time pow'r, the Pen-te-cost-al pow'r,

That sin-ners be con-vert-ed and Thy name glo-ri-fied!

Spirit Of The Living God

Arr. by B. B. McKinney

Spir-it of the liv-ing God, fall fresh on me; Spir-it of the

liv-ing God, fall fresh on me. Break me, melt me, mold me,

fill me. Spir-it of the liv-ing God, fall fresh on me.

Let The Fire Fall

H. Tee   H. Tee

1. They were gath-er'd in an up-per cham-ber, As com-mand-ed by the
2. As E-li-jah we would raise the al-tar, For our tes-ti-mo-ny
3. 'Tis the cov-e-nant-ed prom-ise giv-en, To as man-y as the
4. With a liv-ing coal from off Thy al-tar, Touch our lips to swell Thy

ris-en Lord, and the prom-ise of the Fa-ther, there they sought with
clear and true, Christ the Sav-iour, lov-ing Heal-er, com-ing Lord, Bap-
Lord shall call, To the fa-thers, and their chil-dren, to Thy peo-ple
won-drous praise To ex-tol Thee, bless, a-dore Thee and our songs of

one ac-cord, oh, hal-le-lu-jah; When the Ho-ly Ghost from heav'n de-
tiz-er too, oh, hal-le-lu-jah; Ev-er flow-ing grace and full sal-
one and all, oh, hal-le-lu-jah; So re-joic-ing in Thy Word un-
wor-ship raise, oh, hal-le-lu-jah; Let the clouds of glo-ry now de-

scend-ed, Like a rush-ing wind and tongues of fire, So, dear Lord, we
va-tion, For a ru-in'd race Thy love has plann'd, For this bless-ed
fail-ing, We draw nigh in faith Thy pow'r to know, Come, O come Thou
scend-ing, Fill our hearts with ho-ly ec-sta-sy, Come in all Thy

seek Thy bless-ing, Come with glo - ry now our hearts in - spire.
rev - e - la - tion, For Thy writ-ten Word we dare to stand.
burn-ing Spir - it, Set our hearts with heav'n-ly fire a - glow. Let the
glo - rious ful - ness, Bless-ed Ho - ly Spir - it have Thy way.

fire fall, let the fire fall, Let the heav-n'ly fire fall, We are wait - ing

and ex - pect - ing, While in faith dear Lord, we call, dear Lord, we call, Oh,

let the fire fall, let the fire fall, On Thy prom - ise we de - pend,

From the glo - ry of Thy pres - ence let the Pen - te - cost-al fire de - scend.

Waiting On The Lord

C. F. Weigele   C. F. Weigele

1. Wait - ing on the Lord, for the prom - ise giv - en; Wait - ing
2. Wait - ing on the Lord, giv - ing all to Je - sus; Wait - ing
3. Wait - ing on the Lord, long - ing to mount high - er; Wait - ing

on the Lord, to send from heav - en; Wait - ing on the Lord,
on the Lord, till from sin He frees us; Wait - ing on the Lord,
on the Lord, hav - ing great de - sire; Wait - ing on the Lord,

by our faith re - ceiv - ing;
for the heav'n - ly breez - es; Wait - ing in the up - per room.
for the heav'n - ly fire;

REFRAIN

The pow - - - er! the pow - - - er! Gives
The Pen - te - cos - tal pow'r! the Pen - te - cos - tal pow'r!

vic - t'ry o - ver sin and pu - ri - ty with - in; The pow - - - -
The Pen - te - cos - tal

er! the pow - - - - er! The pow'r they had at Pen - te - cost.
pow'r! the Pen - te - cos - tal pow'r!

100   Breathe On Me, Breath Of God

Edwin Hatch

Robert Jackson

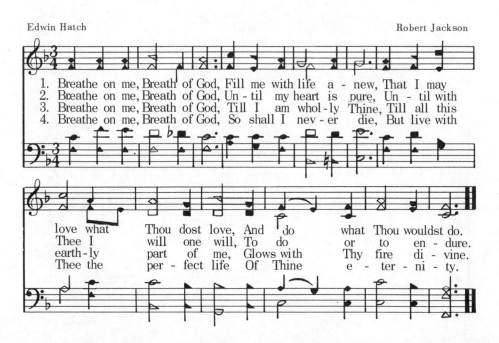

1. Breathe on me, Breath of God, Fill me with life a - new, That I may
2. Breathe on me, Breath of God, Un - til my heart is pure, Un - til with
3. Breathe on me, Breath of God, Till I am whol - ly Thine, Till all this
4. Breathe on me, Breath of God, So shall I nev - er die, But live with

love what Thou dost love, And I do what Thou wouldst do.
Thee I will one will, To do or to en - dure.
earth - ly part of me, Glows with Thy fire di - vine.
Thee the per - fect life Of Thine e - ter - ni - ty.

Send The Fire

1. Thou Christ of burn-ing, cleans-ing flame,
2. God of E - li - jah, hear our cry, Send the fire,
3. 'Tis fire we want, for fire we plead,

send the fire, send the fire! Thy blood bo't gift to -
He'll make us fit to
The fire will meet our

day we claim,
live or die, Send the fire, send the fire, send the fire;
ev - 'ry need,

Look down and see this wait - ing host, Give us
To burn up ev - 'ry trace of sin, To bring
For strength to ev - er do the right, For grace

the prom - ised Ho - ly Ghost, We want an - oth - er
the light and glo - ry in, The rev - o - lu - tion
to con - quer in the fight, For pow'r to walk the

Pen - te - cost,
now be - gin,   Send the fire, send the fire, send the fire.
world in white,

102   **O Blessed Holy Spirit**

Vep Ellis   Vep Ellis

(CHORUS)

O bless - ed Ho - ly Spir - it,   cleans-ing thru and thru,

O'er my tongue it's flood-ing like a riv - er ev - er new;

A lan - guage heav-en hear-eth,   though to earth un - known,

Sweet com-mun-ion, ho - ly un - ion, God and   His own.

'Tis Burning In My Soul

Delia T. White

Wm. J. Kirkpatrick

1. God sent His might - y pow'r To this poor, sin - ful heart,
2. Be - fore the cross I bow, Up - on the al - tar lay
3. No good that I have done, His prom - ise I em - brace;

To keep me ev - 'ry hour, And need - ful grace im - part;
A will - ing of - f'ring now, My all from day to day.
Ac - cept - ed in the Son, He saves me by His grace.

And since His Spir - it came, To take su - preme con - trol,
My Sav - iour paid the price, My name He sweet - ly calls;
All glo - ry be to God! Let hal - le - lu - jahs roll;

The love - en - kin - dled flame Is burn - ing in my soul.
Up - on the sac - ri - fice The fire from heav - en falls.
His love is shed a - broad, The fire is in my soul.

'Tis burn - ing in my soul, 'Tis burn - ing in my soul;

The fire of heav'n - ly love is burn - ing in my soul,
burn - ing in my soul,

The Ho - ly Spir - it came, All glo - ry to His name!

The fire of heav'n - ly love is burn - ing in my soul.
burn - ing in my soul.

The Fire Is Burning

Rev. Johnson Oatman, Jr.

Geo. C. Hugg

1. I've been on Mount Pis-gah's loft-y height, And I've sat-is-fied my
2. I will walk with Je-sus, bless His name, And to be like Him I
3. I my all up-on the al-tar lay, As I to my clos-et
4. By faith's eye I scan the o-cean's foam, And be-yond I see the

long-ing heart's de-sire; For I caught a glimpse of glo-ry bright,
ev-'ry day as-pire; For His love is like a heav'n-ly flame,
lov-ing-ly re-tire; And the flame con-sumes whi le there I pray,
ha-ven I de-sire; There I view the bea-con lights of home,

REFRAIN

And my soul is burn-ing with the fire. Oh, the

fire is burn-ing, yes, 'tis bright-ly burn-ing, Oh, 'tis burn-ing,

burn-ing in my soul; Oh, the fire is burn-ing, yes, 'tis

bright-ly burn-ing, Oh, 'tis burn-ing, burn-ing in my soul.
burn-ing in my soul.

105   Give Me Oil In My Lamp

Arr. by Adger M. Pace

1. Give me oil in my lamp, oil in my lamp, Give me
2. Give me joy in my soul, joy in my soul, Give me

oil in my lamp I pray; Give me oil in my lamp,
joy in my soul I pray; Give me joy in my soul,

keep me shin-ing in the camp, Un-til the break of day.
hal-le-lu-jahs then will roll, Un-til the break of day.

He Abides

Herbert Buffum

D. M. Shanks

1. I'm re-joic-ing night and day, As I walk the pil-grim way,
2. Once my heart was full of sin, Once I had no peace with-in,
3. He is with me ev-'ry-where, And He knows my ev-'ry care,
4. There's no thirst-ing for the things Of the world, they've taken wings,

For the hand of God in all my life I see; And the rea-son
Till I heard how Je-sus died up-on the tree; Then I fell down
I'm as hap-py as a bird and just as free; For the Spir-it
Long a-go I gave them up, and in-stant-ly; All my night was

of my bliss, Yes, the se-cret all is this: That the Com-fort-er a-
at His feet, And there came a peace so sweet, Now the Com-fort-er a-
has con-trol, Je-sus sat-is-fies my soul, Since the Com-fort-er a-
turned to day, All my bur-dens rolled a-way, Now the Com-fort-er a-

REFRAIN

bides with me.
bides with me. He a-bides, He a-bides,
bides with me. He a-bides, He a-bides,
bides with me.

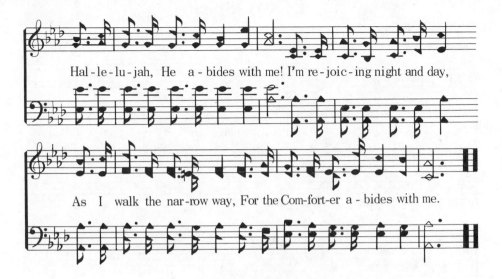

Hal-le-lu-jah, He a-bides with me! I'm re-joic-ing night and day,

As I walk the nar-row way, For the Com-fort-er a-bides with me.

107 Without Him

Unknown

(CHORUS)

With-out Him I could do noth-ing, With-out Him

I'd sure-ly fail; With-out Him I would be

drift-ing, Like a ship with-out a sail.

By My Spirit

Almeda Herrick   Almeda Herrick

1. Is there a moun-tain in your way? Do doubts and fears a-bound?
2. Is there a riv-er in your path, A riv-er deep and wide?
3. Is there a fier-y fur-nace trial Far more than you can bear?
4. Then trust a-lone the might-y God, He speaks, the winds o-bey;

Press on, oh, hear the Spir-it say, This moun-tain shall come down.
Step in, the wa-ters will roll back, You'll reach the oth-er side.
Be-hold the bless-ed Son of God, Is walk-ing with you there.
Take cour-age, then, O faint-ing heart, For you He'll make a way.

REFRAIN

"Not by might, not by pow'r, by my
"Not by might, not by pow'r,

Spir-it saith the Lord of hosts," "Not by might,
"Not by might

not by pow'r, not by pow'r, by my Spir - it saith the

Lord;'' Lord of hosts;'' This moun - tain shall be re - moved.

this moun - tain shall be re - moved, This moun - tain shall

be re - moved, "by My Spir - it" saith the Lord.

Holy Spirit, Use Me

Leon H. Ellis

Leon H. Ellis

Slowly with consecration

1. I would serve Thee, Je - sus, I would be like Thee,
2. Ho - ly Spir - it use me, I sur - ren - der now,

Thy Word is pre - cious, so real to me;
I want to serve Thee, please show me how;

There is on - ly one aim in this life worth - while,
I will wait in pa - tience till I hear from Thee,

To be like Je - sus and be His child.
O Ho - ly Spir - it, grant this, my plea.

Ho - ly Spir - it use me, use me now, take my life to - day,

Use me in Thy serv - ice, pre - cious Lord, this I dai - ly pray;

Make my life a bless - ing, as I go, fill me with Thy fire,

Ho - ly Spir - it use me, use me now, that's my de - sire.

110 Break Thou The Bread Of Life

Mary A. Lathbury

William F. Sherwin

1. Break Thou the bread of life, Dear Lord to me,
2. Bless Thou the truth, dear Lord, To me, to me,
3. Thou art the bread of life, O Lord, to me,
4. O send Thy Spir - it, Lord, Now un - to me,

As Thou didst break the loaves Be - side the sea;
As Thou didst bless the bread By Gal - i - lee;
Thy ho - ly Word the truth That sav - eth me;
That He may touch mine eyes, And make me see:

Be - yond the sa - cred page I seek Thee, Lord;
Then shall all bond - age cease All fet - ters fall;
Give me to eat and live With Thee a - bove;
Show me the truth con - cealed With - in Thy Word,

My spir - it pants for Thee, O liv - ing Word.
And I shall find my peace, My all in all.
Teach me to love Thy truth, For Thou art love.
And in Thy Book re - vealed I see the Lord.

O Word Of God Incarnate

William W. How

Arr. by Felix Mendelssohn

1. O   Word of   God In - car - nate, O Wis - dom from   on high,
2. The   church from   Thee, her Mas - ter, Re - ceived the gift   di - vine,
3. It   float - eth   like a ban - ner Be - fore God's host   un - furled;
4. O   make Thy   church, dear Sav-iour, A lamp of   pur - est gold,

O   Truth un-changed, un - chang-ing, O Light of   our   dark sky:
And   still that light she   lift - eth O'er all the   earth   to shine:
It   shin - eth like a   bea - con A - bove the   dark - ling world:
To   bear be - fore the   na - tions Thy true light as   of   old:

We praise Thee for the ra - diance That from the   hal - lowed   page,
It   is   the   sa-cred cas - ket, Where gems of   truth are   stored;
It   is   the chart and com-pass That o'er life's surg - ing   sea,
O   teach Thy wan - dering pil-grims By this their   path to   trace,

A   lan - tern to   our   foot - steps, Shines on from age   to   age.
It   is   the heav'n-drawn   pic - ture Of Thee, the liv - ing Word.
'Mid mists and rocks and   quick - sands, Still guides, O Christ,   to Thee.
Till clouds and dark-ness   end - ed, They see Thee face   to face.

Wonderful Words Of Life

Philip P. Bliss

Philip P. Bliss

1. Sing them o-ver a-gain to me, Won-der-ful words of life;
2. Christ, the bless-ed One, gives to all, Won-der-ful words of life;
3. Sweet-ly ech-o the gos-pel call, Won-der-ful words of life;

Let me more of their beau-ty see, Won-der-ful words of life;
Sin-ner, list to the lov-ing call, Won-der-ful words of life;
Of-fer par-don and peace to all, Won-der-ful words of life;

Words of life and beau-ty, Teach me faith and du-ty;
All so free-ly giv-en, Woo-ing us to heav-en;
Je-sus, on-ly Sav-iour, Sanc-ti-fy for-ev-er,

REFRAIN

Beau-ti-ful words, won-der-ful words, Won-der-ful words of life;

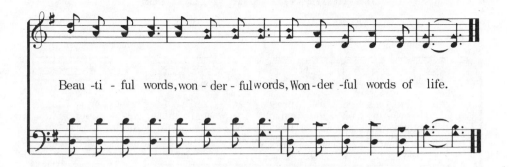

Beau-ti-ful words, won-der-ful words, Won-der-ful words of life.

113 Holy Bible, Book Divine

John Burton, Sr.   William B. Bradbury

1. Ho - ly Bi - ble, Book di - vine, Pre - cious
2. Mine to chide me when I rove, Mine to
3. Mine to com - fort in dis - tress, Suf - fering
4. Mine to tell of joys to come, And the

trea - sure, thou art mine: Mine to tell me whence
show a Sav - iour's love; Mine thou art to guide
in this wil - der - ness; Mine to show, by liv -
reb - el sin - ner's doom; O thou ho - ly Book

I came: Mine to teach me what I am.
and guard; Mine to pun - ish or re - ward.
ing faith, Man can tri - umph o - ver death.
di - vine, Pre - cious treas - ure, thou art mine.

Standing On The Promises

R. Kelso Carter

R. Kelso Carter

114

1. Stand-ing on the prom-is-es of Christ my King,
2. Stand-ing on the prom-is-es that can-not fail,
3. Stand-ing on the prom-is-es of Christ the Lord,
4. Stand-ing on the prom-is-es I can-not fall,

Thru e-ter-nal a-ges let His prais-es ring;
When the howl-ing storms of doubt and fear as-sail,
Bound to Him e-ter-nal-ly by love's strong cord,
Lis-tening ev-ery mo-ment to the Spir-it's call,

Glo-ry in the high-est, I will shout and sing,
By the liv-ing word of God I shall pre-vail,
O-ver-com-ing dai-ly with the Spir-it's Sword,
Rest-ing in my Sav-iour as my all in all,

Stand-ing on the prom-is-es of God.

Stand - ing, stand - ing,
Stand - ing on the prom - is - es, stand - ing on the prom - is - es,

Stand - ing on the prom - is - es of God my Sav - iour;

Stand - ing, stand - ing,
Stand - ing on the prom - is - es, stand - ing on the prom - is - es,

I'm stand - ing on the prom - is - es of God.

A Glorious Church

R. E. Hudson   R. E. Hudson

1. Do you hear them com - ing, broth - er, Throng-ing up the steeps of
2. Do you hear the stir - ring an - thems Fill-ing all the earth and
3. Nev - er fear the clouds of sor - rows, Nev - er fear the storms of
4. Wave the ban - ner, shout His prais - es, For our vic - to - ry is

light, Clad in glo - rious shin-ing gar - ments, Blood-washed, garments
sky, 'Tis a grand, vic - to - rious ar - my, Lift its ban - ner
sin, We shall tri - umph on the mor - row, E - ven now our
nigh! We shall join our con - qu'ring Sav-iour, We shall reign with

REFRAIN

pure and white?
up on high! 'Tis a glo - rious church with-out spot or wrin - kle,
joys be - gin.
Him on high!

Washed in the blood of the Lamb, 'Tis a glo - rious church, with-

out spot or wrin - kle Washed in the blood of the Lamb.

The Church's One Foundation

Samuel J. Stone

Samuel S. Wesley

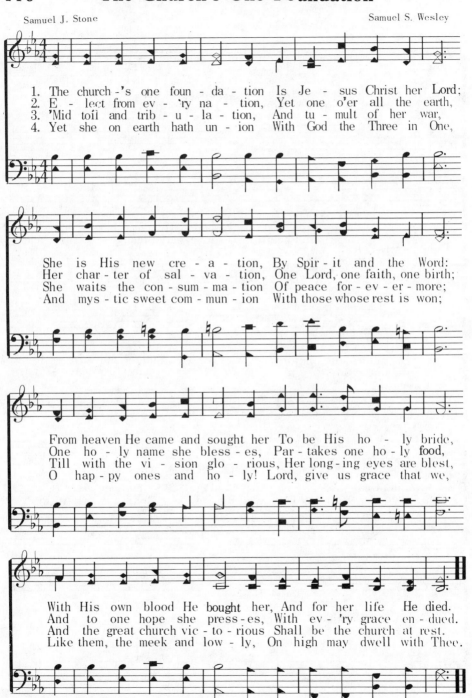

1. The church-'s one foun - da - tion Is Je - sus Christ her Lord;
2. E - lect from ev - 'ry na - tion, Yet one o'er all the earth,
3. 'Mid toil and trib - u - la - tion, And tu - mult of her war,
4. Yet she on earth hath un - ion With God the Three in One,

She is His new cre - a - tion, By Spir - it and the Word:
Her char - ter of sal - va - tion, One Lord, one faith, one birth;
She waits the con - sum - ma - tion Of peace for - ev - er - more;
And mys - tic sweet com - mun - ion With those whose rest is won;

From heaven He came and sought her To be His ho - ly bride,
One ho - ly name she bless - es, Par - takes one ho - ly food,
Till with the vi - sion glo - rious, Her long - ing eyes are blest,
O hap - py ones and ho - ly! Lord, give us grace that we,

With His own blood He bought her, And for her life He died.
And to one hope she press - es, With ev - 'ry grace en - dued.
And the great church vic - to - rious Shall be the church at rest.
Like them, the meek and low - ly, On high may dwell with Thee.

117 Head Of The Church Triumphant

Delton L. Alford

Tune adapted from J. F. Lampe
Delton L. Alford

Joyfully and vigorously

1. Head of the church tri - um - phant, We joy - ful - ly a -
2. O Lord, with joy we praise Thee, For all Thy boun - t'ous

dore Thee, Till Thou ap - pear, Thy mem - bers here, shall
bless - ings, With hearts of love, give thanks to Thee, and

sing like those in glo - ry; We lift our hearts and voic - es
of - fer ad - o - ra - tion; We lift our song to heav - en,

with blest an - tic - i - pa - tion, And cry a - loud and give to
in hon - or to Thy pow - er, We ev - er long to be with

God, the praise of our sal - va - tion.
Thee, and wait for Thy re - turn - ing.

Rise Up, O Men Of God

William P. Merrill

William H. Walter

1. Rise up, O men of God! Have done with less-er things; Give
2. Rise up, O men of God! His king-dom tar-ries long: Bring
3. Rise up, O men of God! The Church for you doth wait, Her
4. Lift high the cross of Christ! Tread where His feet have trod: As

heart and soul and mind and strength To serve the King of kings.
in the day of broth-er-hood And end the night of wrong.
strength un- e -qual to her task: Rise up, and make her great!
broth-ers of the Son of Man Rise up, O men of God.

119 The Church Of God Shall Ever Stand

Harvey Tallent

Harvey Tallent

1. The Church of God shall ev - er stand, This prom-ise Christ hath made;
2. Though all the hosts of hell as - sail, It shall for - e'er en - dure;
3. Some day He'll come to claim His bride, Oh! what re - joic - ing then;

En - dured by God's own might - y hand, For on the rock 'tis laid.
Through storm-y blasts it shall pre-vail And ev - er rest se - cure.
With Him for-ev - er to a - bide Free from the foes of sin.

120 Like A Mighty Army

C. S. Grogan

C. S. Grogan

1. Like a might-y ar-my moves the Church of God,
2. Might-i-er than weap-ons made by men of earth,
3. We will take Her mes-sage far a-cross the sea,

O'er the pow'rs of e-vil we have brave-ly trod;
Is our faith in Je-sus born of vir-gin birth;
Tell each fall-en broth-er Christ doth make men free;

We will press for vic-'try on each bat-tle line,
When the storms are rag-ing fierce on ev-'ry hand,
Shout a-loud the Gos-pel, this our bat-tle cry,

'Til at last we con-quer in this cause di-vine.
An-chored in the Sav-iour, we shall ev-er stand.
Raise the blood-stained ban-ner, keep it wav-ing high.

REFRAIN

Like a might-y ar-my moves the
Like a might-y Chris-tian ar-my moves the

How Firm A Foundation

George Keith

Anna Steck

1. How firm a foun - da - tion, ye saints of the Lord,
2. In ev - 'ry con - di - tion, in sick - ness and health,
3. Fear not, I am with thee; O be not dis - mayed;
4. E'en down to old age all my peo - ple shall prove
5. The soul that on Je - sus doth lean for re - pose,

Is laid for your faith in His ex - cel - lent Word;
In pov - er - ty's vale, or a - bound - ing in wealth,
For I am thy God, and will still give thee aid;
My con - stant e - ter - nal un - change - a - ble love;
I will not, I will not de - sert to his foes;

What more can He say, than to you He hath said,
At home or a - broad, on the land, on the sea,
I'll strength - en thee, help thee, and cause thee to stand,
And when hoar - y hairs shall their tem - ples a - dorn,
That soul, though all hell should en - deav - or to shake,

Ye who un - to Je - sus for ref - uge have fled!
As thy days may de - mand shall thy strength ev - er be.
Up - held by my right - eous om - nip - o - tent hand.
Like lambs they shall still on my bos - om be borne.
I'll nev - er, no nev - er, no nev - er for - sake.

I Know Whom I Have Believed

Daniel W. Whittle

James McGranahan

1. I know not why God's won-drous grace To me He hath made known;
2. I know not how this sav-ing faith To me He did im - part;
3. I know not how the Spir - it moves, Con-vinc-ing men of sin;
4. I know not when my Lord may come, At night or noon-day fair;

Nor why, un-wor - thy, Christ in love Re-deemed me for His own.
Nor how be-liev - ing in His Word Wrought peace with-in my heart.
Re - veal-ing Je - sus thro' the Word, Cre-at-ing faith in Him.
Nor if I'll walk the vale with Him, Or meet Him in the air.

REFRAIN

But "I know whom I have be - liev - ed, and am per -

suad - ed that He is a - ble To keep that which

I've com - mit - ted Un - to Him a - gainst that day."

123 Trust And Obey

John H. Sammis

Daniel B. Towner

1. When we walk with the Lord in the light of His Word
2. Not a bur - den we bear, Not a sor - row we share,
3. But we nev - er can prove The de - lights of His love
4. Then in fel - low -ship sweet We will sit at His feet

What a glo - ry He sheds on our way! While we do His good will,
But our toil He doth rich - ly re - pay; Not a grief or a loss,
Un - til all on the al - tar we lay; For the fa - vor He shows
Or we'll walk by His side in the way; What He says we will do,

He a-bides with us still, And with all who will trust and o - bey.
Not a frown or a cross, But is blest if we trust and o - bey.
And the joy He be-stows Are for them who will trust and o - bey.
Where He sends we will go; Nev - er fear, on - ly trust and o - bey.

REFRAIN

Trust and o - bey, for there's no oth - er way To be

hap - py in Je - sus, But to trust and o - bey.

Faith For Today

Leon H. Ellis

Leon H. Ellis

1. There is a high-way of faith for to-day, Lead-ing a-bove all our
2. Thou-sands be-fore us have trav-eled this road, High a-bove moun-tains of
3. Faith gives us vic - t'ry o'er all of our fears, Free-dom from sick-ness and

fears;　For those who dare here to trav - el its way, Je - sus will
sin;　Press-ing their jour-ney tho' heav - y the load, Striv-ing a
sin;　Faith brings the pres-ence of Je - sus so near, Bless-ing a -

REFRAIN

ev - er be near.
life crown to win.　Faith for to - day, faith all the
gain and a - gain.

way,　Now and for e - ter - ni - ty;　Faith in the

Lord, faith in His Word, Liv - ing thru Cal - va - ry.

My Hope Is Built

125

Edward Mote

William B. Bradbury

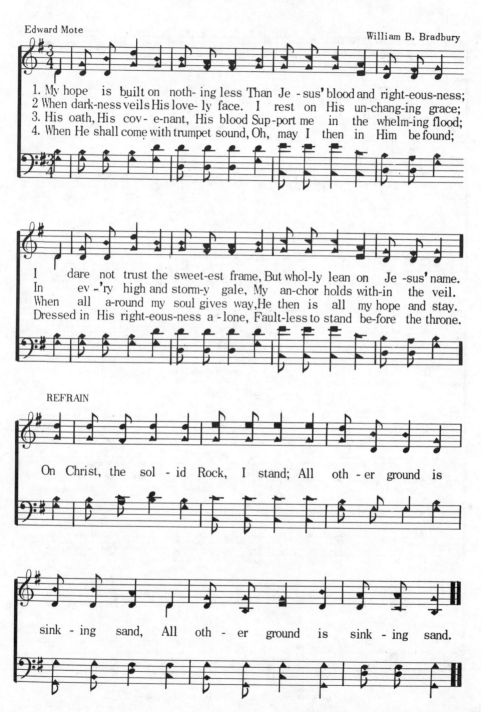

1. My hope is built on noth- ing less Than Je -sus' blood and right-eous-ness;
2. When dark-ness veils His love- ly face. I rest on His un-chang-ing grace;
3. His oath, His cov - e-nant, His blood Sup-port me in the whelm-ing flood;
4. When He shall come with trumpet sound, Oh, may I then in Him be found;

I dare not trust the sweet-est frame, But whol-ly lean on Je -sus' name.
In ev -'ry high and storm-y gale, My an-chor holds with-in the veil.
When all a-round my soul gives way, He then is all my hope and stay.
Dressed in His right-eous-ness a -lone, Fault-less to stand be-fore the throne.

REFRAIN

On Christ, the sol - id Rock, I stand; All oth - er ground is

sink - ing sand, All oth - er ground is sink - ing sand.

126 A Deep, Settled Peace

(HIDDEN PEACE)

John S. Brown

L. O. Brown

1. I can-not tell thee whence it came, This peace with-in my breast;
2. Be-neath the toil and care of life, This hid-den stream flows on;
3. I can-not tell the half of love, Un-feigned, supreme di-vine,
4. I can-not tell thee why He chose To suf-fer and to die,

But this I know, there fills my soul A strange and tran-quil rest.
My wea-ry soul no long-er thrists, Nor am I sad and lone.
That caused my dark-est in-most self With beams of hope to shine.
But if I suf-fer here with Him I'll reign with Him on high.

REFRAIN

There's a deep set-tled peace in my soul, (in my soul,) There's a

deep set-tled peace in my soul; (in my soul;) Tho' the

bil-lows of sin near me roll, He a-bides, Christ a-bides.

He Leadeth Me!

Joseph H. Gilmore

William B. Bradbury

1. He lead - eth me! O bless - ed tho't! O words with heav'n - ly
2. Some-times 'mid scenes of deep-est gloom, Some-times where Eden's
3. Lord, I would clasp Thy hand in mine, Nor ev - er mur - mur
4. And when my task on earth is done, When, by Thy grace, the

com - fort fraught! Whate'er I do, wher-e'er I be, Still 'tis God's
bow-ers bloom, By wa-ters still, o'er trou - bled sea, Still 'tis His
nor re - pine, Con - tent, what-ev - er lot I see, Since 'tis Thy
vic - t'ry's won, E'en death's cold wave I will not flee, Since God thro'

REFRAIN

hand that lead - eth me!
hand that lead - eth me!
hand that lead - eth me! He lead-eth me, He lead-eth me,
Jor - dan lead - eth me!

By His own hand He lead - eth me: His faith-ful fol - l'wer

I would be, For by His hand He lead - eth me.

Christt The Lord Shall Triumph

Edward L. Williams

Edward L. Williams

1. The Lord is my for-tress strong, And might-y is He to save;
2. The Lord ev-'ry bat-tle wins, For He's ev-'ry day the same;
3. Oh, come ye and praise the Lord, And bring forth the di-a-dem;

He holds the pow-er, O'er death, hell, and o'er the grave.
Vic-t'ry is prom-ised, Be-lieve on His pre-cious name.
Oh hal-le-lu-jah, All pow-er be-longs to Him.

REFRAIN

The Lord shall o-ver-come, The true way shall pre-vail;
The Lord The true

And all oth-er foes will fail, For Christ, the Lord, shall tri-umph.

Have Faith In God

B. B. McKinney

B. B. McKinney

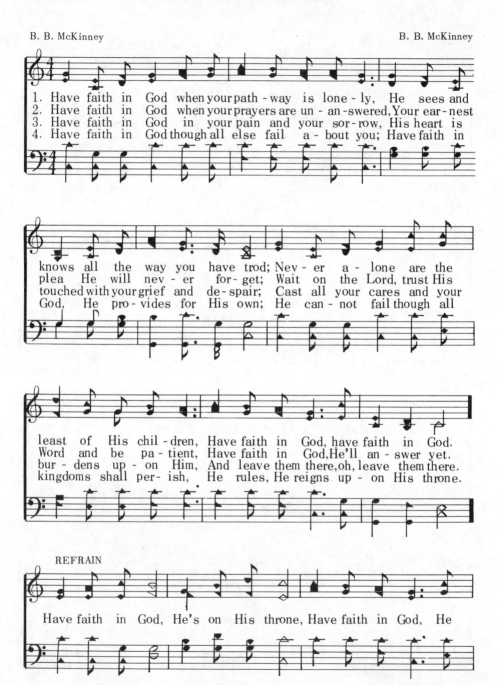

1. Have faith in God when your path-way is lone-ly, He sees and
2. Have faith in God when your prayers are un-an-swered, Your ear-nest
3. Have faith in God in your pain and your sor-row, His heart is
4. Have faith in God though all else fail a-bout you; Have faith in

knows all the way you have trod; Nev-er a-lone are the
plea He will nev-er for-get; Wait on the Lord, trust His
touched with your grief and de-spair; Cast all your cares and your
God, He pro-vides for His own; He can-not fail though all

least of His chil-dren, Have faith in God, have faith in God.
Word and be pa-tient, Have faith in God, He'll an-swer yet.
bur-dens up-on Him, And leave them there, oh, leave them there.
kingdoms shall per-ish, He rules, He reigns up-on His throne.

REFRAIN

Have faith in God, He's on His throne, Have faith in God, He

watch - es o'er His own; He can - not fail,

He must pre - vail, Have faith in God, have faith in God.

130

John Fawcett

Blest Be The Tie

Arr. by Lowell Mason

1. Blest be the tie that binds Our hearts in
2. Be - fore our Fa - ther's throne We pour our
3. We share our mu - tual woes, Our mu - tual
4. When we a - sun - der part, It gives us

Chris - tian love; The fel - low - ship of
ar - dent pray'rs; Our fears, our hopes, our
bur - dens bear; And of - ten for each
in - ward pain; But we shall still be

kin - dred minds Is like to that a - bove.
aims are one, Our com - forts and our cares.
oth - er flows The sym - pa - thiz - ing tear.
joined in heart, And hope to meet a - gain.

It Is Well With My Soul

Horatio G. Spafford

Philip P. Bliss

1. When peace, like a riv - er, at - tend - eth my way,
2. Though Sa - tan should buf - fet, though tri - als should come,
3. My sin -- oh, the bliss of this glo - ri - ous thought,
4. And, Lord, haste the day when the faith shall be sight,

When sor - rows like sea bil - lows roll; What - ev - er my lot,
Let this blest as - sur - ance con - trol; That Christ has re - gard-
My sin not in part, but the whole Is nailed to the cross
The clouds be rolled back as a scroll; The trump shall re - sound

Thou hast taught me to say, It is well, it is well
ed my help - less es - tate, And hath shed His own blood
and I bear it no more, Praise the Lord, praise the Lord,
and the Lord shall de - scend, "E - ven so," it is well

REFRAIN

with my soul.
for my soul. It is well with my
oh my soul. It is well
with my soul.

soul,   It is well, it is well with my soul.
with my soul,

132   I Can, I Will, I Do Believe

Traditional

1. I'm kneel-ing at the mer-cy seat,   I'm kneel-ing
2. Re-fin-ing fire, go thru my heart,   Re-fin-ing
3. O that it now from heav'n might fall,   O that it

REF - I can, I will, I do be-lieve,   I can, I

at the mer-cy seat,   I'm kneel-ing at the
fire, go thru my heart,   Re-fin-ing fire, go
now from heav'n might fall,   O that it now from

will, I do be-lieve,   I can, I will, I

FINE
D. C. for Ref.

mer-cy seat,   Where Je-sus an-swers pray'r.
thru my heart,   Il-lu-mi-nate my soul.
heav'n might fall,   And all my sins con-sume.

do be-lieve,   That Je-sus saves me now.

Blessed Assurance

Fanny J. Crosby

Mrs. Joseph F. Knapp

1. Bless - ed as - sur - ance, Je - sus is mine! Oh, what a
2. Per - fect sub - mis - sion, per - fect de - light, Vi - sions of
3. Per - fect sub - mis - sion, all is at rest, I in my

fore - taste of glo - ry di - vine! Heir of sal - va - tion,
rap - ture now burst on my sight: An - gels de - scend - ing
Sav - iour am hap - py and blest: Watch - ing and wait - ing,

pur - chase of God, Born of His Spir - it, wash'd in His blood.
bring from a - bove Ech - oes of mer - cy, whis - pers of love.
look - ing a - bove, Fill'd with His good-ness, lost in His love.

REFRAIN

This is my sto - ry, this is my song, Prais - ing my

Sav - iour all the day long; This is my sto - ry, this is my

song, Prais - ing my Sav - iour all the day long.

134   Jesus Is The Sweetest Name I Know

CHORUS

Lela Long

Je - sus is the sweet - est name I know, And He's just the same

as His love - ly name, And that's the rea - son why I love Him so;

Rall.

Oh, Je - sus is the sweet - est name I know.

He'll Keep Me

Bennie S. Triplett

Bennie S. Triplett

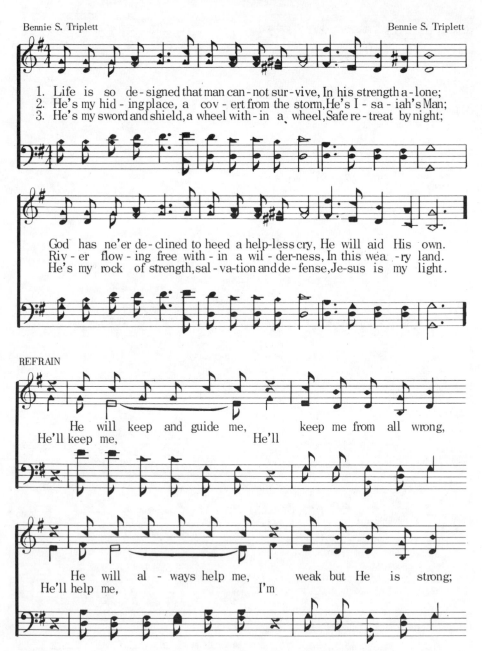

1. Life is so de-signed that man can-not sur-vive, In his strength a-lone;
2. He's my hid-ing place, a cov-ert from the storm, He's I-sa-iah's Man;
3. He's my sword and shield, a wheel with-in a wheel, Safe re-treat by night;

God has ne'er de-clined to heed a help-less cry, He will aid His own.
Riv-er flow-ing free with-in a wil-der-ness, In this wea-ry land.
He's my rock of strength, sal-va-tion and de-fense, Je-sus is my light.

REFRAIN

He will keep and guide me, keep me from all wrong,
He'll keep me, He'll

He will al-ways help me, weak but He is strong;
He'll help me, I'm

He knows how to show me the path that leads a - bove,
He'll show me the

Keep me in His arms, He'll keep me in His love.
He'll keep me safe in His love.

136

Jesus Never Fails

(CHORUS)

A. A. Luther   A. A. Luther

Je - sus nev - er fails, Je - sus nev - er fails;

Heav'n and earth may pass a - way, But Je - sus nev - er fails.

Trusting Jesus

T. L. Gilley, Jr.   T. L. Gilley, Jr.

1. I am fac - ing home at last, my wand'ring days are past,
2. He will lead me by the hand, straight to the prom - ised land,

And my load of sin is cast on Christ the bless - ed Lord;
At His side I then shall stand with saints at home a - bove;

I was weak but now I'm strong, while march - ing with the throng,
In the pal - ace of the king, where joy - bells ev - er ring,

Go - ing to the land of song, Re - ceive a great re - ward.
Soon my hap - py soul will sing, Where all is peace and love.

REFRAIN

I'm com - plete - ly trust - ing Je - sus, Ev - 'ry hour of ev - 'ry day; For He'll for-sake me nev-er, But go with me all the way.

138 All I Need

C. P. Jones

C. P. Jones

1. Je - sus Christ is made to me,
2. He re - deemed me when he died,
3. To my Sav - iour will I cleave,
4. Glo - ry, glo - ry to the Lamb,

All I need, all I need;

He a - lone is all my plea,
I with Him was cru - ci - fied,
He will not His ser - vant leave,
By His Spir - it sealed I am,

He is all I need.

REFRAIN

Wis - dom, righteous - ness and pow'r, Ho - li - ness for - ev - er - more,

My re - demp - tion full and sure, He is all I need.

Whispering Hope

Alice Hawthorne

Arr. John T. Cook

1. Soft as the voice of an an - gel, Breath - ing a les - son un -
2. If in the dusk of the twi - light, Dim be the re - gion a -
3. Hope as an an - chor so stead - fast, Rends the dark veil for the

heard, Hope with a gen - tle per - sua - sion, Whis - pers her
far, Will not the deep - en - ing dark - ness bright - en the
soul, Whith - er the Mas - ter has en - tered, Rob - bing the

com - fort - ing word; Wait till the dark - ness is
glim - mer - ing star? Then when the night is up -
grave of its goal; Come, then, O come glad fru -

o - ver, Wait till life's tem - pest is done,
on us, Why should the heart sink a - way?
i - tion, Come to my sad wea - ry heart,

Arr. Copyright 1947 by The Stamps Quartet Music Co., Inc., in "World Wide Church Songs."

Hope for the sun-shine to-mor-row, Aft - er the show - er is
When the dark mid - night is o - ver, Watch for the break - ing of
Come, O Thou blest hope of glo - ry Nev - er, O nev - er de -

REFRAIN

gone. Whis - - per - ing hope, O how
day. Whis - per - ing hope, whis - per - ing hope,
part.

wel - - - come Thy voice; Mak - - -
Wel - come Thy voice, O how wel - come Thy voice; Mak - ing my heart,

ing my heart in its sor - row re - joice.
mak - ing my heart in its sor - row re - joice.

Go To Jesus

Delma Day

T. W. Day

1. When the cares of life get heav-y, and there seems to be no way,
2. Earth-ly friends may all for-sake you, and you feel you're all a - lone,
3. Je - sus un - der-stands your problems, He has passed this way be-fore,

Go to Je-sus, trust in Him;
Je - sus, go to Je-sus, al - ways trust in Him;

He is al-ways near to help you, turn your dark-est night to day,
He is clos-er than a broth-er, you can claim Him as your own,
He will be your guide and captain, from this earth to heav-en's shore,

Go to Je-sus, trust in Him.
Je - sus, go to Je-sus, trust in Him, trust in Him.

REFRAIN

What He has done for oth - ers, He'll sure-ly do for you,

Just trust in Him com-plete-ly, and He will see you through;

Wor-ry not a-bout the fu - ture, don't give up when things look dim,

Go to Je-sus, trust in Him.
Je-sus, go to Je-sus, trust in Him, trust in Him.

In The Shadow Of The Cross

Berniece M. Brostrom

Wesley H. Daniel

1. As we jour-ney on t'ward heav-en's shin-ing goal,
2. On that tree of sor-row Je-sus died for all,
3. There are souls to res-cue, there are souls to save,

We may suf-fer pain and loss;
Took up-on Him-self our dross;
On the sea of life they toss;

Bur-dens on-ly bring us bless-ings if we live,
As I see Him there I long to ev-er live,
May we be a light and teach them how to live,

In the shad-ow of the cross.

Are you liv - ing in the shad - ow of the cross,

Where the Sav - iour took your place?

By the cross He'll lead us to that home a - bove,

There we'll see Him face to face.

He Hideth My Soul

Fanny J. Crosby

William J. Kirpatrick

1. A won-der-ful Sav-iour is Je-sus my Lord, A won-der-ful
2. A won-der-ful Sav-iour is Je-sus my Lord, He tak-eth my
3. With num-ber-less bless-ings each mo-ment He crowns, And filled with His
4. When clothed in His bright-ness, trans-port-ed I rise To meet Him in

Sav-iour to me; He hid-eth my soul in the cleft of the rock,
bur-den a-way; He hold-eth me up, and I shall not be moved,
full-ness di-vine, I sing in my rap-ture, oh, glo-ry to God
clouds of the sky, His per-fect sal-va-tion, His won-der-ful love

REFRAIN

Where riv-ers of pleas-ure I see.
He giv-eth me strength as my day.
For such a Re-deem-er as mine! He hid-eth my soul
I'll shout with the mil-lions on high.

in the cleft of the rock that shad-ows a dry, thirst-y land;

He hid-eth my life in the depths of His love, And cov-ers me

there with His hand, And cov-ers me there with His hand.

143 ## Oh, How I Love Jesus

CHORUS

Oh, how I love Je-sus, Oh, how I love Je-sus,

Oh, how I love Je-sus, Be-cause He first loved me.

144 Come And Dine

Words and melody by C. C. Widmeyer

S. H. Bolton

1. Je - sus has a ta - ble spread Where the saints of God are fed
2. The dis - ci - ples came to land, Thus o - bey - ing Christ's com - mand
3. Soon the Lamb will take His bride To be ev - er at His side,

He in - vites His chos - en peo - ple, "Come and dine;"
For the Mas - ter called un - to them, "Come and dine;"
All the host of heav - en will as - sem - bled be;

With His man - na He doth feed And sup - plies our ev - 'ry need:
There they found their hearts'de - sire, Bread and fish up - on the fire;
O, 'twill be a glo - rious sight, All the saints in spot - less white;

O 'tis sweet to sup with Je - sus all the time!
Thus He sat - is - fies the hun - gry ev - 'ry - time.
And with Je - sus they will feast e - ter - nal - ly.

REFRAIN

"Come and dine," the Mas-ter call-eth, "Come and dine;"
O come and dine;

You may feast at Je-sus' ta-ble all the time;
O come and dine;

He who fed the mul-ti-tude, Turned the wa-ter in-to wine,

To the hun-gry call-eth now, "Come and dine."

145 He Keeps Me Singing

Luther B. Bridgers

Luther B. Bridgers

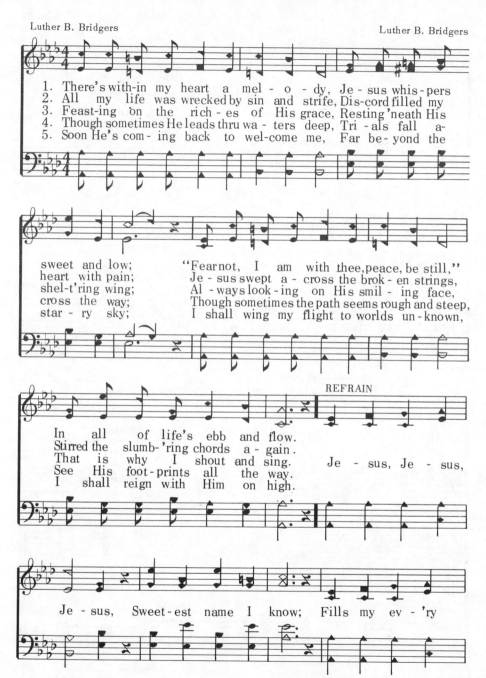

1. There's with-in my heart a mel - o - dy, Je - sus whis-pers
2. All my life was wrecked by sin and strife, Dis-cord filled my
3. Feast-ing on the rich - es of His grace, Resting 'neath His
4. Though sometimes He leads thru wa - ters deep, Tri - als fall a-
5. Soon He's com - ing back to wel-come me, Far be - yond the

sweet and low; "Fear not, I am with thee, peace, be still,"
heart with pain; Je - sus swept a - cross the brok - en strings,
shel-t'ring wing; Al - ways look - ing on His smil - ing face,
cross the way; Though sometimes the path seems rough and steep,
star - ry sky; I shall wing my flight to worlds un - known,

REFRAIN

In all of life's ebb and flow.
Stirred the slumb- 'ring chords a - gain.
That is why I shout and sing. Je - sus, Je - sus,
See His foot - prints all the way.
I shall reign with Him on high.

Je - sus, Sweet - est name I know; Fills my ev' - 'ry

Copyright 1909, Renewal 1937. Broadman Press. Used by permission.

long - ing, Keeps me sing - ing as I go.

146   Friendship With Jesus

Major Ludgate

Arr. from Foster

1. A friend of Je - sus! Oh, what bliss That one so vile as I
2. A Friend when oth - er friendships cease, A Friend when oth - ers fail,
3. A Friend when life's short race is o'er, A Friend when earth is past,

Should ev - er have a Friend like this To lead me to the sky!
A Friend who gives me joy and peace A Friend when foes as - sail.
A Friend to meet on heav - en's shore, A Friend when home at last.

REFRAIN

Friend - ship with Je - sus! Fel - low - ship di - vine!

Oh, what bless - ed, sweet com - mun - ion! Je - sus is a Friend of mine.

Count Your Blessings

Johnson Oatman, Jr.

Edwin O. Excell

1. When up - on life's bil - lows you are tem - pest tossed,
2. Are you ev - er bur - dened with a load of care?
3. When you look at oth - ers with their lands and gold,
4. So, a - mid the con - flict, wheth - er great or small,

When you are dis - cour - aged, think - ing all is lost,
Does the cross seem heav - y you are called to bear?
Think that Christ has prom - ised you His wealth un - told;
Do not be dis - cour - aged, God is o - ver all;

Count your man - y bless - ings, name them one by one,
Count your man - y bless - ings, ev - 'ry doubt will fly,
Count your man - y bless - ings, mon - ey can - not buy
Count your man - y bless - ings, an - gels will at - tend,

And it will sur - prise you what the Lord hath done.
And you will be sing - ing as the days go by.
Your re - ward in heav - en, nor your home on high.
Help and com - fort give you to your jour - ney's end.

REFRAIN

Count _____ your bless-ings, name them one _____ by _____ one;
Count your man -y bless-ings, _____ name them one by _____ one;

Count _____ your bless-ings, See what God _____ hath _____ done;
Count your man - y bless - ings, _____ see what God hath _____ done;

rit. . . . .

Count _____ your bless-ings, _____ name them one by _____ one;
Count your man - y bless-ings,

a tempo

Count your man - y bless - ings, see what God hath done.

He Included Me

Johnson Oatman, Jr.
Hampton H. Sewell

1. I am so hap-py in Christ to-day, That I go sing-ing a-
2. Glad-ly I read, who-so-ev-er may Come to the foun-tain of
3. Ev-er God's Spir-it is say-ing, Come! Hear the Bride say-ing, no
4. Free-ly come drink words the soul to thrill! O with what joy they my

long my way; Yes, I'm so hap-py to know and say,
life to-day; But when I read it I al-ways say,
long-er roam; But I am sure while they're call-ing home,
heart do fill! For when He said, "Who-so-ev-er will,"

REFRAIN

"Je-sus in-clud-ed me too." Je-sus in-clud-ed me, Yes,

He in-clud-ed me, When the Lord said "Who-so-ev-er," He in-

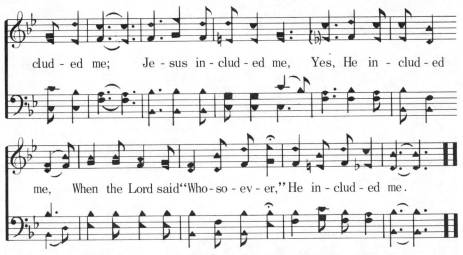

clud - ed me; Je - sus in - clud - ed me, Yes, He in - clud - ed

me, When the Lord said "Who - so - ev - er," He in - clud - ed me.

149   There's A Wideness In God's Mercy

Frederick W. Faber

Lizzie S. Tourjee

1. There's a   wide - ness in God's   mer - cy, Like the wide -
2. There is   wel - come for the   sin - ner, And more grac -
3. If   our   love were but more   sim - ple We should take

ness   of   the sea; There's a   kind - ness   in His
es   for   the good; There is   mer - cy   with the
Him   at   His word; And our   lives would   be all

jus - tice, Which   is   more   than   lib - er - ty.
Sav - iour; There   is   heal - ing   in   His   blood.
sun - shine In   the   sweet - ness   of   our   Lord.

150 Tell Me The Old, Old Story

Kate Hankey

W. H. Doane

1. Tell me the Old, Old Sto - ry, Of un - seen things a - bove,
2. Tell me the sto - ry slow - ly, That I may take it in,
3. Tell me the sto - ry soft - ly, With ear - nest tones and grave;
4. Tell me the same old sto - ry, When you have cause to fear

Of Je - sus and His glo - ry, Of Je - sus and His love;
That won - der - ful re - demp - tion, God's rem - e - dy for sin;
Re - mem - ber I'm the sin - ner Whom Je - sus came to save;
That this world's emp - ty glo - ry Is cost - ing me too dear;

Tell me the sto - ry sim - ply, As to a lit - tle child,
Tell me the sto - ry of - ten, For I for - get so soon,
Tell me the sto - ry al - ways, If you would real - ly be,
Yes, and when that world's glo - ry Is dawn - ing on my soul,

For I am weak and wea - ry, And help - less and de - filed.
The "ear - ly dew" of morn - ing Has passed a - way at noon.
In an - y time of trou - ble, A com - fort - er to me.
Tell me the Old, Old Sto - ry: "Christ Je - sus makes thee whole."

Tell me the Old, Old Sto - ry, Tell me the Old, Old Sto - ry,

Tell me the Old, Old Sto - ry Of Je - sus and His love.

151   Jesus Loves The Little Children

George F. Root   George F. Root

1. Je - sus loves the lit - tle chil - dren, All the chil - dren of the
2. Je - sus died for all the chil - dren, All the chil - dren of the

world, Red and yel - low, black and white, All are pre - cious in His
world, Red and yel - low, black and white, All are pre - cious in His

sight, Je - sus loves the lit - tle chil - dren of the world.
sight, Je - sus died for all the chil - dren of the world.

I Love To Tell The Story

Katherine Hankey

William G. Fischer

1. I love to tell the sto - ry Of un - seen things a - bove,
2. I love to tell the sto - ry; 'Tis pleas - ant to re - peat
3. I love to tell the sto - ry; For those who know it best

Of Je - sus and His glo - ry, Of Je - sus and His love:
What seems each time I tell it, More won - der - ful - ly sweet:
Seem hun - ger - ing and thirst - ing To hear it, like the rest:

I love to tell the sto - ry Be - cause I know 'tis true;
I love to tell the sto - ry, For some have nev - er heard
And when in scenes of glo - ry I sing the new, new song,

It sat - is - fies my long - ings As noth - ing else can do.
The mes - sage of sal - va - tion From God's own ho - ly Word.
'Twill be the old, old sto - ry That I have loved so long.

REFRAIN

I love to tell the sto - ry, 'Twill be my theme in glo - ry,

To tell the old, old sto - ry of Je - sus and His love.

153   Enough For Me

Rev. E. A. Hoffman   Rev. E. A. Hoffman

1. O love sur - pass-ing knowledge! O grace, so full and free!
2. O won - der - ful sal - va - tion! From sin He makes me free!
3. O blood of Christ, so pre - cious, Poured out on Cal - va - ry!

I know that Je - sus saves me,
I feel the sweet as - sur - ance, And that's e - nough for me.
I feel its cleans-ing pow - er,

REFRAIN

And that's e - nough for me, O that's e - nough for me;

I know that Je - sus saves me, And that's e - nough for me.

154   The Way Of The Cross Leads Home

Jessie Brown Pounds

Charles H. Gabriel

1. I must needs go home by the way of the cross, There's no oth-er
2. I must needs go on in the blood-sprinkled way, The path that the
3. Then I bid fare-well to the way of the world, To walk in it

way but this; I shall ne'er get sight of the gates of light,
Sav - iour trod, If I ev - er climb to the heights sub-lime,
nev - er - more; For my Lord says "Come," and I seek my home,

REFRAIN

If the way of the cross I miss.
Where the soul is at home with God.
Where He waits at the o - pen door.

The way of the cross leads

home,   The way of the cross leads home;   It is
leads home,   leads home;

sweet to know as I on-ward go, The way of the cross leads home.

155   O Master, Let Me Walk With Thee

Washington Gladden   H. Percy Smith

1. O, Mas-ter, let me walk with Thee In low-ly paths
2. Help me the slow of heart to move By some clear, win-
3. Teach me Thy pa-tience; still with Thee In clos-er, dear-
4. In hope that sends a shin-ing ray Far down the fu-

of serv - ice free; Tell me Thy se - cret, help
ning word of love; Teach me the way - ward feet
er com - pa - ny, In work that keeps faith sweet
ture's broad' - ning way, In peace that on - ly Thou

me bear The strain of toil, the fret of care.
to stay, And guide them in the home - ward way.
and strong, In trust that tri - umphs o - ver wrong.
canst give, With Thee, O, Mas - ter, let me live.

156 Take The Name Of Jesus With You

Lydia Baxter   William H. Doane

1. Take the name of Je-sus with you, Child of sor-row and of woe;
2. Take the name of Je-sus ev-er As a shield from ev-'ry snare;
3. O the pre cious name of Je-sus! How it thrills our souls with joy,
4. At the name of Je-sus bow-ing, Fall-ing pros-trate at His feet,

It will joy and com-fort give you, Take it then wher-e'er you go.
If temp-ta-tions round you gath-er, Breathe that ho-ly name in pray'r.
When His lov-ing arms re-ceive us, And His songs our tongues employ.
King of kings in heav'n we'll crown Him, When our jour-ney is com-plete.

REFRAIN

Pre-cious name, O how sweet!
Pre-cious name, O how sweet!

Hope of earth and joy of heav'n; Pre-cious name, O how
Pre-cious name, O how

sweet! Hope of earth and joy of heav'n.
sweet, how sweet!

Stand Up For Jesus

George Duffield, Jr.   George J. Webb

1. Stand up, stand up for Je - sus, Ye sol - diers of the cross;
2. Stand up, stand up for Je - sus, Stand in His strength a - lone;
3. Stand up, stand up for Je - sus, The strife will not be long;

Lift high His roy - al ban - ner, It must not suf - fer loss:
The arm of flesh will fail you, Ye dare not trust your own:
This day the noise of bat - tle, The next the vic - tor's song:

From vic - t'ry un - to vic - t'ry His ar - my shall He lead.
Put on the gos - pel ar - mor, Each piece put on with prayer;
To him that o - ver - com - eth A crown of life shall be;

Till ev - 'ry foe is van - quished, And Christ is Lord in - deed.
Where du - ty calls or dan - ger, Be nev - er want - ing there.
He, with the King of glo - ry, Shall reign e - ter - nal - ly.

Onward, Christian Soldiers

Sabine Baring-Gould

Arthur S. Sullivan

1. On - ward Chris - tian sol - diers, March - ing as to war,
2. At the sign of tri - umph Sa - tan's host doth flee;
3. Like a might - y ar - my Moves the church of God;
4. On - ward, then, ye peo - ple, Join our hap - py throng,

With the cross of Je - sus Go - ing on be - fore!
On, then, Chris - tian sol - diers, On to vic - to - ry!
Broth - ers, we are tread - ing Where the saints have trod;
Blend with ours your voic - es In the tri - umph song;

Christ, the roy - al Mas - ter, Leads a - gainst the foe;
Hell's foun - da - tions quiv - er At the shout of praise;
We are not di - vid - ed; All one bod - y we,
Glo - ry, laud, and hon - or, Un - to Christ the King;

For - ward in - to bat - tle, See His ban - ner go!
Broth - ers, lift your voic - es, Loud your an - thems raise!
One in hope and doc - trine, One in char - i - ty.
This thro' count - less a - ges Men and an - gels sing.

REFRAIN

On - ward, Chris-tian sol - diers, March-ing as to war, With the cross of Je - sus Go - ing on be - fore!

159   March On, O Church Of God

Rev. James C. Moore   Rev. James C. Moore

March on, O church of God, March on to vic - to - ry; The pow'r of Tho foes as -
Our God is

sail, thou'lt nev - er fail,
God your strenght shall be, O church of God march on.
sure, thou'lt e'er en - dure,

We're Marching To Zion

160

Issac Watts
Refrain by Robert Lowry

Robert Lowry

1. Come, we that love the Lord, And let our joys be
2. Let those re - fuse to sing Who nev - er knew our
3. The hill of Zi - on yields A thou - sand sa - cred
4. Then let our songs a - bound, And ev - 'ry tear be

known; Join in a song with sweet ac - cord, Join in a
God; But chil - dren of the heav'n - ly King, But chil - dren
sweets, Be - fore we reach the heav'n - ly fields, Be - fore we
dry; We're march - ing thro' Im - man - uel's ground, We're march - ing

song with sweet ac - cord, And thus sur - round the throne, And thus sur -
of the heav'n - ly King, May speak their joys a - broad, May speak their
reach the heav'n - ly fields, Or walk the gold - en streets, Or walk the
thro' Im - man - uel's ground, To fair - er worlds on high, To fair - er

REFRAIN

round the throne.
joys a - broad.   We're march - ing to Zi - on, Beau - ti - ful
gold - en streets.   We're march - ing on to Zi - on,
worlds on high.

beau - ti - ful Zi - on; We're march - ing up - ward to

Zi - on, The beau - ti - ful cit - y of God.
Zi - on, Zi - on,

161   **Faith Of Our Fathers**   Henri F. Hemy

Frederick W. Faber   Ad. by James G. Walton

1. Faith of our fa - thers! liv - ing still In spite of dun - geon, fire, and sword,
2. Faith of our fa - thers! we will strive To win all na - tions un - to thee,
3. Faith of our fa - thers! we will love Both friend and foe in all our strife,

O how our hearts beat high with joy When-e'er we hear that glo - rious word!
And through the truth that comes from God Mankind shall then be tru - ly free:
And preach thee, too, as love knows how By kind - ly words and vir - tuous life:

Faith of our fa - thers, ho - ly faith! We will be true to thee till death.
Faith of our fa - thers, ho - ly faith! We will be true to thee till death.
Faith of our fa - thers, ho - ly faith! We will be true to thee till death.

Victory Ahead

Rev. William Grum   Rev. William Grum

1. When the hosts of Is - ra - el, led by God, Round the walls of
2. Da - vid, with a shep-herd's sling and five stones, Met the gi - ant
3. Dan - iel prayed un - to the Lord thrice each day, Then un - to the
4. Oft - en with the car - nal mind I was tried, Ask - ing for de -
5. When like those who've gone be-fore to that land, By death's riv - er

Jer - i - cho soft - ly trod; Trust - ing in the Lord, they
on the field all a - lone; Trust - ing · in the Lord, he ·
li - on's den led the way; Trust - ing in the Lord, he
liv - er - ance oft I cried; Trust - ing in the Lord, I
cold and dark I shall stand; Trust - ing in the Lord, I

felt the con-qu'ror's tread, By faith they saw the vic - to - ry a-head.
knew what God had said, By faith he saw the vic - to - ry a-head.
did not fear or dread, By faith he saw the vic - to - ry a-head.
reck-oned I was dead, By faith I saw the vic - to - ry a-head.
will not fear or dread, By faith I see the vic - to - ry a-head.

REFRAIN

Vic - to - ry a - head! Vic - to - ry a - head! Thro' the blood of

Je - sus, vic - to - ry a - head; Trust - ing in the Lord, I

hear the con - qu'ror's tread, By faith I see the vic - to - ry a - head.

163   Fight The Good Fight

John S. B. Monsell

William Boyd

1. Fight the good fight with all thy might! Christ is thy
2. Run thou the race through God's good grace, Lift up thine
3. Faint not nor fear, His arms are near, He chang - eth

strength, and Christ thy right; Lay hold on life, and it
eyes, and seek His face; Life with its way be - fore
not and thou art dear; On - ly be - lieve, and thou

shall be Thy joy and crown e - ter - nal - ly.
us lies, Christ is the path, and Christ the prize.
shalt see That Christ is all in all to thee.

164 Who Is On The Lord's Side?

Frances R. Havergal

Arr. John Goss

1. Who is on the Lord's side? Who will serve the King? Who will be His
2. Je - sus, Thou hast bought us, Not with gold or gem, But with Thine own
3. Fierce may be the con - flict, Strong may be the foe, But the King's own

help - ers, Oth - er lives to bring? Who will leave the world's side?
life - blood, For Thy di - a - dem: With Thy bless - ing fill - ing
ar - my None can o - ver - throw:'Round His stand - ard rang - ing,

Who will face the foe? Who is on the Lord's side? Who for
Each who comes to Thee, Thou hast made us will - ing, Thou hast
Vic - t'ry to se - cure; For His truth un - chang - ing Makes the

Him will go? By Thy call of mer - cy, By Thy grace di - vine,
made us free. By Thy grand re - demp - tion, By Thy grace di - vine,
tri - umph sure. Joy - ful - ly en - list - ing, By Thy grace di - vine,

We are on the Lord's side, Sav - iour, we are Thine.

165 The Haven Of Rest

Henry L. Gilmour

George D. Moore

1. My soul in sad ex - ile was out on life's sea, So bur-dened with
2. I yield-ed my - self to His ten - der em - brace, And faith tak-ing
3. Oh, come to the Sav-iour, He pa - tient - ly waits To save by His

sin and dis-tressed, Till I heard a sweet voice say-ing "Make Me your choice,"
hold of the word, My fet - ters fell off and I an - chored my soul:
pow - er di - vine; Come, an - chor your soul in the ha - ven of rest,

REFRAIN

And I en - tered the ha - ven of rest.
The ha - ven of rest is my Lord. I've an-chored my soul in the
And say, "My Be - lov - ed is mine."

ha - ven of rest, I'll sail the wide seas no more; The tem - pest may

sweep o'er the wild storm - y deep, In Je - sus I'm safe ev - er - more.

166 Love Lifted Me

James Rowe

Howard E. Smith

1. I was sink- ing deep in sin, Far from the peace- ful shore,
2. All my heart to Him I give, Ev - er to Him I'll cling,
3. Souls in dan - ger, look a - bove, Je - sus com- plete- ly saves;

Ver - y deep - ly stained with- in, Sink- ing to rise no more;
In His bless- ed pres - ence live, Ev - er His prais- es sing;
He will lift you by His love Out of the an - gry waves;

But the Mas- ter of the sea Heard my de - spair- ing cry,
Love so might - y and so true Mer - its my soul's best songs;
He's the Mas- ter of the sea, Bil - lows His will o - bey;

From the wa - ters lift - ed me, Now safe am I.
Faith - ful, lov - ing serv - ice, too, To Him be - longs.
He your Sav - iour wants to be, Be saved to - day.

REFRAIN

The Love Of God

Vep Ellis   Vep Ellis

1. The love of God has been ex-tend-ed to a fall-en
2. It goes be-neath the deep - est stain that sin could ev - er
3. The flow-ers bloom-ing in the spring, the heav-ens up a-

race; Thru Christ, the Sav-iour of all men, there's hope in sav-ing
leave; Re-deem-ing souls to live a-gain, who will on Christ be-
bove; In si-lent dec-la-ra-tion bring the sto-ry of God's

REFRAIN

grace, sav - ing grace.
lieve, will be - lieve.   The love   of   God   is
love, match-less love.

Love of   God

great - er   far,   gold or   sil - ver
great - er   far than gold   or   sil - ver

wealth af-

ev - er could af-ford,   It   Reach - es   past
ford,   It reach - es   past the

high-est star, cov-ers, yes, it
high-est star and cov-ers all the
cov-ers

cov-ers all the world; Pow-er is e-ter-nal, e-
world; Its pow-er is e-ter-nal,

ter-nal, Its glo-ry is su-per-nal, su-per-nal, When
Its glo-ry is su-per-nal, When

all this earth pass a-way,
all this earth shall pass a-way,

Al-ways be the love of God.
There'll al-ways be the pre-cious love of God.

God Is Love

C. S. Grogan

C. S. Grogan
V. B. (Vep) Ellis

1. For ev - 'ry bit - ter tear I shed, and ev - 'ry wea - ry
   Bit - ter tear I shed,
2. No art - ist ev - er could por - tray, no mor - tal tongue could
   Ev - er could por - tray,

mile I tread, I'll be re - paid in
wea - ry mile I tread, I'll be re - paid
ev - er say, Just what we gained thru
tongue could ev - er say, Just what we gained

heav'n a - bove; For ev - 'ry an - gry word I hear, I'll
An - gry word I hear,
Cal - va - ry; But ev - 'ry trust - ing heart can feel, and
Trust - ing heart can feel,

see a mil - lion smiles up there, Be - cause my
mil - lion smiles up there, Be - cause
know that His great love is real, I know it's
His great love is real, I know

God is love. God is love, yes,
my God
real to-day. God is love, God is love,
it's real

God is love, I'll tell the world
God is love, God is love, Tell the world, tell the world

my God is love; His Son He gave the world
Son He gave, Son He gave, world to save,

to save, I know my God is love.
world to save, I know my God

169 O Happy Day

Philip Doddridge

Arr. by L. B. Harris

1. O hap-py day . . . . that fixed my choice . . . .
2. O hap-py bond . . . . that seals my vows . . . .
3. 'Tis done, the great . . . . trans-ac-tion's done! . . . .

On Thee, my Sav - - - - - - - iour and my God! the liv - ing God!
To Him who mer - - - - - - its all my love! yes, all my love!
I am my Lord's . . . . and He is mine, He's tru - ly mine;

Well may this glow - - - - - - ing heart re - joice, ...
Let cheer-ful an - - - - - - thems fill His house, ...
He drew me and . . . . I fol-lowed on, ...

And tell its rap - - - - - - - - - tures all a - broad, a-broad.
While to that sa - - - - - - - - cred shrine I move, I move.
Charmed to con-fess . . . . the voice di - vine, di - vine.

REFRAIN

He taught me how to watch and pray,
He taught me how to pray, to watch and pray,
He taught me how to pray, to watch and pray,
He taught me how to pray, to watch and pray,

And live re-joic - - - - - - - - ing ev-'ry day;
And live re - joic - ing ev -'ry day;
And live re - joic-ing ev -'ry pass-ing day;
And live re - joic - ing ev -'ry pass-ing day;

O hap-py day, O hap-py day,
O hap-py day, O hap-py day,
O hal - - - le-lu - jah, O hap-py day,
Hap-py day, blest hap-py day,

When Je-sus washed my sins a-way.
When Je-sus washed my sins a-way, my sins a-way.

The Message Of The Cross

C. S. Grogan   C. S. Grogan

1. Once I was in bond-age was a slave to sin,
2. Je - sus went to Cal - v'ry, paid the debt for me,
3. Now the won - drous sto - ry, let me tell to you,

Had no one to help me e - ven my best friend;
Gave me life e - ter - nal, par - don full and free;
Full of grace and glo - ry it is ev - er new;

Then I heard the sto - ry, the mes - sage of the cross,
He knew I was guilt - y and yet He paid my cost,
I know you will love it, the mes - sage of the cross,

Now I know the Sav - iour and I'm no long - er lost.
What a bless - ed sto - ry, the mes - sage of the cross.
There is none a - bove it, it saves you when you're lost.

REFRAIN

Thru the mes - sage of the cross I found Je - sus,

Thru the blood He bought my soul at Cal - va - ry;

Now the chains that fet - tered me are gone for - ev - er,

Thru the mes - sage of the cross I've been set free.

171 **Am I A Soldier Of The Cross?**

Isaac Watts

Thomas A. Arne

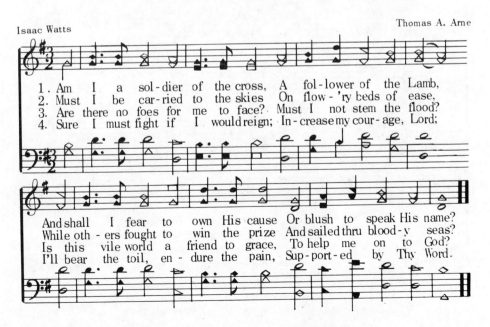

1. Am I a sol-dier of the cross, A fol-lower of the Lamb,
2. Must I be car-ried to the skies On flow-'ry beds of ease,
3. Are there no foes for me to face? Must I not stem the flood?
4. Sure I must fight if I would reign; In-crease my cour-age, Lord;

And shall I fear to own His cause Or blush to speak His name?
While oth - ers fought to win the prize And sailed thru blood-y seas?
Is this vile world a friend to grace, To help me on to God?
I'll bear the toil, en - dure the pain, Sup-port-ed by Thy Word.

Jesus Passed By

Marvin P. Dalton, legato

Marvin P. Dalton

1. There is a sto-ry of long a-go, Men roamed in
2. Men found com-pas-sion, hun-gry were fed, Some saw their
3. One day a sin-ner, I found re-lief, Gone was my

dark - ness no where to go; One day the scene changed,
loved ones bro't from the dead; They found great com - fort
bur - den, gone was my grief; An - gels were sing - ing,

they ceased to cry, There was a rea - son,
came from on high, There was a rea - son,
and so was I, There was a rea - son,

REFRAIN

Je - sus passed by. Glo - ry and hon - or be to the

King, Shout hal - le - lu - jah, make prais - es ring;

Look to the fu - ture home in the sky,

There is a rea - son, Je - sus passed by.

173　　**Jesus, The Very Thought Of Thee**

Bernard of Clairvaux
Tr. by Edward Caswall

John B. Dykes

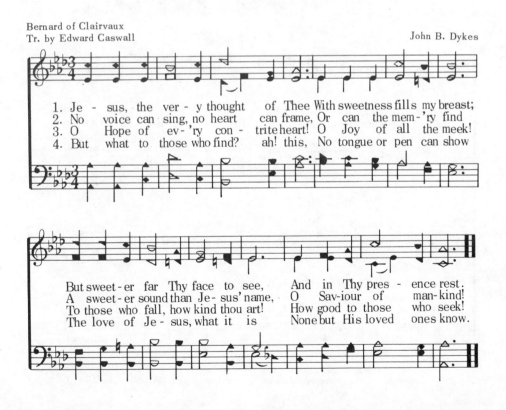

1. Je - sus, the ver - y thought of Thee With sweetness fills my breast;
2. No voice can sing, no heart can frame, Or can the mem-'ry find
3. O Hope of ev-'ry con - trite heart! O Joy of all the meek!
4. But what to those who find? ah! this, No tongue or pen can show

But sweet - er far Thy face to see, And in Thy pres - ence rest.
A sweet-er sound than Je- sus' name, O Sav-iour of man-kind!
To those who fall, how kind thou art! How good to those who seek!
The love of Je - sus, what it is None but His loved ones know.

174   Christ The Lord Was Really There

C. L. Wright, Jr.   C. L. Wright, Jr.

1. Let me tell you how the Lord came in - to my heart to stay,
2. When I knelt there on my knees some-thing new came o - ver me,

How He cast all my sins far a - way;
It was peace, joy and won - der - ful love;

How He took a way-ward heart and He made it pure a - gain,
I can shout the vic - to - ry since He set this sin - ner free,

How He spoke peace and changed me with - in.
When He spoke peace from heav - en a - bove.

REFRAIN

I was on my knees in pray'r, Christ the Lord was real - ly there,

And He flood - ed my soul, made the joy bil - lows roll;

Yes, the Lord was real - ly there, to re - lieve my ev - 'ry care,

And He spoke sweet peace to my soul.

175

Saved, Saved!

Jack P. Scholfield   Jack P. Scholfield

1. I've found a friend who is all to me, His
2. He saves me from ev-'ry sin and harm, Se-
3. When poor and need-y and all a-lone, In

love is ev-er true;
cures my soul each day;
love He said to me;

I love to tell how He lift-ed me, And
I'm lean-ing strong on His might-y arm; I
"Come un-to Me and I'll lead you home, To

what His grace can do for you.
know He'll guide me all the way.
live with Me e-ter-nal-ly."

Saved   by His pow'r di-vine, Saved   to new life sub-
Saved by His pow-er,   Saved to new life,

lime! Life now is sweet and my joy is com-plete, For I'm saved, saved, saved.

176   I Will Praise Him

Mrs. M. J. Harris   Mrs. M. J. Harris

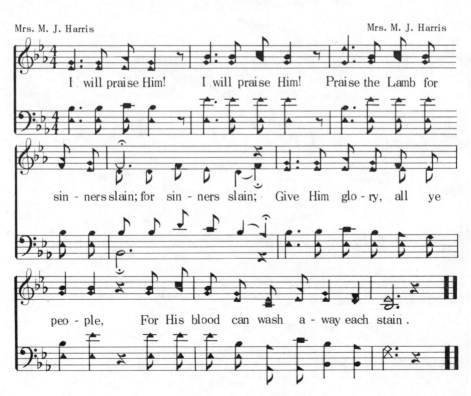

I will praise Him! I will praise Him! Praise the Lamb for

sin - ners slain; for sin - ners slain; Give Him glo - ry, all ye

peo - ple, For His blood can wash a - way each stain.

Happy Day

Philip Doddridge

Ad. from Edward F. Rimbault

1. O hap - py day that fixed my choice On Thee, my Sav-iour and my God!
2. 'Tis done the great trans - ac - tion's done I am my Lord's and He is mine;
3. Now rest, my long di - vid - ed heart, Fixed on this bliss-ful cen - ter, rest;
4. High heav'n that hears the solemn vow, That vow re - newed shall dai - ly hear;

Well may this glow-ing heart re - joice, And tell its rap - tures all a - broad.
He drew me and I fol - lowed on, Re - joiced to own the call di - vine.
Here have I found a no - bler part, Here heav'nly pleas-ures fill my breast.
Till in life's lat-est hour I bow, And bless, in death, a bond so dear.

REFRAIN

Hap - py day, hap - py day, When Je - sus washed my sins a - way!

He taught me how to watch and pray, And live re - joic-ing ev - 'ry day;

Hap - py day, hap - py day, When Je - sus washed my sins a - way!

His Blood Is On My Soul

R. E. Winsett

R. E. Winsett

1. Dear Je - sus all my sins for - gave, And washed and made me whole;
2. The temp-ter can - not o - ver-come, Or gain the least con-trol;
3. I have His Spir- it now with- in, My life in His con-trol;
4. I am de - ter-mined by His grace, To reach bright heaven's goal;

I have sweet peace and joy with- in, His blood is on my soul.
I have God's ev - er-last- ing seal, Christ's blood is on my soul.
I'm read - y for the crown-ing day, His blood is on my soul.
And reign with Je - sus on His throne, His blood is on my soul.

REFRAIN

His blood is on my soul, my soul, His blood is on my soul;

I rest se - cure - ly in His hand, His blood is on my soul.

179
I'm Glad He Lifted Me Out

W. L. (Bill) Hopper

W. L. (Bill) Hopper

Not too fast

1. I'll nev - er for - get that day when I heard the dear
2. I trav - eled on sin's broad road, far a - way from that
3. If you are a - way from God, in the path - way of

Sav - iour say, I'll take all your fears a - way, your trou - bles and
blest a - bode, And bent 'neath my heav - y load, but now I can
sin you trod, Let Him be your staff and rod, and turn you a -

doubts, your trou - bles and doubts; My feet were on sink - ing sand
shout, oh yes, I can shout; For Je - sus, the Sav - iour came
bout, He'll turn you a - bout; From sin He will set you free,

and I knew that I could not stand, Then I felt His
when I called on His pre - cious name, He took all my
and the path - way of life you'll see, Then just as He

precious hand as He lift - ed me out, as He lift - ed me out.
sin and shame and He lift - ed me out, yes, He lift - ed me out.
did for me, He will lift you right out, He will lift you right out.

D.S.- loved me so that He lift - ed me out, yes, He lift - ed me out.

REFRAIN

He lift - ed me out
He lift - ed me out
of the deep mir - y

clay,
of the deep mir - y clay,
He plant - ed my feet
He plant - ed my feet

on the heav - en - ly way;
on the heav - en - ly way;
I'll tell it wher -

D.S.

e'er I go, for I want the whole world to know, I'm glad that He

What A Change In My Life

Charles B. Wycuff

Charles B. Wycuff

1. I wan-dered a-long the down-ward road in sin and dark-ness,
2. The storms may come and winds may blow but I'll not wa-ver,
3. One day we shall see the Lord re-turn in clouds of glo-ry,

My soul was lost and I was sink-ing in de-spair;
The cap-tain is Je-sus, He's the Mas-ter of the sea;
The graves will burst and all the dead in Christ will rise;

But kneel-ing one day in hum-ble pray'r down at the al-tar,
No long-er I sail in doubt for I know where I am go-ing,
My bod-y will then be made like my Lord's glo-r'ous bod-y,

My life was changed and I've had joy be-yond com-pare.
With Him I know I am safe, thru-out e-ter-ni-ty.
And with the an-gels we'll go sail-ing thru the skies.

REFRAIN

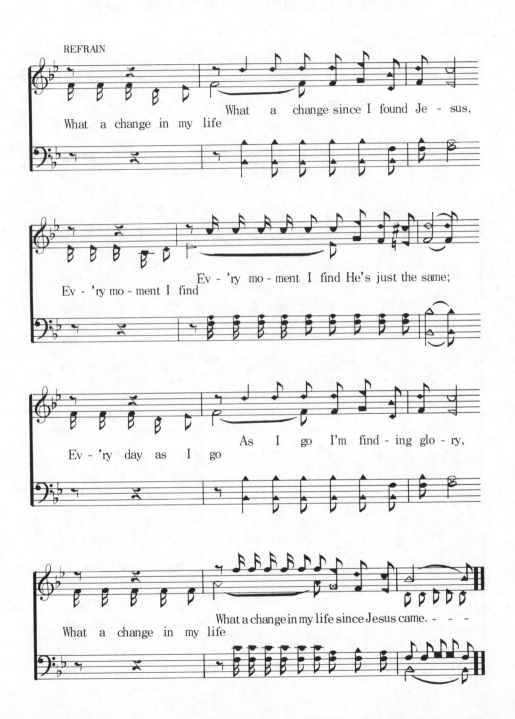

What a change since I found Je - sus,
What a change in my life

Ev - 'ry mo - ment I find He's just the same;
Ev - 'ry mo - ment I find

As I go I'm find - ing glo - ry,
Ev - 'ry day as I go

What a change in my life since Jesus came. - - - -
What a change in my life

181 I Never Lived Until I Lived For Jesus

T. W. Day

T. W. Day

1. In this world I've tried most ev - 'ry - thing to find peace for my soul,
2. I have found in Him a sat - is - fac - tion, tongue can not ex - press,
3. Just to feel His pres-ence by my side brings com-fort to my soul,

I've gone here and there and ev - 'ry - where that I could think to go;
That true joy and peace now flood my soul with last - ing hap - pi - ness;
Just to know that He will e'er a - bide is bet - ter felt than told;

Yet I nev - er thought of do - ing right, I nev - er stopped to pray,
Now the Lord sup - plies my ev - 'ry need, a - long life's pil - grim way,
And it brings me com - fort, con - so - la - tion, joy be - yond com - pare,

But then Je - sus came and saved my soul, I can't for - get that day.
Now I am so glad He lives with - in, with all my heart I say.
Just to have such blest as - sur - ance and to know He's al - ways there.

I nev - er lived   un - til I lived for Je - sus,
     Nev - er lived   Je - sus Christ, my Lord,

He par - doned me,   put peace and joy with - in;
     Par - doned me,   put peace and joy with - in;

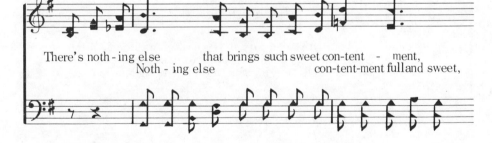

There's noth - ing else   that brings such sweet con - tent - ment,
     Noth - ing else   con - tent - ment full and sweet,

I'll walk with Him,   He'll keep me till the end, till the end.

Victory In Jesus

E. M. Bartlett

E. M. Bartlett

1. I heard an old, old sto - ry, how a Sav - iour came from glo - ry,
2. I heard a - bout His heal - ing, of His cleans-ing pow'r re - veal-ing,
3. I heard a - bout a man - sion He has built for me in glo - ry,

How He gave His life on Cal - va - ry to save a wretch like me;
How He made the lame to walk a - gain and caused the blind to see;
And I heard a - bout the streets of gold be - yond the crys - tal sea;

I heard a - bout His groan-ing, of His pre - cious blood's a-ton - ing,
And then I cried, "Dear Je- sus, come and heal my bro-ken spir - it",
A - bout the an - gels sing-ing, and the old re - demp-tion sto - ry,

Then I re - pent - ed of my sins and won the vic - to - ry.
And some-how Je - sus came and bro't to me the vic - to - ry.
And some sweet day I'll sing up there the song of vic - to - ry.

O vic - to - ry in Je - sus, my Sav - iour, for - ev - er,

He sought me and bo't me with His re - deem - ing blood;

He loved me ere I knew Him, and all my love is due Him,

He plunged me to vic - to - ry, be - neath the cleans - ing flood.

It's Real

H. L. Cox   H. L. Cox

1. Oh, how well do I re-mem-ber how I doubt-ed day by day,
2. When the truth came close and searching, all my joy would dis-ap-pear,
3. When the Lord sent faith-ful ser-vants who would dare to preach the truth,
4. But at last I tired of liv-ing such a life of fear and doubt,
5. So I prayed to God in ear-nest, and not car-ing what folks said,

For I did not know for cer-tain that my sins were washed a-way;
For I did not have the wit-ness of the Spir- it bright and clear;
How my heart did so con-demn me as the Spir- it gave re-proof!
For I want-ed God to give me something I would know a-bout;
I was hun-gry for the bless-ing, my poor soul it must be fed;

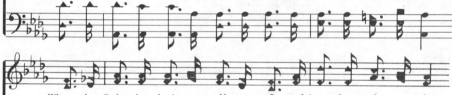

When the Spir- it tried to tell me, I would not the truth re-ceive,
If at times the com-ing judg-ment would ap-pear be-fore my mind,
Sa-tan said at once, "'Twill ru-in you to now con-fess your state,
So the truth would make me hap-py, and the light would clear-ly shine,
Then at last by faith I touched Him, and, like sparks from smit-ten steel,

I en-deav-ored to be hap-py, and to make my-self be-lieve.
Oh, it made me so un-eas-y, for God's smile I could not find.
Keep on work-ing and pro-fess-ing, and you'll en-ter heav-en's gate."
And the Spir- it gave as-sur-ance that I'm His and He is mine.
Just so quick sal-va-tion reached me, oh, bless God, I know it's real!

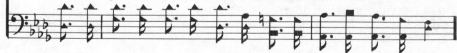

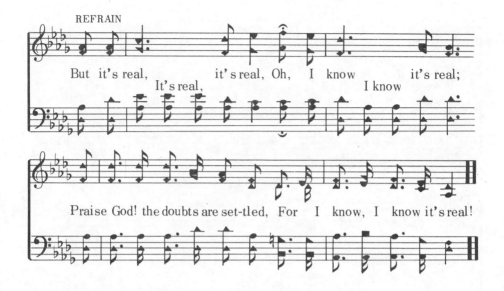

But it's real,　　it's real, Oh, I know　　it's real;

It's real,　　　　　　　　　　I know

Praise God! the doubts are set-tled, For I know, I know it's real!

184　Jesus, Thou Joy Of Loving Hearts

Tr. by Ray Palmer　　　　　　　　　　　　　　　　　　Henry Baker

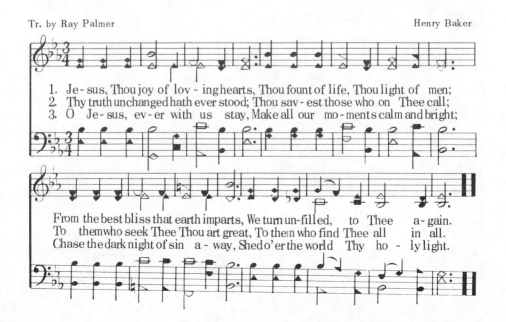

1. Je-sus, Thou joy of lov-ing hearts, Thou fount of life, Thou light of men;
2. Thy truth unchanged hath ever stood; Thou sav-est those who on Thee call;
3. O Je-sus, ev-er with us stay, Make all our mo-ments calm and bright;

From the best bliss that earth imparts, We turn un-fill-ed, to Thee a-gain.
To them who seek Thee Thou art great, To them who find Thee all in all.
Chase the dark night of sin a-way, Shed o'er the world Thy ho-ly light.

Calvary Covers It All

Mrs. Walter G. Taylor

Mrs. Walter G. Taylor

1. Far dear-er than all that the world can im-part, Was the
2. The stripes that He bore and the thorns that He wore, Told His
3. How matchless the grace when I looked in the face, Of this
4. How bless-ed the thought that my soul by Him bought, Shall be

mes-sage that came to my heart, to my heart; How that
mer-cy and love ev-er-more, ev-er-more; And my
Je-sus, my cru-ci-fied Lord, of my Lord; My re-
His in the glo-ry on high, His on high; Where with

Je-sus a-lone for my sin did a-tone,
heart bowed in shame as I called on His name,
demp-tion com-plete I then found at His feet,
glad-ness and song I'll be one of the throng,
And Cal-va-ry

REFRAIN

cov-ers it all.
cov-ers it all. Cal-va-ry cov-ers it all,

My past with its sin and stain; My guilt and de-spair

Je-sus took on Him there, And Cal-va-ry cov-ers it all.

186   Amazing Grace

John Newton   Early American Melody

1. A - maz - ing grace! how sweet the sound, That saved a
2. 'Twas grace that taught my heart to fear, And grace my
3. Thro' man - y dan - gers, toils, and snares, I have al -
4. When we've been there ten thou - sand years, Bright shin-ing

wretch like me! I once was lost, but
fears re - lieved; How pre - cious did that
read - y come; 'Tis grace hath bro't me
as the sun, We've no less days to

now am found, Was blind, but now I see.
grace ap - pear The hour I first be - lieved!
safe thus far, And grace will lead me home.
sing God's praise Than when we first be - gun.

187

Because Of Calvary

Charles L. Towler

Charles L. Towler

1. No tongue can ev - er tell of the pow'r in Je - sus' blood,
2. To those who are a - stray in the black - en'd fields of sin,

One drop was suf - fi - cient for me;
He calls, yes, He beck - ons for thee;

Sal - va - tion for the soul and heal - ing for the bod - y
The vil - est sin - ners come and re - ceive their full sal - va - tion

REFRAIN

Are gained thru Cal - va - ry. Be - cause of Cal -
Be - cause of Cal - va - ry.

va - ry, now my life is worth - while, Be - cause of

Cal - va - ry, I can wear a sun - ny smile; O

Je - sus gave His life that I might live, I'll live in

heav - en some day, be - cause of Cal - v'ry, Cal - va - ry.

Since I Have Been Redeemed

188

Edwin O. Excell   Edwin O. Excell

1. I have a song   I love to sing, Since I have been re-deemed,
2. I have a Christ   who sat-is-fies, Since I have been re-deemed,
3. I have a wit - ness bright and clear, Since I have been re-deemed,
4. I have a home   pre-pared for me, Since I have been re-deemed,

Of my Re - deem - er, Sav - iour, King, Since I have been re - deemed.
To do His will   my high - est prize, Since I have been re - deemed.
Dis - pell-ing ev - ery doubt and fear, Since I have been re - deemed.
Where I shall dwell e - ter - nal - ly, Since I have been re - deemed.

REFRAIN

Since   I   have been re - deemed,
Since   I have been re - deemed, Since   I have been re - deemed,

Since   I have been re - deemed, I will glo - ry in His name;

Since I have been re-deemed,
Since I have been re-deemed, Since I have been re-deemed,

I will glo-ry in my Sav-iour's name.

189 I Love Thy Kingdom, Lord

Timothy Dwight

Handel

1. I love Thy king-dom Lord, The house
2. I love Thy Church, O God! Her walls
3. Sure as Thy truth shall last, To Zi-

of Thine a - bode, The Church our blest
be - fore Thee stand, Dear as the ap-
on shall be giv'n, The high-est glo-

Re - deem - er saved With His own pre - cious blood.
ple of Thine eye, And grav - en on Thy hand.
ries earth can yield; And bright - er bliss of heav'n.

190

I Sing Because I'm Happy

Harvey A. Everette

L. O. Sanderson

1. I sing be - cause I am hap - py, I once by the world was en - ticed, But I found the pow'r to sal - va - tion, The un - search - a - ble rich - es of Christ.
2. I sing be - cause I am hap - py, In Je - sus my hope and my stay, And the joy of last - ing as - sur - ance, I pos - sess by His truth in His way.
3. I sing be - cause I am hap - py, In tell - ing the sto - ry of love, And in bid - ding all to sub - mis - sion, To be sure of a hav - en a - bove.

REFRAIN

I'll sing be - cause I'm hap - py, And I'll sing be - cause I'm free, I'll sing God's praise thru all my days, And sing e - ter - nal - ly.

O Say, But I'm Glad

Rev. James P. Sullivan

Mildred Ellen Sullivan

1. There is a song in my heart to-day, Some-thing I nev-er had;
2. Won-der-ful, mar-vel-ous love He brings In-to a heart that's sad;
3. Won't you come to Him with all your care, Wea-ry and worn and sad?

Je-sus has tak-en my sins a-way— O say, but I'm glad!
Thru dark-est tun-nels the soul just sings, "O say, but I'm glad!"
You too will sing as His love you share, "O say, but I'm glad!"

REFRAIN

O say, but I'm glad, I'm glad, O say, but I'm glad;

Je-sus has come and my cup's o-ver-run, O say, but I'm glad!

Wonderful Joy

Shirley Wilson
Elsie W. Murphy

Shirley Wilson
Elsie W. Murphy

1. When I was sink - ing in de - spair, Je - sus heard my ear - nest pray'r,
2. Some of these days I'm go - ing there, and with loved ones I shall share,

Saved my soul, - - - - made me whole; - - - -
Heav - en's land, - - - - 'twill be grand; - - - -

Oh, such joy He did im - part, placed His love with - in my heart,
We shall all be hap - py there, nev - er have a pain or care,

Then He took my sins a - way and gave me joy.
And we'll rest from all our strife and live in joy.

Won - der - ful joy, un - speak - a - ble joy,

I have joy the world can nev - er take a - way;

Some sweet day I'm go - ing home, and I nev - er more shall roam,

I'll have joy, joy, joy, won - der - ful joy, won - der - ful joy.

193 The Fountain That Will Never Run Dry

C. L. Wright, Jr.   C. L. Wright, Jr.

1. I am drink-ing to-day from the foun-tain of life,
2. From this foun-tain I find won-drous peace for my soul,

And the wa-ter flows free from on high, from on high;
And a joy that my cup can-not hold, can-not hold;

There is plen-ty for all who will drink of the flow,
So re-fresh-ing to me I will ev-er re-ly,

From the foun-tain that will nev-er run dry.
On   nev-er run dry.

REFRAIN

I'm drink - ing of wa - ter from the foun - tain that will nev - er

run dry, No more will I hun - ger for the things that will die;

I'm drink - ing of cool pure wa - ter my Fa - ther doth sup - ply,

I'm drink - ing of wa - ter that will nev - er run dry.

nev - er run dry.

Living In Christ

Harvey A. Everette

Adger M. Pace

1. Liv - ing in Christ .... from day un - to day, ...
2. Dai - ly I try ...... to help some lost soul, ...
3. Liv - ing in Christ .... and He lives in me, ...

Hon - or - ing Him ...... each step of my way; ....
Point-ing them to ...... the heav - en - ly goal; ....
Cleans-ing my heart ..... and mak - ing me free; ....

Walk - ing in light ..... He sends from a - bove, ...
Tell - ing them of ...... the joys that a - wait, ...
Mov - ing a - long ...... I've noth - ing to fear, ...

Guid - ing me on ...... thru won - der - ful love. ....
Saved ones in-side ...... the beau - ti - ful gate. ....
Liv - ing in Christ, ... sweet heav - en is near. ....

REFRAIN

Liv - ing in Christ, He's liv-ing in me,
Liv-ing in Christ, He's liv-ing in me,

Makes me re-joice, I'm hap-py and free;
Makes me re-joice, I'm hap-py and free;

Giv - ing Him all my tal - ents in love,
Giv - ing Him all my tal-ents in love,

Go - ing with Him to heav-en a - bove,
Go - ing with Him to heav - en a - bove.

195 For Me To Live Is Christ

Phil. 1:21

Leon H. Ellis

Leon H. Ellis

March Rhythm

1. Some men live for wealth and world - ly fame, Oth - ers live to build up their own name; My de - sire as on thro' life I go, Is to live a life that all may see and know.
2. Say my friend, if you would have suc - cess, Live a life that's full of hap - pi - ness; You must bow your knee in hum - ble prayer, Then He'll lift you up from all your dark de - spair.
3. Why not look un - to the Lord to - day, Why not let Him take your cares a - way; Je - sus Saves! why not be - lieve to - day, Then re - deemed from sin you'll join with us to say.

REFRAIN

For me to live is Christ! And to die is gain,

I'm Walking With Jesus

Horace L. Mauldin

Horace L. Mauldin

1. This world is not my home, I may leave most an - y time,
2. This earth - ly life is short, soon my jour - ney here will end,
3. Just think what lies a - head when I cross the Jor - dan wide,

I'm read - y now and wait - ing to leave this world be - hind;
It can - not be much long - er, I'll leave this world of sin;
It makes me trav - el on - ward to reach the oth - er side;

There are man - y man - sions yon - der be - yond the mys - tic foam,
Soon the bat - tle will be o - ver, the vic - t'ry's al - most won,
There is noth - ing here to stop me, in sin no more I'll roam,

I'm walk - ing with Je - sus, I'm on my jour - ney home.
I'm walk - ing with Je - sus, I see the set - ting sun.
I'm walk - ing with Je - sus, I know I'll make it home.

REFRAIN

I'm walk-ing with Je - sus   Walk - ing with Him each step of the

In The Garden

C. Austin Miles

C. Austin Miles

1. I come to the gar-den a-lone, While the dew is still on the
2. He speaks, and the sound of His voice Is so sweet the birds hush their
3. I'd stay in the gar-den with Him, Tho the night a-round me be

ros - es; And the voice I hear fall - ing on my ear, The
sing - ing; And the mel - o - dy that He gave to me, With-
fall - ing; But He bids me go through the voice of woe, His

REFRAIN

Son of God dis-clos - es.
in my heart is ring - ing. And He walks with me, and He
voice to me is call - ing.

talks with me, And He tells me I am His own; And the

joy we share as we tar - ry there, None other has ev - er known.

Heavenly Sunlight

H. J. Zelley

G. H. Cook

1. Walk-ing in sun-light, all of my jour-ney, O - ver the moun-tains,
2. Shad-ows a-round me, shad-ows a-bove me, Nev - er con-ceal my
3. In the bright sun-light, ev - er re - joic -ing, Press-ing my way to

thro' the deep vale; Je - sus has said "I'll nev - er for - sake thee,"
Sav - iour and guide; He is the light, in Him is no dark-ness,
man-sions a -bove; Sing-ing His prais - es, glad -ly I'm walk- ing,

Prom-ise di - vine that nev - er can fail.
Ev - er I'm walk-ing close to His side.
Walk-ing in sun -light,sun-light of love.

REFRAIN

Heav -en - ly sun -light,
heav - en - ly sun-light,flood-ing my soul with glo - ry di - vine; Hal - le-
lu - jah, I am re -joic -ing, Sing-ing His prais - es, Je - sus is mine.

199 The Lord Is My Shepherd

Ardon A. Hollis

Ardon A. Hollis

1. I wan - dered a - lone — — — — — — — down sin's lone - some
2. A pil - grim down here — — — — — — — tho foot - sore and

val - ley, lone - ly and sad, Till I heard a sweet voice, - - - - say - ing
wea - ry, wea - ry with care, I will nev - er turn back - - - - till the

sin - ner come home; - - - - - I heed - ed the call - - - -
set - ting of sun; - - - - - Some won - der - ful day - - - -

came to Him and re - pent - ed, now I'm so glad, I am hap - py to -
in that beau - ti - ful cit - y, cit - y so fair, All my trav - el - ing

day, - - - - - for I'm one of His own. - - - - -
days - - - - - on this earth will be run. - - - - -

REFRAIN

The Lord is my Shep-herd, - - - - - - - and I shall not want, In pas - tures so green, - - - - He mak - eth me lie; - - - - - Be - side the still wa - ters, the cool and still wa - ters, He re - stor - eth my soul, my poor hun - gry soul, O glo - ry to God I am free and made whole.

O glo-ry to God I'm so hap - py and whole.

200 Jesus Is Precious To Me

Mary Lewis

Jimi Hall

1. How precious is the name of Jesus, How it ever
2. He gives us faith to trust His promise, He sustains us
3. 'Twas sad He had to go to Cal-v'ry, But it opened

thrills my happy soul; It brings such joy and sweet-est
in the hour of test; His precious promise He doth
up a way for man; And that is why I tell the

comfort, Since that day the Saviour made me whole.
give us, We should nev-er of-fer less than our best.
sto-ry, For He gave us our re-demp-tion plan.

REFRAIN   *Ladies Only*   *Parts*

He's precious to me, He's precious to me, My Jesus is

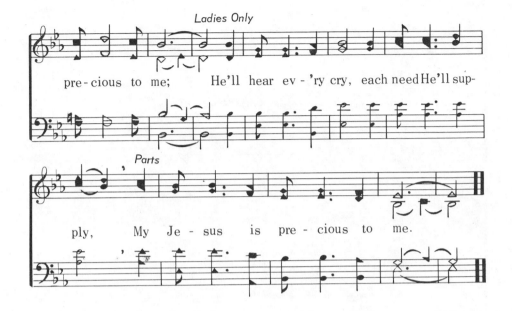

Ladies Only

pre - cious to me; He'll hear ev - 'ry cry, each need He'll sup-

Parts

ply, My Je - sus is pre - cious to me.

201 **Begin, My Tongue**

Isaac Watts
From Henry W. Greatorex's "Collection"

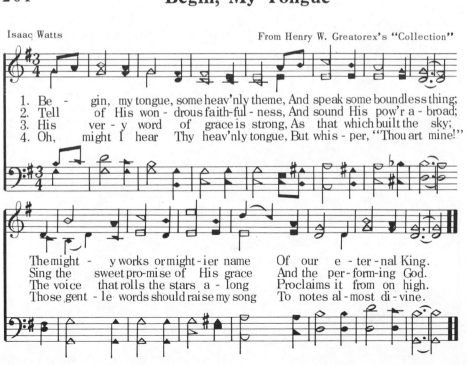

1. Be - gin, my tongue, some heav'nly theme, And speak some boundless thing;
2. Tell of His won - drous faith-ful - ness, And sound His pow'r a - broad;
3. His ver - y word of grace is strong, As that which built the sky;
4. Oh, might I hear Thy heav'nly tongue, But whis - per, "Thou art mine!"

The might - y works or might-ier name Of our e - ter-nal King.
Sing the sweet pro-mise of His grace And the per-form-ing God.
The voice that rolls the stars a - long Proclaims it from on high.
Those gent - le words should raise my song To notes al-most di - vine.

202 The Spirit Of The Lord Is Upon Me

T. W. Day   T. W. Day

1. Since Je - sus saved my soul from Sa - tan's bond - age,
2. In sick - ness or in health He's al - ways near me,
3. I know that God is real I feel His pres - ence,

'Twas then He set my wea - ry spir - it free;
He nev - er leaves me here to walk a - lone;
And He'll sup - ply my ev - 'ry earth - ly need;

Sweet peace and joy He gave and sat - is - fac - tion,
My dear - est friend and clos - er than all oth - ers,
I put my trust in Him now and the fu - ture,

Oh what a bless - ed friend is He.
I know I am His ver - y own.
From earth to heav - en's shore He'll lead.

The spir - it of the Lord is up - on me,

The spir - it of the Lord is here;

The spir - it of the Lord is up - on me,

It drives a - way all doubt and fear, doubt and fear.

I'd Tell The World

C. S. Grogan   C. S. Grogan

1. If I could count my bless-ings, and name them one by one,
2. I'm thru with sin-ful pleas-ures, I've left them all be-hind,
3. If I could speak like an - gels, and have a mil - lion years

I'd write a book so ev-'ry one could read; so all could read;
They on - ly give con-tent-ment for a while, but for a while;
On earth to talk a - bout my Sav-iour's love, His bound-less love;

I'd start each line with "Glo - ry", and end with "Praise the Lord",
I gave them up for Je - sus, He means so much to me,
When time for me had end - ed, and Je - sus called me home,

I'd tell how Je - sus fills my ev - 'ry need, my ev - 'ry need.
While a - ges roll His love will still a - bide, will still a - bide.
I'd still have much to tell in heav'n a - bove, in heav'n a - bove.

REFRAIN

I'd tell the world how Je - sus saved me,
I'd tell the world saved my soul,

I'd tell the world He set me free;
I'd tell the world and made me whole;

O yes, if I could count my bless-ings and name them one by one,

I'd tell the world what Je-sus is to me, He is to me.

204 Somewhere In Heaven

C. L. Wright, Jr.

C. L. Wright, Jr.

1. Some - where in heav-en my prayer was heard, I can feel it through and through; Bur - dens have been lift-ed, gone is all my care, Makes my heart with- in feel new.

2. Some - where in heav-en my prayer was heard, I can feel it in my soul; Sa - tan had to give way as I made my plea, And the Sav-iour washed me whole.

REFRAIN

Somewhere in heav - en my prayer was heard, As I looked to-ward that shore; Heav-en I did feel, that's why I know it's real, I will praise Him ev - er - more.

An-gels sang a glad new song; And some morning fair, I'll sing with them up there, With the Sav-iour's blood-washed throng.

When We All Get To Heaven

Eliza E. Hewitt

Emily D. Wilson

1. Sing the won-drous love of Je-sus, Sing His mer-cy and His grace:
2. While we walk the pil-grim path-way Clouds will o-ver-spread the sky;
3. Let us then be true and faith-ful, Trust-ing serv-ing ev-'ry day;
4. On-ward to the prize be-fore us! Soon His beau-ty we'll be-hold;

In the man-sions bright and bless-ed, He'll pre-pare for us a place.
But when trav'ling days are o-ver, Not a shad-ow, not a sigh.
Just one glimpse of Him in glo-ry Will the toils of life re-pay.
Soon the pearl-y gates will o-pen; We shall tread the streets of gold.

1. for us a place.

REFRAIN

When we all get to heav-en, What a day of re-
When we all What a

joic-ing that will be! When we all see
day of re-joic-ing that will be When we all

Je-sus, We'll sing and shout the vic-to-ry.
and shout the vic-to-ry.

206 When The Roll Is Called Up Yonder

James M. Black   James M. Black

1. When the trum-pet of the Lord shall sound, and time shall be no more,
2. On that bright and cloud-less morn-ing when the dead in Christ shall rise,
3. Let us la-bor for the Mas-ter from the dawn till set-ting sun,

And the morn-ing breaks, e-ter-nal, bright, and fair;
And the glo-ry of His res-ur-rec-tion share;
Let us talk of all His won-drous love and care;

When the saved of earth shall gath-er o-ver on the oth-er shore,
When His cho-sen ones shall gath-er to their home be-yond the skies,
Then when all of life is o-ver, and our work on earth is done,

And the roll is called up yon-der, I'll be there.

REFRAIN

When the roll   is called up yon - - - der,
When the roll   is called up yon - der, I'll be there,

When the roll   is called up yon - - - - der,
When the roll is called up yon - der I'll be there,

When the roll   is called up yon - der,
When   the   roll

When the roll is called up yon - der, I'll be there.

207 When They Ring The Golden Bells

Dion DeMarbelle   Dion DeMarbelle

1. There's a land be - yond the riv - er, That we call the sweet for -
2. We shall know no sin nor sor - row, In that ha - ven of to -
3. When our days shall know their num - ber, When in death we sweet - ly

ev - er, And we on - ly reach that shore by faith's de - cree;
mor - row, When our barque shall sail be - yond the sil - ver sea;
slum - ber, When the King com - mands the spir - it to be free;

One by one we'll gain the por - tals, There to dwell with the im -
We shall on - ly know the bless - ing Of our Fa - ther's sweet ca -
Nev - er - more with an - guish la - den, We shall reach that love - ly

mor - tals,
ress - ing, When they ring the gold - en bells for you and
ai - den,

REFRAIN

me, you and me. Don't you hear the bells now ring-ing? Don't you

hear the an-gels sing-ing? 'Tis the glo-ry hal-le-

lu-jah ju-bi-lee, ju-bi-lee, In the far-off sweet for-

ev-er, Just be-yond the shin-ing riv-er. When they

ring the gold-en bells for you and me, you and me.

208 My Saviour First Of All

(I SHALL KNOW HIM)

Fanny J. Crosby

John R. Sweney

1. When my life-work is end-ed, and I cross the swelling tide, When the bright and glo-rious morn-ing I shall see; I shall know my Re-deem-er when I reach the oth-er side, And His smile will be the first to wel-come me.

2. Oh, the soul-thrill-ing rap-ture when I view His bless-ed face, And the lus-ter of His kind-ly beam-ing eye; How my full heart will praise Him for the mer-cy, love, and grace That pre-pared for me a man-sion in the sky.

3. Oh, the dear ones in glo-ry, how they beck-on me to come, And our part-ing at the riv-er I re-call; To the sweet vales of E-den they will sing my wel-come home, But I long to meet my Sav-iour first of all.

4. Thro' the gates to the cit-y in a robe of spot-less white, He will lead me where no tears will ev-er fall; In the glad song of a-ges I shall min-gle with de-light, But I long to meet my Sav-iour first of all.

REFRAIN

I shall know Him, I shall know Him, I shall know Him,

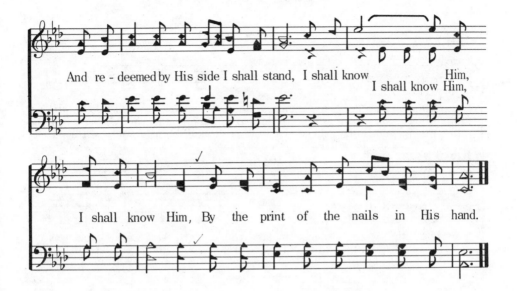

And re-deemed by His side I shall stand, I shall know Him, I shall know Him,

I shall know Him, By the print of the nails in His hand.

209   **Praise The Saviour**

Thomas Kelly   German

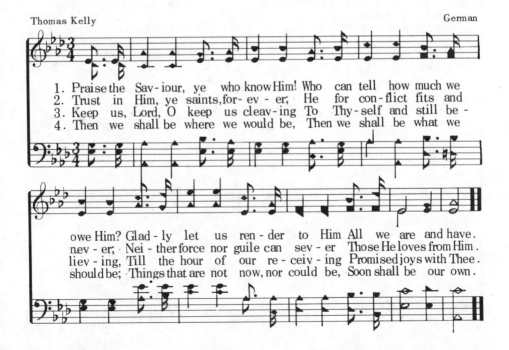

1. Praise the Sav-iour, ye who know Him! Who can tell how much we
2. Trust in Him, ye saints, for-ev-er; He for con-flict fits and
3. Keep us, Lord, O keep us cleav-ing To Thy-self and still be-
4. Then we shall be where we would be, Then we shall be what we

owe Him? Glad-ly let us ren-der to Him All we are and have.
nev-er; Nei-ther force nor guile can sev-er Those He loves from Him.
liev-ing, Till the hour of our re-ceiv-ing Promised joys with Thee.
should be; Things that are not now, nor could be, Soon shall be our own.

Look For Me

A. A. Payn

C. Austin Miles

1. When you get to heav - en, as you sure - ly will
2. When you roam with friends a - cross the heav'n - ly fields,
3. When you hear them sing - ing, 'round the great white throne,

If the Sav - iour's name you own; Aft - er you have
Ev - er find - ing treas - ures new; When you stand in
Songs of praise un - to the Lamb; When you hear the

greet - ed those you love the best, Who are stand - ing round the
rap - ture on some star - ry height, Gaz - ing on some glo - rious
ran - somed, with their harps of gold, Shouting, "Glo - ry to His

REFRAIN

throne.
view. Hal - le - lu - jah! You may look for me, for I'll be
name!"

there, I'll be there, I'll be
I'll be there, I'll be there,

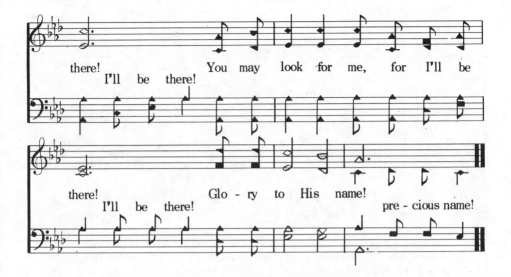

there! I'll be there! You may look for me, for I'll be

there! I'll be there! Glo-ry to His name! pre-cious name!

211   I Shall Reach Home

James Rowe   Howard E. Smith

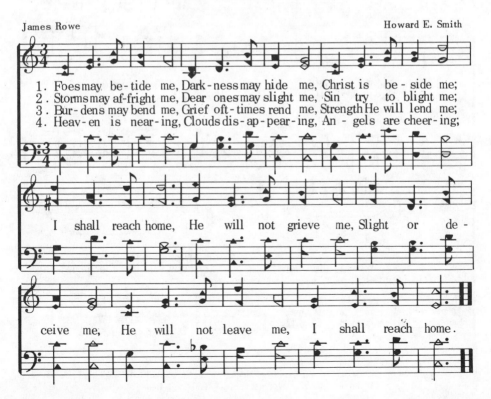

1. Foes may be-tide me, Dark-ness may hide me, Christ is be-side me;
2. Storms may af-fright me, Dear ones may slight me, Sin try to blight me;
3. Bur-dens may bend me, Grief oft-times rend me, Strength He will lend me;
4. Heav-en is near-ing, Clouds dis-ap-pear-ing, An-gels are cheer-ing;

I shall reach home, He will not grieve me, Slight or de-

ceive me, He will not leave me, I shall reach home.

I'll Meet You In The Morning

Albert E. Brumley   Albert E. Brumley

1. I will meet you in the morn-ing, by the bright riv-er side, When all
2. I will meet you in the morn-ing, in the sweet by and by, And ex-
3. I will meet you in the morn-ing, at the end of the way, On the

sor-row has drift-ed a-way; I'll be stand-ing at the por-tals
change the old cross for a crown; There will be no dis-ap-point-ments
streets of that cit-y of gold; Where we all can be to-geth-er

when the gates o-pen wide, At the close of life's long, drear-y day.
and no-bod-y shall die, In that land ere the sun go-eth down.
and be hap-py for aye, While the years and the a-ges shall roll.

REFRAIN

Meet you in the morn-ing,   meet you in the morn-ing,
I'll meet   you in the morn-ing
Know me in the morn-ing,   know me in the morn-ing,
You'll know   me in the morn-ing

That Glad Reunion Day

Adger M. Pace

Adger M. Pace

1. There will be a hap - py meet - ing in heav - en I know,
2. There with - in the ho - ly cit - y we'll sing and re - joice,
3. When we live a mil - lion years in that won - der - ful place,

When we see the man - y loved ones we've known here be - low;
Prais - ing Christ the bless - ed Sav - iour with heart and with voice;
Bask - ing in the love of Je - sus, be - hold - ing His face;

Gath - er on the bless - ed hill - tops with hearts all a - glow,
Tell Him how we came to love Him and make Him our choice,
It will seem but just a mo - ment of prais - ing His grace,

That will be a glad re - un - ion day.

REFRAIN

Glad day, a won-der-ful day,
That will be a hap-py day, yes, a won-der-ful day,

Glad day, a glo-ri-ous day;
That will be a hap-py day, yes, a glo-ri-ous day;

There with all the ho-ly an-gels and loved ones to stay,

That will be a glad re-un-ion day.

214 Will You Meet Me In Heaven?

T. L. Gilley, Jr.   T. L. Gilley, Jr.

1. Will you meet me up in heav-en when the saints are gath-ered home,
2. No fare-wells will e'er be spok-en, nev-er take the part-ing hand,
3. I am wait-ing, watching, long-ing, for that bless-ed day to come,

In that love-ly land so bright and fair, so bright and fair;
And no bur-dens there will be to bear, no long-er bear;
When my spir-it shall be free from care, free from all care;

There will nev-er be a heart-ache, and no sor-row ev-er comes,
Earth-ly ties will then be brok-en o-ver in the glo-ry-land,
And the strains of heav'n-ly mu-sic fill the air with joy-ful song,

Oh, my broth-er, will you meet me there?
Meet me o-ver there?

REFRAIN

Will you meet me up in heav-en some glad day,
Meet me, heav-en, meet me some glad day,

When the shad-ows all have passed a-way, have passed a-way;

May we gath-er by the riv-er bright and fair,
Gath-er, riv-er, by the riv-er fair,

Oh, my broth-er, will you meet me there?
Meet me o-ver there?

215 Where The Shades Of Love Lie Deep

O. A. Parris   Eugene Wright

1. We are oft-en bowed   with a load   of   sor-row, When our
2. With the cares of life   we   are al - ways bend-ed, And the
3. We will have more faith   on   the pil - grim jour - ney, And our

loved   ones fall a - sleep;   But we'll meet   a - gain,
hills   are rough and steep; Praise the Lord   we   know
vows   to Je - sus keep;   He will wel - come   us

on   the glad to - mor - row,
it will   all be   end - ed, Where the shades of love lie deep.
to   the   land of   E - den,

REFRAIN

It   will   be   a grand to - mor - row, to - mor - row, In that land

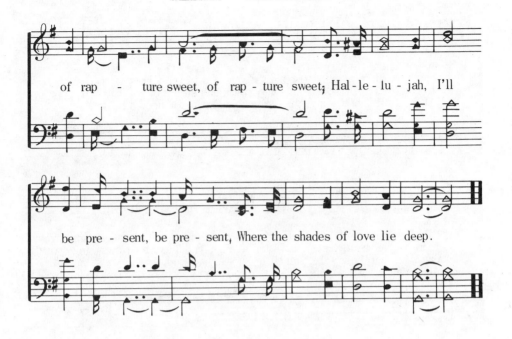

of rap - ture sweet, of rap - ture sweet; Hal - le - lu - jah, I'll

be pre - sent, be pre - sent, Where the shades of love lie deep.

216   Rest Beyond

A. J. Showalter   A. J. Showalter

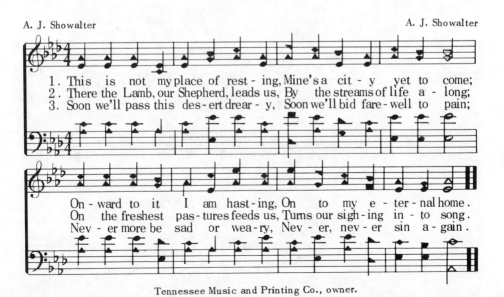

1. This is not my place of rest - ing, Mine's a cit - y yet to come;
2. There the Lamb, our Shepherd, leads us, By the streams of life a - long;
3. Soon we'll pass this des - ert drear - y, Soon we'll bid fare - well to pain;

On - ward to it I am hast - ing, On to my e - ter - nal home.
On the freshest pas - tures feeds us, Turns our sigh - ing in - to song.
Nev - er more be sad or wea - ry, Nev - er, nev - er sin a - gain.

When I Can Read My Title Clear

Issac Watts

J. C. Lowry

1. When I can read my ti - tle clear to man-sions in the skies,
2. Should earth a-gainst my soul en-gage and fi - ery darts be hurled,
3. Let cares like a wild del - uge come, and storms of sor-row fall,
4. There shall I bathe my wea-ry soul in seas of heav'n-ly rest.

I'll bid fare-well to ev - 'ry fear, and wipe my weep-ing eyes;
Then I can smile at Sa - tan's rage, and face a frown - ing world;
May I but safe - ly reach my home, my God, my Heav'n, my all;
And not a wave of trou-ble roll a - cross my peace-ful breast;

And wipe my weep-ing eyes, and wipe my weep-ing eyes,
And face a frown - ing world and face a frown - ing world,
My God, my Heav'n, my all, my God, my Heav'n, my all,
A - cross my peace-ful breast, a - cross my peace-ful breast,

I'll bid fare-well to ev - 'ry fear, and wipe my weep-ing eyes.
Then I can smile at Sa - tan's rage, and face a frown - ing world.
May I but safe - ly reach my home, My God, my Heav'n, my all.
And not a wave of trou-ble roll a - cross my peace-ful breast.

218   Heaven Will Surely Be Worth It All

W. Oliver Cooper

Minzo C. Jones

1. Of - ten I'm hin - dered on my way, Bur - dened so heav - y I
2. Man - y the tri - als, toils and tears, Man - y a heart - ache may
3. Toil - ing and pain I will en - dure, Till I shall hear the death

al - most fall; Then I hear Je - sus sweet - ly say,
here ap - pall; But the dear Lord so tru - ly says, "Heav - en will
an - gel call; Je - sus has prom - ised and I'm sure,

REFRAIN

sure - ly be worth it all." Heav - en will sure - ly be worth it all,

Worth all the sor - rows that here be - fall; Aft - er this life with

all its strife, Heav - en will sure - ly be worth it all.

Naturalized For Heaven

Adger M. Pace

Otis L. McCoy

1. I've been sing-ing and re - joic - ing since the Sav-iour heard my plea,
2. Though a stran - ger and an al - ien, yet He knew me, called my name,
3. Now my soul finds pleasant pas - tures in this land of corn and wine,
4. When we reach that love - ly coun - try there will be no tear-dimmed eyes,

And placed His hand, and placed His hand, up - on my brow, up - on my brow;
I trem - bling said, I trem - bling said, Lord who art Thou? Lord who art Thou;
In Christ I am, in Christ I am a fruit - ful bough, a fruit - ful bough;
No dev - il there, no dev - il there to start a row, to start a row;

Blot - ting out my sins for - ev - er, free - ly jus - ti - fy - ing me,
"I am Christ who died to save you and to cleanse you from all sin,"
Joined with Him in ho - ly un - ion, I can sing and shout and shine,
So I've bought a one - way tick - et for a man - sion in the skies,

I'm nat - ural - ized - - - - for heav - en now.
I'm nat - ural - ized

REFRAIN

I'm nat - ural - ized - - - for heav - en now, - -
I'm nat - ural - ized - - - for heav - en now,

To Christ my King - - - I've made my vow; - - -
To Christ my King - - - I've made my vow;

Let come what may - - - - I care not how, - - -
Let come what may - - - - I care not how,

I'm nat - ural - ized - - - for heav - en now.
I'm nat - ural - ized - - - for heav - en now.

The Homecoming Week

Rev. Raymond Browning

Adger M. Pace

Slow with feeling

1. Up - on our jour - ney here be - low we meet with pain and loss,
2. The shad-ows now be - gin to fall, the time is draw-ing nigh,
3. The pre - cious blood of God's own Son has saved and sanc - ti - fied,

Some - times there is a crown of thorns, some-times the heav - y cross;
When Christ our Lord shall come a - gain like light-ning from the sky;
A won - drous peo - ple for His name and they are called the bride;

The drear - y road to Cal - va - ry, the bit - ter goad and sting,
And while we wait and suf - fer here, praise God, we'll shout and sing,
Tho' here neg-lect-ed and de - spised, one day the Lord will bring,

But what's in - side those gates of pearl will be worth ev - 'ry - thing.
For one glimpse thro' those gates of pearl will be worth ev - 'ry - thing.
His chos - en ones with - in the gates, and that's worth ev - 'ry - thing.

When we're in-side the gates of pearl, We'll learn a lot of things,

We'll have a harp that's made of gold, Per-haps a thou-sand strings;

We'll sing and shout and dance a-bout, The Lamb will dry our tears,

We'll have a grand home-com-ing week, The first ten thou-sand years.

221 Have You Heard About That City?

Words & Melody
C. S. Grogan

V. B. (Vep) Ellis

1. I heard a sto - ry (and it told) of man-sions wait-ing streets of gold,
2. There's ev - er flow-ing (deep and wide) a crys-tal riv - er by your side,
3. There'll be no cry - ing (no more tears) there'll be no sor-rows no more fears,

They call it heav - en the prom - ised land, the prom - ised land;
God's light is shin - ing so bright and fair, so bright and fair;
We'll live in splen-dor and ne'er grow old, and ne'er grow old;

They say there's glo - ry (o - ver there) and cel - e - brat-ing (ev - 'ry-where)
That's where I'm go - ing (some glad day) to live for - ev - er (yes, for aye)
There'll be no dy - ing (no one sad) in that to - mor-row (we'll be glad)

And ev - 'ry-thing a - bout that place is real - ly grand, is real - ly grand.
With friends and loved ones now a - wait-ing me up there, a - wait-ing there.
We'll walk and talk with Christ up - on the streets of gold, the streets of gold.

REFRAIN

Have you heard, Have you heard,
Heard the won - drous sto - ry of the man - sions up in glo - ry,

Have you heard a - bout that cit - y in the sky, Up in the sky;

Have you heard, Have you heard,
Heard a - bout the riv - er that is flow - ing free for - ev - er,

That the saints shall live up there and nev - er die, And nev - er die?

I See Jesus

Charles B. Wycuff

Charles B. Wycuff

1. Once a man named Ste-phen, preached a-bout the Lord,
2. As the stones fell on him, beat-ing out his life,
3. Thro' the gates of glo-ry, down the streets of gold,

Folks were saved and folks were healed, as they heard his word;
Ste-phen knew he'd soon be thro' with all toil and strife;
Marched a he-ro of the Lord, in-to heav-en's fold;

Sa-tan did not like it, soon he had his crowd,
So much like the Mas-ter, with a heart so true,
When he met the Sav-iour, at the great white throne,

And as he was tried they heard Ste-phen cry a-loud.
He prayed "Lord, for-give for they know not what they do".
I be-lieve He smiled and said, "Ste-phen, wel-come home"

"I see Je - sus, stand - ing at the Fa - ther's right hand,

I see Je - sus, yon - der in the prom - ised land;

Work is o - ver, Now I'm com - ing to Thee,

I see Je - sus, stand - ing, wait - ing for me."

I'll Thank Him, I'll Praise Him

Joan Morris

Max M. Morris

1. When I get to heav - en and see my Sav - iour's face,
2. When my life has end - ed, be - fore Him I shall stand,

I'll thank Him, I'll praise Him for won - drous sav - ing grace;
I'll thank Him, I'll praise Him for sav - ing fall - en man;

As I sit be - side Him 'neath heav - en's shin - ing throne,
Up in that fair cit - y we'll nev - er have a care,

I'll thank Him, I'll praise Him for lead - ing me home.
I'll thank Him, I'll praise Him for He will be there.

When I get to heav - en, I'll lay my bur-dens down,
Yes, when I get to heav'n,

I'll see the King of glo - ry, re - ceive my home, my robe and crown;

I'll thank Him, I'll praise Him for - ev - er and ev - er,

I'll thank Him, I'll praise Him for sav - ing my soul.

At The Crowning

Mrs. Ida McCoy

Mrs. Ida McCoy

1. I would like to be at the crown-ing Of my Sav - iour and my King,
2. I would like to be with the mar - tyrs, As He calls them to His side,
3. I would like to be in the rap - ture, When the saints meet in the air,

I would like to stand at the por - tals, As the saints come marching in;
And to hear the words of the wel - come, Come and with Me e'er a - bide;
I would like to go to the sup - per, Oh, what joy be - yond com-pare;

I would like to hear the mu - sic Of the white-robed an-gel band,
I would like to be at the ban-quet, When the Lord shall serve His own,
I ex - pect to be in the num-ber That walk the street of gold,

I would like to join in their num-ber I know it will be grand.
I would like to stand with the mil - lions That sing a - round the throne.
I ex - pect to be with my Sav-iour, And His dear face be - hold.

Oh, what joy 'twill be, When we gath - er in the air;
Joy great joy, it will be,

Friends and loved ones see, Oh, the joy be - yond com - pare.
Friends and loved ones we'll see,

225 The Lord Will Come

John Milton   Jeremiah Clark

1. The Lord will come and not be slow, His foot - steps can - not err;
2. Truth from the earth, like to a flower, Shall bud and blos - som then;
3. Rise, God, judge Thou the earth in might, This wick - ed earth re - dress;
4. For great Thou art, and won - ders great, By Thy strong hand are done;

Be - fore Him righteous - ness shall go, His roy - al har - bin - ger.
And jus - tice, from her heav'n - ly pow'r, Look down on mor - tal men.
For Thou art He who shall by right, The na - tions all pos - sess.
Thou in Thy ev - er - last - ing seat Re - main - est God a - lone.

I'll Be At Home

C. S. Grogan

C. S. Grogan

1. I fell up-on my knees one day and re-pent-ed of my sins,
2. We know not when our Lord will come to catch His saints a-way,
3. The first ten thou-sand years up there, let me look up-on His face,

By faith I o-pened up my heart and let the Sav-iour in;
He on-ly told us in His Word to work and watch and pray;
I'll need that long to thank my Lord for His a-maz-ing grace;

He blot-ted out my sin-ful past and claimed me as His own,
As light-ning flash-es from the sky, He will come and we'll be gone,
I'll then have time to meet my friends as through that land I roam,

He's com-ing back for me some day and then I'll be at home.
At last we'll have a home with Him that we can call our own.
I'll have a grand e-ter-ni-ty in heav-en, my new home.

REFRAIN

Oh, yes, I'll be at home, I know I'll be at home,
Yes, I'll be at home, know I'll be at home,

To live up there for-ev-er, no more in sin to roam;
Live up there for aye, no more in sin to roam;

I'm hap-py on my way, I'm near-er ev-'ry day,
Hap-py on my way, near-er ev-'ry day,

I'll soon reach heaven's pearly gates and then I'll be at home.
Soon reach heaven's gates and then I'll be at home.

I'm Moving Up Some Day

Rev. & Mrs. Jack W. Simmons   Rev. & Mrs. Jack W. Simmons

1. I've start-ed on a jour-ney to a cit-y bright and fair,
2. So oft-en here we move a-bout, no place to call our home,
3. I've made my prep-a-ra-tion I'm just wait-ing for the time,

No sor-row there, I'll nev-er know a care, no pain nor care;
But o-ver there no more we'll have to roam, we'll nev-er roam;
To soar a-way to that fair home of mine, that home of mine;

I'll soon be home with loved ones true with Christ I'll live for aye,
We'll set-tle down for our last time and nev-er move a-way,
And as I jour-ney thru this land I'm glad that I can say,

I'm mov-ing up to glo-ry-land some day, I'll move some day.

REFRAIN

I'm mov - ing up some day to glo - ry, mov - ing up some day,

I'm mov - ing up to glo - ry - land to stay, to ev - er stay;

I'm glad that I can know that I am read - y now to go,

I'm mov - ing up to glo - ry - land some day, some hap - py day.

228 I Wouldn't Miss It For The World

Charles B. Wycuff

Charles B. Wycuff

1. I've start - ed out to win a place when I have run this earth - ly race, In heav - en where with the Lord I'll be; In that land far be - yond the sun where sor - row nev - er more can come, From pain and care we'll be ev - er free, ev - er free.

2. 'Tho Sa - tan comes to hin - der me I know that I have been set free, And I am un - der his pow'r no more; I'll keep my trust in Christ, my Lord and rest on His e - ter - nal word, And I'll land safe - ly on heav - en's shore, heaven's shore.

3. When time has come for me to go from this vain world of sin be - low, And I have told those I love good - bye; I'll take my flight to worlds un - known to heav - en's bright and star - ry dome, My home in heav - en be - yond the sky, past the sky.

REFRAIN

By His grace I'll make it   I shall make it thru,
By His grace I   shall reach heav-en,

Want to see what waits in-side those gates of   pearl;
Oh, I

No more pain and heart-ache   we shall ev-er know,
No more heart-aches,   pain or sor-row,

No, I would not miss it for the   world.
Oh, I know

If I Knew Of A Land

W. L. (Bill) Hopper

W. L. (Bill) Hopper

1. If I knew of a land where no sor - row ev - er came,
2. If I knew of a land where no dark clouds ev - er came,
3. If I knew of a land where my dreams would all come true,

Where the weath - er was just right and there were no sick or lame;
Where the sky was al - ways bright and there'd be no storm or rain;
Where the things of life were free and there'd be no work to do;

Where there'd be no good - bys and the peo - ple lived for aye,
Where our loved ones were true and would not a trust be - tray,
Where no war e'er could come and we'd live in peace for aye,

I would sell all I have and move to - day.

REFRAIN

Well, I know of a land where joys are wait - ing,

Where the peo - ple live for - ev - er and for aye;

'Twill be one e - ter - nal day with - out a sor - row,

And some morn - ing when He calls I'll move a - way.

230

Over Yonder

C. S. Grogan

C. S. Grogan

1. Soon I'll come to cross the might-y Jor-dan riv-er,
2. Ev-'ry time I pray I feel a lit-tle near-er,
3. As I read the Word of Life I'm grow-ing strong-er,

Soon I'll sail a-way be-yond the roll-ing tide;
To my home e-ter-nal just a-cross the sea;
I am search-ing for the things that sat-is-fy;

Then I'll be with Christ in par-a-dise for-ev-er,
Ev-'ry time I speak His name, my Lord is dear-er,
If I'm true to Him but just a lit-tle long-er,

O-ver yon-der on the hal-le-lu-jah side.
O-ver yon-der by His side I long to be.
O-ver yon-der I will find them by and by.

REFRAIN

O - ver yon - der, o - ver yon - der,
O - ver yon - der, o - ver yon - der,

Par - a - dise is just be - yond the roll - ing tide;

Oh how glad I'll be to see the face of Je - sus,

O - ver yon - der on the hal - le - lu - jah side.

231 There Will Dawn A Brighter Day

Edward L. Williams

Edward L. Williams

1. When I get to heav-en some sweet day, my cares will all be o'er,
2. God has prom-ised in His bless-ed Word, He has pre-pared a place,
3. Man-y things in life we do not know, rea-sons are hard to find,

Then I'll see my Sav-iour, praise His name, on that e-ter-nal shore;
If I will His Ho-ly Word o-bey, He will sup-ply the grace;
Why we're burdened dai-ly and de-pressed, why life has been un-kind;

I will shout the vic-t'ry, I have won a won-drous crown of life,
I must reach that land of end-less day, what-e'er the cost may be,
Mys-ter-ies of life will be re-vealed, we'll know as we are known,

I will trust in Him to lead me thru this world of sin and strife.
What a won-drous land of beau-ty rare, from cares I will be free.
What a hap-py day I know 'twill be, nev-er to be a-lone.

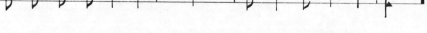

REFRAIN

I'll nev-er-more be lone-ly, I'll nev-er-more be
No, nev-er-more,

blue, I'm trust-ing in my Je-sus
nev-er be blue, I'm trust-ing Him

to guide me safe - ly thru; There'll nev-er be a
to guide me safe-ly thru;

heart-ache or sor-row, all tears dried a-way, When

Sa-tan comes, re-sist Him, There will dawn a bright-er day.

That Heavenly Home

Frank White

Frank White

1. I'm look-ing a - way - - - be-yond the dark stream, - -
2. That won-der-ful home - - - will nev-er be sold, - -
3. That heav-en-ly home - - - has man-sions of light, - -

To heav-en's fair home, - - - - of which I oft dream; - - -
We'll ev - er live there, - - - where no one grows old; - - -
No storm clouds will rise, - - - - no shad-ows of night; - - -

There mil - lions have gone, - - - its glo - ry to share, - - -
The cit - y's bright spires - - - the sun will out-shine, - - -
No sor-row, no pain, - - - all sin will be gone, - - -

Get read - y my friend, - - - - to live o - ver there.
With all of the saved, - - - - that home shall be mine.
We'll live with the Lord - - - - - while a - ges roll on.

REFRAIN

That heav-en-ly home   lies o-ver death's sea,

That heav-en-ly home   lies o-ver death's sea,

There loved ones I know, are wait-ing for me, are wait-ing for me;

There loved ones I know,   are wait-ing for me;

With Je - sus we'll live - - - in glo - ry di - vine, - - -

That heav - en - ly home - - - - - will sure - ly be mine .

233 Remember

M. S. Lemons

R. E. Winsett

1. I re-mem-ber how my Sav-iour died for me, died for me,
2. I re-mem-ber how He blessed and broke the bread, broke the bread,
3. I re-mem-ber how He blessed the cup of wine, cup of wine,
4. Just re-mem-ber how they pierced Him in the side, in the side,

On the rug-ged cross of dark Mount Cal-va-ry; Cal-va-ry;
Sig-ni-fies my bro-ken bod-y, thus He said, thus He said;
That which is the pre-cious fruit-age of the vine, of the vine;
From which flowed the pre-cious heal-ing cleans-ing tide; cleansing tide;

I re-mem-bered how He cried, How He bowed His head and died,
Bro-ken on the cru-el tree, Hang-ing there for you and me,
O this is My blood, He said, And for man-y it was shed,
It was shed for you and me, That from sin we might be free,

I re-mem-ber dark Cal-va-ry, dark Cal-va-ry.

REFRAIN

I re - mem - ber how He paid the debt for me, debt for me,

How His blood was shed on dark Cal - va - ry, Cal - va - ry;

O the blood of Cal - 'ry's brow, I can see it flow - ing now,

I re - mem - ber dark Cal - va - ry, dark Cal - va - ry.

We Gather At Thy Table, Lord

David Horton

David Horton

1. We gath - er at thy ta - ble, Lord, Thy sac - ri - fice to
2. - Pas - chal Lamb and of - f'ring Priest, Thy - self pre - pared this

bring to mind; With hearts and minds in one ac - cord, We
ho - ly feast; Thou didst or - dain for sac - ra - ment, The

take to - day the bread and wine . As we be - fore Thee hum - bly bow,
blood of Thy new tes - ta - ment. We lift the cup, we take the bread,

Oh, cleanse and pu - ri - fy us now; Pre - pare our hearts
For Thou hast bruised the ser - pent's head; Our soul's de - light,

to see Thy face, By whol - ly trust - ing in Thy grace .
our heart's best praise, O gra - cious, Lord, to Thee we raise.

235

Jesus Saves

Priscilla J. Owens

William J. Kirkpatrick

1. We have heard the joy-ful sound: Je - sus saves! Je - sus saves!
2. Waft it on the roll - ing tide: Je - sus saves! Je - sus saves!
3. Sing a - bove the bat - tle strife: Je - sus saves! Je - sus saves!
4. Give the winds a might - y voice: Je - sus saves! Je - sus saves!

Spread the ti - dings all a - round: Je - sus saves! Je - sus saves!
Tell to sin - ners far and wide: Je - sus saves! Je - sus saves!
By His death and end - less life, Je - sus saves! Je - sus saves!
Let the na - tions now re - joice: Je - sus saves! Je - sus saves!

Bear the news to ev - ery land, Climb the steeps and cross the waves;
Sing, ye is - lands of the sea; Ech - o back, ye o - cean caves;
Sing it soft - ly through the gloom, When the heart for mer - cy craves;
Shout sal - va - tion full and free; High - est hills and deep - est caves;

On - ward! 'tis our Lord's com - mand; Je - sus saves! Je - sus saves!
Earth shall keep her ju - bi - lee: Je - sus saves! Je - sus saves!
Sing in tri - umph o'er the tomb, Je - sus saves! Je - sus saves!
This our song of vic - to - ry: Je - sus saves! Je - sus saves!

Send The Light

Charles H. Gabriel   Charles H. Gabriel

1. There's a call comes ring-ing o'er the rest-less wave,
2. We have heard the Mac-e-do-nian call to-day,
3. Let us pray that grace may ev-'ry-where a-bound;
4. Let us not grow wea-ry in the work of love,

"Send the light! Send the light!"
Send the light! Send the light!

There are souls to res-cue, there are souls to save,
And a gold-en of-f'ring at the cross we lay,
And a Christ-like spir-it ev-'ry-where be found,
Let us gath-er jew-els for a crown a-bove,

Send the light! Send the light!
Send the light! Send the light!

REFRAIN

Send the light! the bless-ed gos-pel light;
Send the light! the bless-ed gos-pel light;

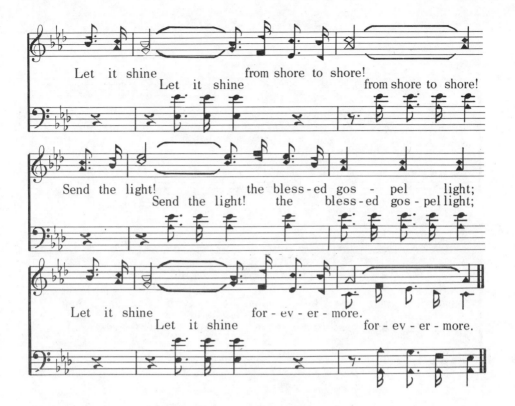

Let it shine   from shore to shore!
Let it shine   from shore to shore!

Send the light!   the bless-ed gos - pel   light;
Send the light!   the   bless-ed gos-pel light;

Let it shine   for - ev - er - more.
Let it shine   for - ev - er - more.

237   A Charge To Keep

Charles Wesley   Lowell Mason

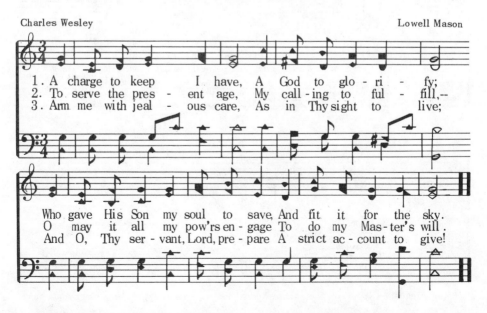

1. A charge to keep   I have, A God to glo-ri - fy;
2. To serve the pres - ent age, My call-ing to ful - fill,--
3. Arm me with jeal - ous care, As in Thy sight to   live;

Who gave His Son   my soul to save, And fit it for the sky.
O may it all   my pow'rs en-gage To do my Mas-ter's will.
And O, Thy ser - vant, Lord, pre-pare A strict ac - count to give!

238 Speak, My Lord

George Bennard

George Bennard

1. Hear the Lord of har-vest sweet-ly call-ing, "Who will go and
2. When the coal of fire — touched the prophet, Mak-ing him as
3. Mil-lions now in sin and shame are dy-ing, Lis-ten to their
4. Soon the time for reap-ing will be o-ver, Soon we'll gath-er

work for Me to-day? Who will bring to Me the lost and
pure, as pure can be, When the voice of God said, "Who'll go
sad and bit-ter cry; Has-ten, broth-er, has-ten to the
for the har-vest-home; May the Lord of har-vest smile up-

REFRAIN

dy-ing? Who will point them to the nar-row way?"
for us?" Then He an-swered, "Here I am, send me!" Speak, my
res-cue; Quick-ly an-swer, "Mas-ter, here am I."
on us, May we hear His bless-ed, "Child, well done."

Lord, speak, my Lord,
Speak, my Lord, speak, my Lord,
Speak, and I'll be

quick to an-swer Thee; Speak, my Lord,
to an-swer Thee; Speak, my Lord,

speak, my Lord, Speak, and I will an-swer, "Lord, send me!"
"Lord, send me!"

239   Lord, Speak To Me

Frances R. Havergal   Robert A. Schumann

1. Lord, speak to me, that   I may   speak In liv - ing
2. Oh! teach me, Lord, that   I may   teach The pre - cious
3. Oh! use me, Lord, use   ev - en   me, Just as Thou

ech - oes of Thy tone; As Thou hast sought, so   let
things Thou dost im - part; And wing my words, that   they
wilt, and when, and where; Un - til Thy bless - ed   face

me   seek, The err - ing chil - dren   lost and lone.
may reach The hid - den depths of   many a heart.
I   see, Thy rest, Thy joy, Thy   glo - ry share.

Win The Lost At Any Cost

Leon H. Ellis

Leon H. Ellis

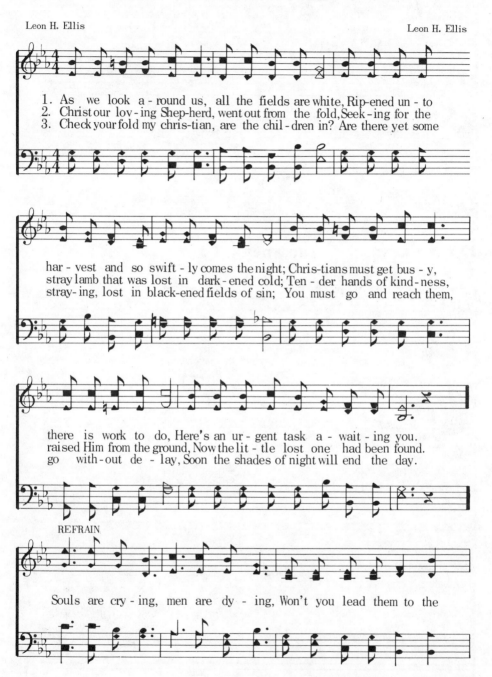

1. As we look a-round us, all the fields are white, Rip-ened un-to
2. Christ our lov-ing Shep-herd, went out from the fold, Seek-ing for the
3. Check your fold my chris-tian, are the chil-dren in? Are there yet some

har-vest and so swift-ly comes the night; Chris-tians must get bus-y,
stray lamb that was lost in dark-ened cold; Ten-der hands of kind-ness,
stray-ing, lost in black-ened fields of sin; You must go and reach them,

there is work to do, Here's an ur-gent task a-wait-ing you.
raised Him from the ground, Now the lit-tle lost one had been found.
go with-out de-lay, Soon the shades of night will end the day.

REFRAIN

Souls are cry-ing, men are dy-ing, Won't you lead them to the

cross?   Go and find them, help to win them,
lead them to the cross?

Win the lost at an - y cost.   Go out and win,   res - cue from

sin, Day's al - most done, low sinks the sun, Souls are cry - ing,

men are dy - ing, Win the lost at an - y cost.

241 Throw Out The Life-Line

Edward S. Ufford

Edward S. Ufford
Arr. by George C. Stebbins

1. Throw out the Life-Line a-cross the dark wave, There is a broth-er whom
2. Throw out the Life-Line with hand quick and strong: Why do you tar-ry, why
3. Throw our the Life-Line to dan-ger-fraught men, Sink-ing in an-guish where
4. Soon will the sea-son of res-cue be o'er, Soon will they drift to e-

some-one should save; Some-bod-y's broth-er! O who then, will dare To
lin-ger so long? See! he is sink-ing; O has-ten to-day—And
you've nev-er been: Winds of temp-ta-tion and bil-lows of woe Will
ter-ni-ty's shore; Haste then, my broth-er, no time for de-lay, But

REFRAIN

throw out the Life-Line, his per-il to share?
out with the Life-Boat! a-way, then, a-way! Throw out the Life-Line!
soon hurl them out where the dark wa-ters flow.
throw out the Life-Line and save them to-day.

Throw out the Life-Line! Some-one is drift-ing a-way; Throw out the

Life-Line! Throw out the Life-Line! Some-one is sink-ing to-day.

We'll Work Till Jesus Comes

Elizabeth Mills

William Miller

1. O land of rest for thee I sigh! When will the mo - ment come
2. To Je - sus Christ I fled for rest; He bade me cease to roam,
3. I sought at once my Sav - iour's side, No more my steps to roam,

When I shall lay my ar - mor by And dwell in peace at home?
And lean for suc - cor on His breast Till he con - ducts me home.
With Him I'll brave death's chilling tide, And reach my heav'n-ly home.

REFRAIN

We'll work till Je - sus comes, We'll work till Je - sus comes,
We'll work   We'll work

We'll work till Je - sus comes, And we'll be gath-ered home.
We'll work

Bringing In The Sheaves

Knowles Shaw

George A. Minor

1. Sow - ing in the morn - ing, sow - ing seeds of kind - ness,
2. Sow - ing in the sun - shine, sow - ing in the shad - ows;
3. Go - ing forth with weep - ing, sow - ing for the Mas - ter,

Sow - ing in the noon - tide and the dew - y eve;
Fear - ing nei - ther clouds nor win - ter's chill - ing breeze;
Tho' the loss sus - tained our spir - it of - ten grieves;

Wait - ing for the har - vest, and the time of reap - ing,
By and by the har - vest, and the la - bor end - ed,
When our weep - ing's o - ver, He will bid us wel - come,

We shall come re - joic - ing, bring - ing in the sheaves.
We shall come re - joic - ing, bring - ing in the sheaves.
We shall come re - joic - ing, bring - ing in the sheaves.

REFRAIN

Bring - ing in the sheaves, bring-ing in the sheaves, We shall

come re - joic - ing, bring - ing in the sheaves; Bring-ing in the sheaves, bring-ing in the sheaves, We shall come re-joic-ing, bring - ing in the sheaves.

244   **Jesus Shall Reign**

Isaac Watts   John Hatton

1. Je - sus shall reign wher - e'er the sun Does his suc - ces - sive jour - neys run; His king - dom spread from shore to shore, Till moons shall wax and wane no more.

2. From north to south the princ - es meet To pay their hom - age at His feet; While west - ern em - pires own their Lord, And sav - age tribes at - tend His Word.

3. Peo - ple and realms of ev - 'ry tongue Dwell on His love with sweet - est song; And in - fant voic - es shall pro - claim Their ear - ly bless - ings on His name.

245 Bring Them In

Alexcenah Thomas   W. A. Ogden

1. Hark! 'tis the Shep-herd's voice I hear, Out in the des-ert dark and drear, Call-ing the sheep who've gone astray Far from the Shepherd's fold a-way.

2. Who'll go and help this Shep-herd kind, Help Him the wand'-ring ones to find? Who'll bring the lost ones to the fold, Where they'll be sheltered from the cold?

3. Out in the des-ert hear their cry, Out on the moun-tains wild and high; Hark! 'tis the Mas-ter speaks to thee, "Go find my sheep wher-e'er they be."

REFRAIN

Bring them in, bring them in, Bring them in from the fields of sin; Bring them in, bring them in, Bring the wand'ring ones to Je-sus.

Rescue The Perishing

Fanny J. Crosby

William H. Doane

1. Res-cue the per-ish-ing, Care for the dy-ing, Snatch them in
2. Tho' they are slighting Him, Still He is wait-ing, Wait-ing the
3. Down in the hu-man heart, Crush'd by the tempt-er, Feel-ings lie
4. Res-cue the per-ish-ing, Du-ty de-mands it; Strength for thy

pit-y from sin and the grave; Weep o'er the err-ing one,
pen-i-tent child to re-ceive; Plead with them ear-nest-ly,
bur-ied that grace can re-store; Touch'd by a lov-ing heart,
la-bor the Lord will pro-vide; Back to the nar-row way

Lift up the fall-en, Tell them of Je-sus the might-y to save.
Plead with them gen-tly, He will for-give if they on-ly be-lieve.
Wak-en'd by kind-ness, Chords that are bro-ken will vi-brate once more.
Pa-tient-ly win them; Tell the poor wan-d'rer a Sav-iour has died.

REFRAIN

Res - cue the per - ish - ing, Care for the dy - ing;

Je - sus is mer - ci - ful, Je - sus will save.

Revive Us Again

William P. Mackay

John J. Husband

1. We praise Thee, O God! for the Son of Thy love,
2. We praise Thee, O God! for Thy Spir - it of light,
3. All glo - ry and praise to the Lamb that was slain,
4. Re - vive us a - gain, fill each heart with Thy love,

For Je - sus who died and is now gone a - bove.
Who hath shown us our Sav - iour and scat - tered our night.
Who hath borne all our sins and hath cleansed ev - 'ry stain.
May each soul be re - kin - dled with fire from a - bove.

REFRAIN

Hal - le - lu - jah! Thine the glo - ry, Hal - le - lu - jah! a - men;

Hal - le - lu - jah! Thine the glo - ry, Re - vive us a - gain.

Revive Thy Work

Alfred Midlane   James McGranahan

1. Re - vive Thy work, O Lord! Thy might - y arm make bare;
2. Re - vive Thy work, O Lord! Dis - turb this sleep of death;
3. Re - vive Thy work, O Lord! Cre - ate soul - thirst for Thee;
4. Re - vive Thy work, O Lord! Ex - alt Thy pre - cious name;

Speak with the voice that wakes the dead, And make Thy peo - ple hear.
Quick - en the smoul - d'ring em - bers now By Thine al - might - y breath.
But hun - g'ring for the bread of life, Oh, may our spir - its be!
And, by the Ho - ly Ghost, our love For Thee and Thine in - flame.

REFRAIN

Re - vive! . . . . . re - vive! . . . . And give re - fresh - ing show'rs;
Re - vive Thy work! re - vive Thy work! And give, oh, give re - fresh - ing show'rs;

The glo - ry shall be all Thine own; The bless - ing shall be ours.

Lord, Send A Revival

B. B. McKinney

B. B. McKinney

1. Send a re-viv-al, O Christ, my Lord, Let it go
2. Send a re-viv-al a-mong Thine own, Help us to
3. Send a re-viv-al to those in sin, Help them, O
4. Send a re-viv-al in ev - 'ry heart, Draw the world

o - ver the land and sea; Send it ac-cord-ing to
turn from our sins a - way; Let us get near - er the
Je - sus, to turn to Thee; Let them the new life in
near - er, O Lord, to Thee; Let Thy sal - va - tion true

Thy dear Word, And let it be - gin in me.
Fa - ther's throne, Re - vive us a - gain, we pray.
Thee be - gin, Oh, give them the vic - to - ry.
joy im - part, And let it be - gin in me.

REFRAIN

Lord, send a re-viv - al, Lord, send a re-viv - al;

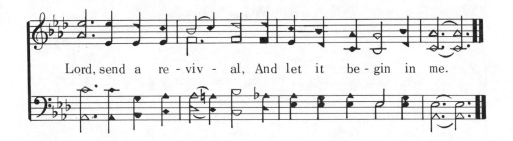

Lord, send a re - viv - al, And let it be - gin in me.

250   What The World Needs Is Jesus

(CHORUS)

Benjamin A. Baur   Benjamin A. Baur

What the world needs is Je - sus, Just a glimpse of Him;

What the world needs is Je - sus, Just a glimpse of Him;

He will bring joy and glad - ness, Take a - way sin and sad - ness;

What the world needs is Je - sus, Just a glimpse of Him.

251   A World–Wide Revival

Mrs. C. H. Morris   Mrs. C. H. Morris

1. For a world-wide re-viv-al, Bless-ed Mas-ter, we pray,
2. Send the "show-ers of bless-ing" as de-clared in Thy Word,
3. There's a "sound of a go-ing in the mul-ber-ry trees"

Let the pow'r of the high-est be up-on us to-day;
Let the "Spir-it of prom-ise" on all flesh be out-poured;
News of na-tions a-wak-ing, borne up-on ev-'ry breeze;

For this world, dear-ly pur-chased by the blood of God's Son,
Send the "lat-ter rain" on us till the land o-ver-flows,
For the prayers of His chil-dren, God in mer-cy doth own,

Back from Sa-tan's do-min-ion and from sin must be won.
Till the des-ert, re-joic-ing, blos-soms forth as the rose.
The re-viv-al's be-gin-ning, and the pow'r's com-ing down.

Send the pow'r, O Lord, send the pow'r, O Lord,

Send the Ho - ly Ghost pow - er, let it now be out-poured;

Send it surg - ing and sweep-ing like the waves of the sea,

Send a world-wide re - viv - al, and be - gin it in me!

Lord, Send A Revival

Bennie S. Triplett

Bennie S. Triplett

1. Send a re-viv-al in me, Lord, I pray, Be - gin to-
2. Lord, wilt Thou not in the midst of these days, Re - vive Thy

day in Thine own way, Take me and use me and
works, re - vive Thy ways, That Thou and Thy peo - ple

make me to be a lamp, a light for Thee; Mold me and
may be em - ployed in cease-less prayer and praise; Pray - ing for

make me, O Mas - ter, to - day, Thou art the pot - ter and
pow - er to come from on high, Prais-ing the Sav - iour who

I am the clay, What - e'er the cost make a chan - nel of
came down to die, That I might live and to Je - sus give

REFRAIN

old time re-viv-al thru me.
all I am or hope to be. Lord, send a re-

viv-al in me, Lord, We need the vic-to-ry;

I'll not re-lease Thee un-til Thou in-crease me with

pow-er and grace full and free, Pour o'er my soul a re-

fresh-ing of old time re-viv-al, re-viv-al from Thee.

253 There Shall Be Showers Of Blessing

El Nathan

James McGranahan

1. "There shall be show-ers of bless - ing:" This is the prom-ise of love;
2. "There shall be show-ers of bless - ing:" Pre - cious re - viv-ing a - gain;
3. "There shall be show-ers of bless - ing:" Send them up-on us, O Lord;
4. "There shall be show-ers of bless - ing:" Oh, that to - day they might fall,

There shall be sea - sons re - fresh - ing, Sent from the Sav - iour a - bove.
O - ver the hills and the val - leys, Sound of a - bun - dance of rain.
Grant to us now a re - fresh - ing, Come, and now hon - or Thy Word.
Now as to God we're con - fess-ing, Now as on Je - sus we call!

REFRAIN

Show - ers of bless - ing, Show-ers of bless - ing we need:
Show-ers, show-ers of bless - ing,

Mer - cy - drops round us are fall - ing, But for the show - ers we plead.

Sweet Hour Of Prayer

William W. Walford

William B. Bradbury

1. Sweet hour of prayer, sweet hour of prayer, That calls me from a world of care,
2. Sweet hour of prayer, sweet hour of prayer, The joys I feel, the bliss I share
3. Sweet hour of prayer, sweet hour of prayer, Thy wings shall my pe-ti-tion bear

And bids me at my Fa-ther's throne, Make all my wants and wish-es known!
Of those whose anx-ious spir-its burn With strong de-sires for thy re-turn!
To Him, whose truth and faith-ful-ness En-gage the wait-ing soul to bless:

In sea-sons of dis-tress and grief, My soul has of-ten found re-lief,
With such I has-ten to the place Where God my Sav-iour shows His face,
And since He bids me seek His face, Be-lieve His word, and trust His grace,

And oft es-caped the temp-ter's snare By thy re-turn, sweet hour of prayer.
And glad-ly take my sta-tion there, And wait for thee, sweet hour of prayer.
I'll cast on Him my ev-'ry care, And wait for thee, sweet hour of prayer.

255 Take It To The Lord In Prayer

V. B. (Vep) Ellis

V. B. (Vep) Ellis

Soprano and Alto Duet

1. If the road be - fore you of - fers naught but toil and pain,
2. When it seems that not a friend on earth can un - der - stand,
3. In your dis - ap - point-ment when your heart is torn with grief,

If the sun is hid - den by dark clouds of rain;
When temp - ta - tion comes to you from ev - 'ry hand;
In your times of sor - row when there's no re - lief;

If with - out a ray of hope your life is filled with care,
When your strength is al - most gone and there's no one to care,
Just re - mem - ber there is One who knows the load you bear,

REFRAIN

Take it to the Lord in prayer. Man - y are the

heart-aches that will come to you, Keep your trust in Je - sus, He will

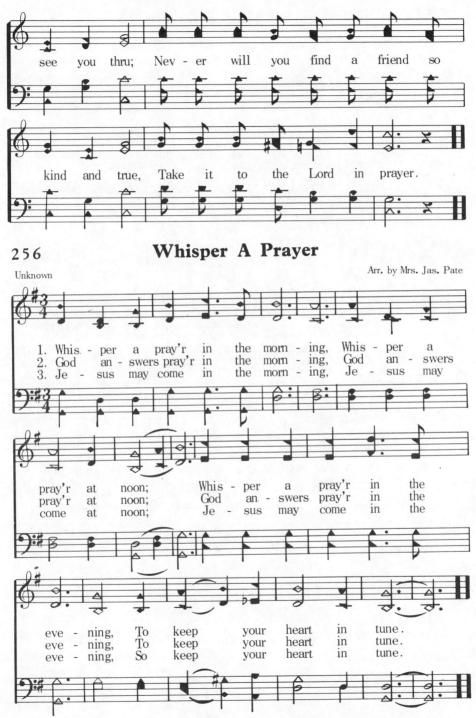

see you thru; Nev - er will you find a friend so

kind and true, Take it to the Lord in prayer.

256 **Whisper A Prayer**

Unknown

Arr. by Mrs. Jas. Pate

1. Whis - per a pray'r in the morn - ing, Whis - per a
2. God an - swers pray'r in the morn - ing, God an - swers
3. Je - sus may come in the morn - ing, Je - sus may

pray'r at noon; Whis - per a pray'r in the
pray'r at noon; God an - swers pray'r in the
come at noon; Je - sus may come in the

eve - ning, To keep your heart in tune.
eve - ning, To keep your heart in tune.
eve - ning, So keep your heart in tune.

I Am Praying For You

S. O'Malley Cluff

Ira D. Sankey

1. I have a Sav-iour, He's plead-ing in glo-ry, A dear
2. I have a Fa-ther; to me He has giv-en A hope
3. I have a robe: 'tis re-splen-dent in white-ness, A-wait-
4. When Christ has found you, tell oth-ers the sto-ry, That my

lov-ing Sav-iour, tho' earth friends be few; And now He is watch-
for e-ter-ni-ty bless-ed and true; And soon will He call
ing in glo-ry my won-der-ing view; Oh, when I re-ceive
lov-ing Sav-iour is your Sav-iour, too; Then pray that your Sav-

ing in ten-der-ness o'er me, And oh, that my Sav-iour were
me to meet Him in heav-en, But, oh, that He'd let me bring
it all shin-ing in bright-ness, Dear friend, could I see you re-
iour may bring them to glo-ry, And prayer will be an-swered; 'twas

REFRAIN

your Sav-iour, too.
you with me, too!
ceiv-ing one, too!   For you I am pray-ing, For you I am
an-swered for you!

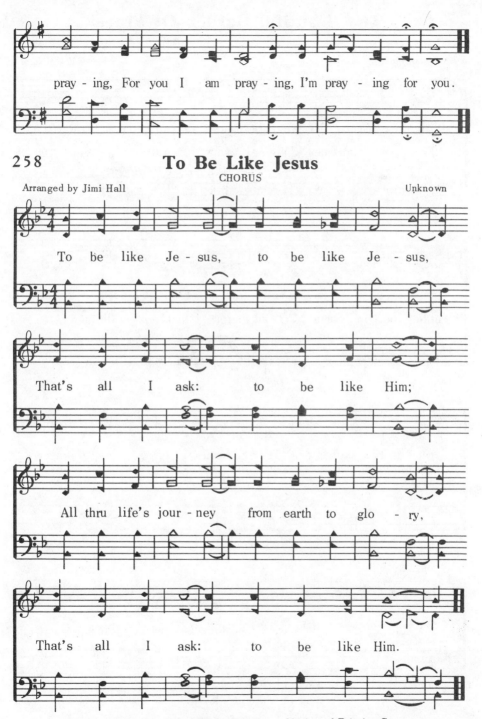

pray - ing, For you I am pray - ing, I'm pray - ing for you.

258

To Be Like Jesus
CHORUS

Arranged by Jimi Hall

Unknown

To be like Je - sus, to be like Je - sus,

That's all I ask: to be like Him;

All thru life's jour - ney from earth to glo - ry,

That's all I ask: to be like Him.

259 The Beautiful Garden Of Prayer

Eleanor A. Schroll

James H. Fillmore

1. There's a gar-den where Je-sus is wait-ing, There's a place that is won-drous-ly fair; For it glows with the light of His pres-ence, 'Tis the beau-ti-ful gar-den of prayer.

2. There's a gar-den where Je-sus is wait-ing, And I go with my bur-den and care; Just to learn from His lips words of com-fort, In the beau-ti-ful gar-den of prayer.

3. There's a gar-den where Je-sus is wait-ing, And He bids you to come meet Him there; Just to walk and to talk with my Sav-iour, In the beau-ti-ful gar-den of prayer.

REFRAIN

O the beau-ti-ful gar-den, the gar-den of prayer, O the

beau - ti - ful gar - den of prayer; There my Sav - iour a - waits,

and He o - pens the gates, To the beau - ti - ful gar - den of prayer.

260   **God Is Present Everywhere**

J. H. Fillmore

J. H. Fillmore

1. They   who seek   the throne of grace Find that throne in   ev - 'ry place;
2. In   our sick - ness, in our health, In   our want   or   in   our wealth;
3. When   our earth - ly com - forts fail, When the woes of life   pre - vail,

If   we live   a   life   of pray'r, God   is   pres - ent   ev - 'ry - where.
If   we look   to God   in pray'r, God   is   pres - ent   ev - 'ry - where.
'Tis the time   for ear - nest pray'r, God   is   pres - ent   ev - 'ry - where.

Whisper The Name Of Jesus

Bennie S. Triplett

Bennie S. Triplett

1. There are some peo - ple who hold the scep - ter high,
2. Why are you seek - ing to sat - is - fy the soul,

Rul - er of sub - jects from birth un - til they die,
In earth - ly treas - ure, in sil - ver and in gold,

Mar - shal - ing ar - mies on near and dis - tant shore,
There's no real joy to be found in such suc - cess,

Con - quer - ing cas - tles un - til they stand no more, Yet there is
World - ly al - loy will not give your spir - it rest, There is a

One who is far a - bove these, Whisper His name, it's Je - sus.
source which will sat - is - fy best, That source is found in Je - sus.

Whis- per the name and the storm will pass a - way,

Whis - per the name, cloud - ed night will turn to day,

Whis - per His name, pain and sick - ness will cease,

Trust in His pow'r and from sin be re - leased, If you be-

live, your de - spair will be peace, Whisper the name of Je - sus.

Yes, God Is Able

Charles L. Towler

Charles L. Towler

1. If God could speak and bring the world in - to ex - is - tence,
2. If God could feed His peo - ple with the bread from heav - en,
3. If God could send down fire to burn up - on the al - tar,

If He could make the light to shine where all was dim;
If He could cause their clothes to nev - er wear a - way;
If He could stop the rain from fall - ing from the sky;

If He de - signed and put the u - ni - verse in mo - tion,
If God could give them wa - ter from a rock - y moun - tain,
If God could cause a man to proph - e - sy the fu - ture,

Then sure - ly there is not a thing too hard for Him.
Then sure - ly He'll sup - ply our needs if we will pray.
Then sure - ly He's the One on whom we should re - ly.

Yes, God is a - ble to do what - so - ev - er we ask,

In the name of His Son, that His will might be done;

And He is a - ble to give what - so - ev - er we need,

If we'll on - ly be - lieve when we pray.

Pray Till Your Prayers Go Through

B. C. Robinson

B. C. Robinson

1. When your life is drear-y and you feel de-spair, Your man-y
2. You may nev-er own a man-sion in this land, Where you'll want for
3. There's a bet-ter day a-wait-ing you and me, If we cling to

trou-bles seem to wor-ry you; It is then you need to
noth-ing and the skies be blue; Yet you look for these
Je-sus, to His word be true; Should we keep on pray-ing

pray a fer-vent pray'r,
on the gold-en strand, Pray till your pray'rs go thru.
and from sin stay free,

REFRAIN

Pray till your pray'rs go thru, go thru, Al-ways pray till your

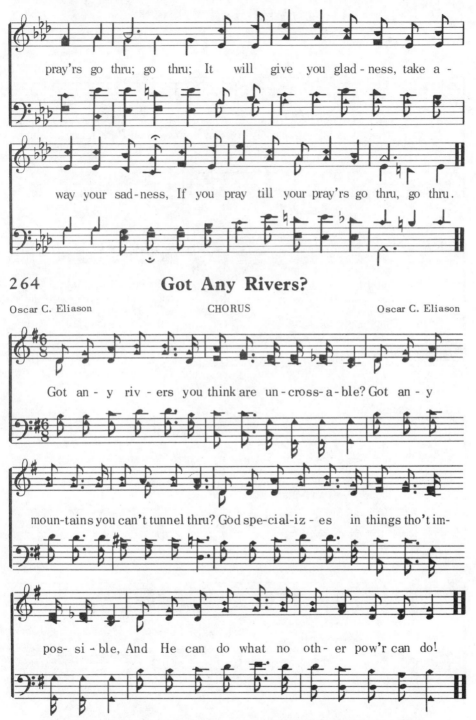

pray'rs go thru; go thru; It will give you glad - ness, take a -

way your sad-ness, If you pray till your pray'rs go thru, go thru.

264

Got Any Rivers?

Oscar C. Eliason

CHORUS

Oscar C. Eliason

Got an - y riv - ers you think are un-cross-a-ble? Got an - y

moun-tains you can't tunnel thru? God spe-cial-iz - es in things tho't im-

pos-si-ble, And He can do what no oth- er pow'r can do!

I Must Tell Jesus

Elisha A. Hoffman

Elisha A. Hoffman

1. I must tell Je - sus all of my tri - als; I can - not bear
2. I must tell Je - sus all of my trou - bles; He is a kind,
3. Tempt-ed and tried, I need a great Sav - iour, One who can help
4. O how the world to e - vil al - lures me! O how my heart

these bur-dens a - lone; In my dis - tress He kind-ly will
com - pas - sion-ate friend; If I but ask Him, He will de -
my bur - dens to bear; I must tell Je - sus, I must tell
is tempt - ed to sin! I must tell Je - sus, and He will

help me; He ev - er loves and cares for His own.
liv - er, Make of my trou - bles quick - ly an end.
Je - sus; He all my cares and sor - rows will share.
help me O - ver the world the vic - t'ry to win.

REFRAIN

I must tell Je - sus! I must tell Je - sus! I can - not bear

my bur - dens a - lone; I must tell Je - sus! I must tell

Je - sus! Je - sus can help me, Je - sus a - lone.

266   Immortal Love, Forever Full

John C. Whittier

William V. Wallace

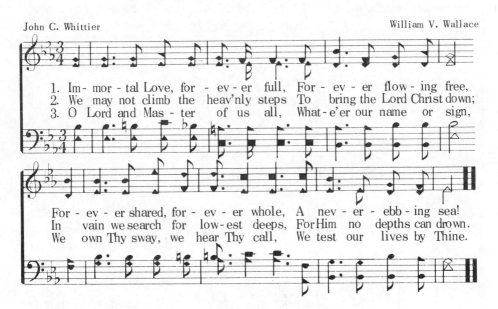

1. Im - mor - tal Love, for - ev - er full, For - ev - er flow - ing free,
2. We may not climb the heav'nly steps To bring the Lord Christ down;
3. O Lord and Mas - ter of us all, What - e'er our name or sign,

For - ev - er shared, for - ev - er whole, A nev - er - ebb - ing sea!
In vain we search for low - est deeps, For Him no depths can drown.
We own Thy sway, we hear Thy call, We test our lives by Thine.

267 Jesus Will Hear Me When I Pray

Edward L. Williams

Edward L. Williams

1. When I'm tried on ev-'ry hand, there is One who'll un-der-stand,
2. There is pow'r in Je-sus' name, hope for all is just the same,
3. When I'm bur-dened and op-pressed, faith will help me stand the test,

Je - sus will hear me when I pray, when I pray;

Vic - to - ry is just a - head, if by Him I will be led,
Free - dom from the guilt of sin, won-drous joy you're sure to win,
That's what gives my heart a song, I can smile when things go wrong,

For Je - sus will hear me when I pray, when I pray.

REFRAIN

Yes, I know He hears my pray'r,
Yes, I sure-ly know Je - sus hears my pray'r,

and He knows my ev-'ry care,
yes, my Sav-iour knows all a-bout my care,

Je - sus will hear me when I pray, when I pray;

If I will o-bey and be - lieve,
If I will o-bey and be - lieve,

the Lord has prom-ised man-y bless-ings that I shall re - ceive,

For Je-sus will hear me when I pray, when I pray.

268 I Need The Prayers

James D. Vaughan With feeling   James D. Vaughan

1. I need the prayers of those I love, While trav-'ling o'er life's rug-ged way, That I may true and faith-ful be, And live for Je-sus ev-'ry day.

2. I need the prayers of those I love, To help me in each try-ing hour, To bear my tempt-ed soul to Him, That He may keep me by His pow'r.

3. I want my friends to pray for me, To hold me up on wings of faith, That I may walk the nar-row way, Kept by our Fa-ther's glo-rious grace.

REFRAIN

I want my friends to pray for me, To bear my tempt-ed soul a-bove, And in-ter-cede with God for me; I need the prayers of those I love.

269 **Higher Ground**

Johnson Oatman, Jr.

Charles H. Gabriel

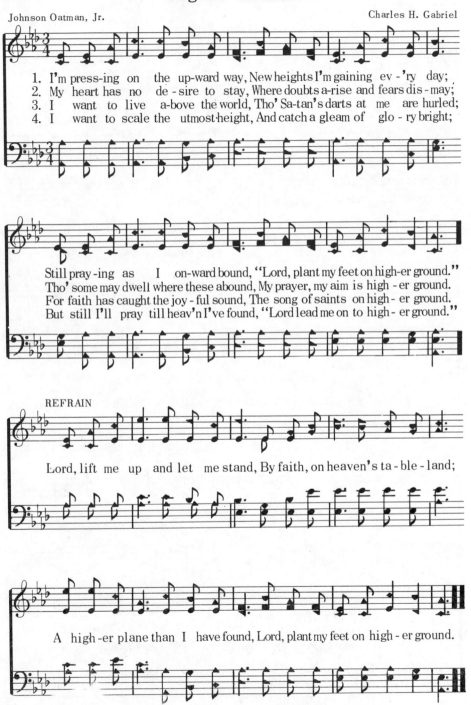

1. I'm press-ing on the up-ward way, New heights I'm gaining ev-'ry day;
2. My heart has no de-sire to stay, Where doubts a-rise and fears dis-may;
3. I want to live a-bove the world, Tho' Sa-tan's darts at me are hurled;
4. I want to scale the utmost height, And catch a gleam of glo-ry bright;

Still pray-ing as I on-ward bound, "Lord, plant my feet on high-er ground."
Tho' some may dwell where these abound, My prayer, my aim is high-er ground.
For faith has caught the joy-ful sound, The song of saints on high-er ground.
But still I'll pray till heav'n I've found, "Lord lead me on to high-er ground."

REFRAIN

Lord, lift me up and let me stand, By faith, on heaven's ta-ble-land;

A high-er plane than I have found, Lord, plant my feet on high-er ground.

Holiness Unto The Lord

Mrs. C. H. Morris   Mrs. C. H. Morris

1. "Called un-to ho-li-ness," Church of our God, Pur-chase of
2. "Called un-to ho-li-ness," chil-dren of light, Walk-ing with
3. "Called un-to ho-li-ness," Bride of the Lamb, Wait-ing the

Je-sus, re-deemed by His blood; Called from the world and its
Je-sus in gar-ments of white; Rai-ment un-sul-lied, nor
Bride-groom's re-turn-ing a-gain; Lift up your heads for the

i-dols to flee, Called from the bond-age of sin to be free.
tar-nished with sin, God's Ho-ly Spir-it a-bid-ing with-in.
day draw-eth near When in His beau-ty the King shall ap-pear.

REFRAIN

"Ho-li-ness un-to the Lord," is our watch-word and song,

"Ho-li-ness un-to the Lord," as we're march-ing a-long;

Sing it, shout it, loud and long,
"Ho - li - ness un - to the Lord," Sing "Ho - li - ness un - to the Lord,"

"Ho - li - ness un - to the Lord," now and for - ev - er.

271   Let The Holy Ghost Come In

R. F. Reynolds   CHORUS   C. W. Rowley

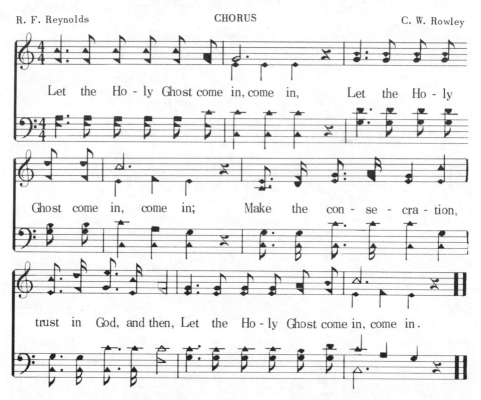

Let the Ho - ly Ghost come in, come in, Let the Ho - ly

Ghost come in, come in; Make the con - se - cra - tion,

trust in God, and then, Let the Ho - ly Ghost come in, come in.

Deeper, Deeper

C. P. Jones

C. P. Jones

1. Deep - er, deep - er in the love of Je - sus Dai - ly let me
2. Deep - er, deep - er! bless-ed Ho - ly Spir - it, Take me deep - er
3. Deep - er, deep - er! tho' it cost hard tri - als, Deep - er let me
4. Deep - er, high - er, ev - 'ry day in Je - sus, Till all con - flict

go; High - er, high - er in the school of wis - dom, More of
still, Till my life is whol - ly lost in Je - sus, And His
go! Root - ed in the ho - ly love of Je - sus, Let me
past, Finds me conqu'ror. and in His own im - age, Per - fect-

REFRAIN

grace to know. Oh, deep - er yet, I
per - fect will. Oh, deep - er yet, I pray,
fruit - ful grow.
ed at last.

pray, And high - er ev - 'ry
deep - er yet, I pray, And high - er ev - 'ry day,

day, And wis - er, bless-ed
high - er ev - 'ry day, And wis - er, bless - ed Lord,

Lord,   In Thy pre - cious ho - ly   Word.
wis - er, bless - ed Lord,

273   ## Take Time To Be Holy

William D. Longstaff   George C. Stebbins

1. Take time to   be   ho - ly, Speak oft with Thy Lord;
2. Take time to   be   ho - ly, The world rush - es on;
3. Take time to   be   ho - ly, Let Him be   Thy guide,
4. Take time to   be   ho - ly, Be   calm in   thy soul;

A - bide in   Him   al - ways, And feed on   His   Word:
Spend much time in   se - cret With Je - sus   a - lone:
And run   not   be - fore Him   What - ev - er   be - tide;
Each tho't and   each mo - tive Be - neath His   con - trol:

Make friends of God's chil - dren, Help those who are   weak;
By   look - ing to   Je - sus   Like Him thou shalt be;
In   joy   or   in   sor - row   Still fol - low thy   Lord,
Thus led   by   His   Spir - it   To   foun - tains of   love,

For - get - ting in   noth - ing His bless - ing to   seek.
Thy friends in   thy   con - duct His like - ness shall see.
And look - ing   to   Je - sus, Still trust in   His   Word.
Thou soon shalt be   fit - ted   For serv - ice a - bove.

274

Jesus Keeps Me Pure Within

J. Newby Thompson   J. Newby Thompson

1. Once I was in bond-age, once I was a slave,
2. Now my soul is hap-py, now my soul is free,
3. "Ho-ly! ho-ly! ho-ly!" in the realms a-bove,

Once I was un-ho-ly, once I was de-praved;
Now my soul is shout-ing, filled with vic-to-ry;
Cry the bless-ed an-gels, tell-ing of His love;

Then I heard how Je-sus from all sin could cure,
Through the blood of Je-sus I am free from sin,
While the heav-ens praise Him, in this world of sin,

When I knelt at Cal-v'ry, Je-sus made me pure.
Je-sus made me ho-ly, made me pure with-in.
I will tell how Je-sus made me pure with-in.

REFRAIN

Glo - ry,
Glo - ry, glo - ry, hal - le - lu - jah, I am saved from sin,

Je - sus
Je - sus Christ, my blest Re - deem - er, keeps me pure with - in;

Since to
Since in hum - ble pray'r and faith to Cal - v'ry I have been,

Je - sus keeps me ho - ly, keeps me pure with - in.

275   I Surrender All

J. W. Van Deventer

W. S. Weeden

1. All to Je - sus I sur - ren - der, All to Him I free - ly give;
2. All to Je - sus I sur - ren - der, Hum - bly at His feet I bow,
3. All to Je - sus I sur - ren - der, Make me, Sav - iour, whol - ly Thine;
4. All to Je - sus I sur - ren - der, Lord, I give my - self to Thee;
5. All to Je - sus I sur - ren - der, Now I feel the sa - cred flame;

I will ev - er love and trust Him, In His pres - ence dai - ly live.
World-ly pleas - ures all for - sak - en, Take me Je - sus, take me now.
Let me feel the Ho - ly Spir - it, Tru - ly know that Thou art mine.
Fill me with Thy love and pow - er, Let Thy bless - ing fall on me.
Oh, the joy of full sal - va - tion! Glo - ry glo - ry to His name!

REFRAIN

I sur - ren - der all,   I sur - ren - der all,
      I sur - ren - der all,   I sur - ren - der all,

All to Thee, my bless - ed Sav - iour, I sur - ren - der all.

276
Take My Life And Let It Be

Frances R. Havergal

William B. Bradbury

1. Take my life, and let it be Con - se - crat - ed, Lord, to
2. Take my feet, and let them be Swift and beau - ti - ful for
3. Take my sil - ver and my gold, Not a mite would I with -
4. Take my will, and make it Thine, It shall be no long - er

Thee; Take my hands and let them move At the
Thee; Take my voice and let me sing Al - ways,
hold; Take my mo - ments and my days, Let them
mine; Take my heart, it is Thine own, It shall

im - pulse of Thy love.
on - ly, for my King.
flow in cease - less praise.
be Thy roy - al throne.

REFRAIN

Lord, I give my life to Thee,

Thine for - ev - er - more to be; Lord, I give my

life to Thee, Thine for - ev - er - more to be.

Cleanse Me

J. Edwin Orr

Maori Melody, arranged

1. Search me, O God, and know my heart to - day;
2. I praise Thee, Lord, for cleans - ing me from sin;
3. Lord, take my life, and make it whol - ly Thine;
4. O Ho - ly Ghost, re - viv - al comes from Thee;

Try me, O Sav - iour, know my thoughts, I pray;
Ful - fill Thy Word, and make me pure with - in;
Fill my poor heart with Thy great love di - vine;
Send a re - viv - al, start the work in me;

See if there be some wick - ed way in me;
Fill me with fire, where once I burned with shame;
Take all my will, my pas - sion, self and pride;
Thy Word de - clares Thou wilt sup - ply our need;

Cleanse me from ev - 'ry sin, and set me free.
Grant my de - sire to mag - ni - fy Thy name.
I now sur - ren - der, Lord, in me a - bide.
For bless - ing now, O Lord, I hum - bly plead.

278 Lord, To Be More Like Thee

Edward L. Williams

Edward L. Williams

1. Lord, be-gin Thy work in me, in me, Help me to be more
2. Fill me with Thy ho - ly fire, Thy fire, Let Thy will be my

like Thee, like Thee; Lord, Thy will I'll do, Let my light shine too,
de - sire, de - sire; Use my life I pray, Point-ing souls the way,

REFRAIN

Lord, to be more like Thee, like Thee. Lord, I come to Thee this

hour, this hour, Fill me with Thy ho - ly pow'r; Cleanse me thru and

thru, make my life a - new, Lord, to be more like Thee, like Thee.

279   I'll Go Where You Want Me To Go

Charles E. Prior

Carrie E. Rounsefell

1. It may not be on the moun-tain's height, Or o-ver the storm-y sea; It may not be at the bat-tle's front My Lord will have need of me; But if by a still, small voice He calls to paths I do not know, I'll an-swer, dear

2. Per-haps to-day there are lov-ing words Which Je-sus would have me speak; There may be now, in the paths of sin, Some wand'rer whom I should seek; O Sav-iour, if Thou wilt be my guide, tho' dark and rug-ged the way, My voice shall

3. There's sure-ly some-where a low-ly place In earth's har-vest fields so wide, Where I may la-bor thro' life's short day, For Je-sus the Cru-ci-fied; So, trust-ing my all un-to Thy care, I know Thou lov-est me, I'll do Thy

Lord, with my hand in Thine, I'll go where You want me to go.
ech - o the mes - sage sweet, I'll say what You want me to say.
will with a heart sin - cere, I'll be what You want me to be.

REFRAIN

I'll go where You want me to go, dear Lord, O'er moun - tain or

plain or sea; I'll say what You want me to

say, dear Lord, I'll be what You want me to be.

Let My Life Be A Light

J. R. Varner

J. R. Varner

1. Let me live, bless - ed Lord, in the light of Thy Word, Let my
2. Give me wis - dom and pow'r ev - 'ry day, ev - 'ry hour, Let me
3. Give me souls for my hire, let my life be on fire, Shin - ing

life be a light on a hill; Lead - ing souls now a - stray
drink from the foun - tain a - bove; Guide my foot - steps a - right
out to the world as a guide; Help me res - cue some one

to the straight nar - row way, Help me do some good deed while I live.
thru the dark storm - y night, Give me peace, give me joy, give me love.
sink - ing now with no hope, That in heav'n we shall ev - er a - bide.

REFRAIN

Let my life be a light shin - ing out thru the night, May I

help strug-gling ones to the fold: Spread-ing cheer ev-'ry-where

to the sad and the lone, Let my life be a light to some soul.

281   I Surrender To Thee

V.B. (Vep) Ellis   CHORUS   V.B. (Vep) Ellis

All that I have, all that I am, All I shall ev-er be;

Can-not re-pay the "love-debt" I owe, I sur-ren-der to Thee.

282 Where He Leads Me

E. W. Blandy

J. S. Norris

1. I can hear my Sav-iour call-ing, I can hear my Sav-
2. I'll go with Him through the gar-den, I'll go with Him through
3. I'll go with Him through the judg-ment, I'll go with Him through
4. He will give me grace and glo-ry, He will give me grace

iour call-ing, I can hear my Sav-iour call-ing, "Take thy
the gar-den, I'll go with Him through the gar-den, I'll go
the judg-ment, I'll go with Him through the judg-ment, I'll go
and glo-ry, He will give me grace and glo-ry, And go

REFRAIN

cross and fol-low, fol-low Me."
with Him, with Him, all the way.
with Him, with Him all the way. Where He leads me I will
with me, with me all the way.

fol-low, Where He leads me I will fol-low, Where He

leads me I will fol-low, I'll go with Him, with Him all the way.

1 Will Follow Thee

Roosevelt Miller

Roosevelt Miller

1. Fol - low Thee is my de - sire, I will fol - low Thee,
2. Thru the pas - ture you may lead, I will fol - low Thee,
3. On the moun - tain near the sky, I will fol - low Thee,

Thru the cold or thru the fire, I will fol - low Thee.
In the val - ley there you be, I will fol - low Thee.
There I'll be and near your side, I will fol - low Thee.

REFRAIN

I will fol - low Thee, dear Lord, I will fol - low Thee,

Whith - er Thou go - est, dear Lord I'll go, I will fol - low Thee.

284

Let Me Touch Him

V.B. (Vep) Ellis   V.B. (Vep) Ellis

1. Let me touch Him, let me touch Jesus, Let me touch Him as He passes by; Then when I shall reach out to others, They shall know Him, they shall live and not die.
2. I was stray-ing so far from Je-sus, I was lone-ly, had no peace with-in; Then the hand of my Sav-iour touched me, Now I'm reach-ing to others in sin.
3. There's a riv-er, a riv-er flow-ing, From with-in and to cleanse my soul; And the flow sets my life to glow-ing, Ho-ly Spir-it, more than sil-ver and gold.

REFRAIN

Oh, to be His hand ex-tend-ed, Reach-ing out

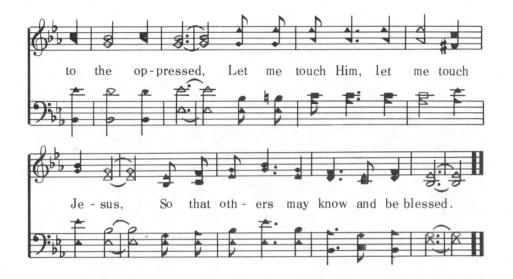

to the op-pressed, Let me touch Him, let me touch

Je - sus, So that oth - ers may know and be blessed.

285 I'll Live For Him

Ralph E. Hudson

C. R. Dunbar

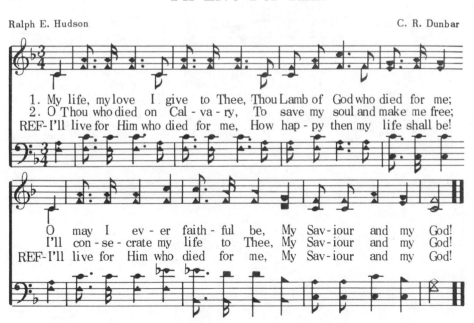

1. My life, my love I give to Thee, Thou Lamb of God who died for me;
2. O Thou who died on Cal - va - ry, To save my soul and make me free;
REF-I'll live for Him who died for me, How hap - py then my life shall be!

O may I ev - er faith - ful be, My Sav - iour and my God!
I'll con - se - crate my life to Thee, My Sav - iour and my God!
REF-I'll live for Him who died for me, My Sav - iour and my God!

Jesus Use Me

Jack and Billy Campbell

Jack and Billy Campbell

1. Dear Lord, I'll be a wit-ness if you will help my weak-ness,
2. I'll stand for Thee, dear Je-sus, tho death may come my way,
3. He's the Lil-y of the Val-ley, the Bright and Morning Star,

I know that I'm not worth-y, Lord, of Thee;
I'll spread the gos-pel to the fall-en here;
He's the fair-est of ten thou-sand to my soul;

By eyes of faith I see Thee up-on the cross of Cal-v'ry,
But if it be Thy will, Lord, to go a-cross the sea,
He's the beau-ti-ful Rose of Shar-on, He's all the world to me,

Dear Lord, I cry, let me Thy ser-vant be.
Lord, help me to be will-ing to say "yes".
But, best of all, He is my com-ing King.

Je - sus, use me, and O Lord, don't re -fuse me,

For sure - ly there's a work that I can do;

And ev - en tho it's hum -ble, Lord, help my will to crum- ble,

'Tho the cost be great, I'll work for you.

287 Give Of Your Best To The Master

Howard B. Grose

Charlotte A. Barnard

1. Give of your best to the Mas-ter, Give of the strength of your youth;
2. Give of your best to the Mas-ter, Give Him first place in your heart;
3. Give of your best to the Mas-ter, Naught else is wor-thy His love;

Throw your soul's fresh, glowing ar-dor In-to the bat-tle for truth:
Give Him first place in your service, Con-se-crate ev - 'ry part:
He gave Him-self for your ransom, Gave up His glo-ry a-bove;

Je - sus has set the ex-am-ple, Dauntless was He, young and brave;
Give, and to you shall be giv-en, God His be-lov-ed Son gave;
Laid down His life with-out mur-mur, You from sin's ru-in to save;

Give Him your loy-al de-vo-tion, Give Him the best that you have.
Grate-ful-ly seek-ing to serve Him, Give Him the best that you have.
Give Him your heart's ad-o-ra-tion, Give Him the best that you have.

REFRAIN

Give of your best to the Mas-ter, Give of the strength of your youth;

Give Of Your Best To The Master

Clad in sal-va-tion's full ar-mor, Join in the bat-tle for truth.

288   Just A Closer Walk With Thee

Arranged by Jimi Hall   Unknown

1. I am weak but Thou art strong, Je-
2. When my fee-ble life is o'er, Time
(Cho.) Just a clos-er walk with Thee, Grant

sus, keep me from all wrong;
for me will be no more;
it Je-sus is my plea;

I'll be sat-is-fied as long,
Guide me gent-ly to that shore,
Dai-ly walk-ing close to Thee,

As I walk, dear Lord, close to Thee.
Let me walk, dear Lord, close to Thee.
Let it be, dear Lord, let it be.

I Am Resolved

Palmer Hartsough

James H. Fillmore

1. I am re-solved no long-er to lin-ger,
2. I am re-solved to go to the Sav-iour,
3. I am re-solved to fol-low the Sav-iour,
4. I am re-solved, and who will go with me?

Charmed by the world's de-light; Things that are high-er,
Leav-ing my sin and strife; He is the true One,
Faith-ful and true each day; Heed what He say-eth,
Come, friends, with-out de-lay, Taught by the Bi-ble,

things that are no-bler, These have al-lured my sight.
He is the just One, He hath the words of life.
do what He will-eth, He is the liv-ing way.
led by the Spir-it, We'll walk the heav'n-ly way.

REFRAIN

I will has-ten to Him, Has-ten so glad and
I will has-ten, has-ten to Him,

free, Je-sus,
Has-ten, glad and free, Je-sus, Je-sus,

greatest, highest, I will come to Thee.

290   O Jesus, I Have Promised

John E. Bode   Arthur H. Mann

1. O Je - sus, I have prom - ised To serve Thee to the end;
2. O Je - sus, Thou hast prom - ised To all who fol - low Thee

Be Thou for - ev - er near me, My Mas - ter and my friend;
That where Thou art in glo - ry There shall Thy serv - ent be;

I shall not fear the bat - tle If Thou art by my side,
And, Je - sus, I have prom - ised To serve Thee to the end;

Nor wan - der from the path - way If Thou wilt be my guide.
O give me grace to fol - low My Mas - ter and my friend.

Near The Cross

Fanny J. Crosby

William H. Doane

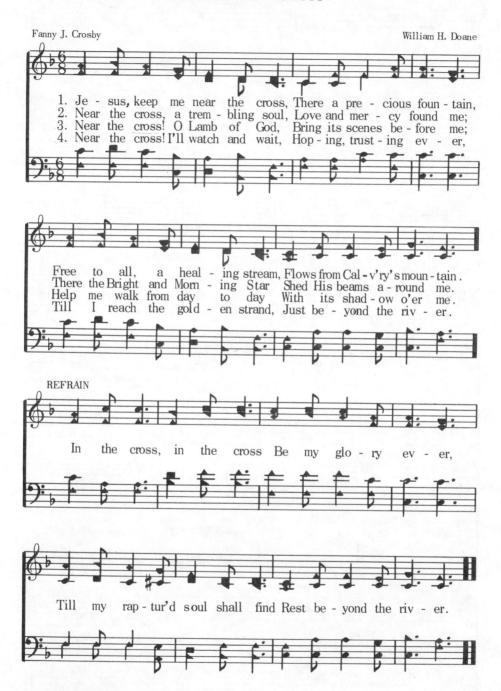

1. Je - sus, keep me near the cross, There a pre - cious foun - tain,
2. Near the cross, a trem - bling soul, Love and mer - cy found me;
3. Near the cross! O Lamb of God, Bring its scenes be - fore me;
4. Near the cross! I'll watch and wait, Hop - ing, trust - ing ev - er,

Free to all, a heal - ing stream, Flows from Cal - v'ry's moun - tain.
There the Bright and Morn - ing Star Shed His beams a - round me.
Help me walk from day to day With its shad - ow o'er me.
Till I reach the gold - en strand, Just be - yond the riv - er.

REFRAIN

In the cross, in the cross Be my glo - ry ev - er,

Till my rap - tur'd soul shall find Rest be - yond the riv - er.

I Need Thee Every Hour

Annie S. Hawks

Robert Lowry

1. I need Thee ev-'ry hour, Most gra - cious Lord;
2. I need Thee ev-'ry hour, Stay Thou near by;
3. I need Thee ev-'ry hour, In joy or pain;
4. I need Thee ev-'ry hour, Most Ho - ly One;

No ten - der voice like Thine Can peace af - ford.
Temp - ta - tions lose their pow'r When Thou art nigh.
Come quick - ly and a - bide, Or life is vain.
O make me Thine in - deed, Thou bless - ed Son.

REFRAIN

I need Thee, O I need Thee; Ev-'ry hour I need Thee!

O bless me now, my Sav - iour, I come to Thee.

Is Your All On The Altar?

Elisha A. Hoffman   Elisha A. Hoffman

1. You have longed for sweet peace, and for faith to in - crease, And have
2. Would you walk with the Lord in the light of His Word, And have
3. Oh, we nev - er can know what the Lord will be - stow Of the
4. Who can tell all the love He will send from a - bove, And how

ear - nest - ly, fer - vent - ly prayed; But you can - not have rest
peace and con - tent - ment al - ways; You must do His sweet will
bless - ings for which we have prayed, Till our bod - y and soul
hap - py our hearts will be made, Of the fel - low - ship sweet

or be per - fect - ly blest Un - til all on the al - tar is laid.
to be free from all ill, On the al - tar your all you must lay.
He doth ful - ly con - trol, And our all on the al - tar is laid.
we shall share at His feet, When our all on the al - tar is laid.

REFRAIN

Is your all on the al - tar of sac - ri - fice laid? Your

heart, does the Spir - it con - trol? You can on - ly be blest

and have peace and sweet rest, As you yield Him your bod - y and soul.

294   Jesus Calls Us

Mrs. Cecil F. Alexander

William H. Jude

1. Je - sus calls us o'er the tu - mult Of our life's wild, rest-less sea;
2. Je - sus calls us from the wor-ship Of the vain world's golden store,
3. In our joys and in our sor-rows, Days of toil and hours of ease,
4. Je - sus calls us: by Thy mer-cies, Sav-iour, may we hear Thy call,

Day by day His sweet voice soundeth, Say-ing, "Christian, fol-low me!"
From each i - dol that would keep us, Say-ing, "Christian, love me more."
Still He calls in cares and pleasures, "Christian, love me more than these."
Give our hearts to Thine o - be - dience, Serve and love Thee best of all.

Have You Counted The Cost?

A. J. Hodge

A. J. Hodge

1. There's a line that is drawn by re - ject - ing our Lord,
2. You may bar - ter your hope of e - ter - ni - ty's morn,
3. While the door of His mer - cy is o - pen to you,

Where the call of His Spir - it is lost;
For a mo - ment of joy at the most;
Ere the depth of His love you ex - haust;

And you hur - ry a - long with the pleas - ure —mad throng,
For the glit - ter of sin and the things it will win,
Won't you come and be healed, won't you whis - per, I yield,

Have you count - ed, have you count - ed the cost?
Have you count - ed, have you count - ed the cost?
I have count - ed, I have count - ed the cost.

REFRAIN

Have you count - ed the cost, if your soul should be lost,

Tho' you gain the whole world for your own?

E - ven now it may be that the line you have crossed,

Have you count - ed, have you count - ed the cost?

How About Your Heart?

Bennie S. Triplett

Bennie S. Triplett

1. How a - bout your heart, Is it right with God?
2. Friend, how would you feel If your heart were made,

That's the thing that counts to - day;
With a win - dow on each side

Is it black by sin? Is it pure with - in?
So that all could see, Not just out - ward charm,

REFRAIN

Could you ask Christ in to stay.
But de - tect if in - ward harm.

Oo ah

Peo - ple of - ten see you As you are out - side,
Oo Oo ah oo

Je - sus real - ly knows you, For He sees in - side;
Oo ah Oo

How a - bout your heart; Is it right with God?

That's the thing that counts to - day.

Lord, I'm Coming Home

Arr. Jimi Hall

William J. Kirkpatrick

1. I've wan-dered far a-way from God, Now I'm com-ing home;
2. I've wast-ed man-y pre-cious years, Now I'm com-ing home;
3. I'm tired of sin and stray-ing, Lord, Now I'm com-ing home;
4. My soul is sick, my heart is sore, Now I'm com-ing home;
5. My on-ly hope, my on-ly plea, Now I'm com-ing home;
6. I need His cleans-ing blood, I know, Now I'm com-ing home;

The paths of sin too long I've trod, Lord, I'm com-ing home.
I now re-pent with bit-ter tears, Lord, I'm com-ing home.
I'll trust Thy love, be-lieve Thy Word, Lord, I'm com-ing home.
My strength re-new, my hope re-store, Lord, I'm com-ing home.
That Je-sus died, and died for me, Lord, I'm com-ing home.
O wash me whit-er than the snow, Lord, I'm com-ing home.

REFRAIN

Com-ing home, com-ing home, Nev-er-more to roam;

O-pen wide Thine arms of love, Now I'm com-ing home.

Arr. Copyright 1963 by Tennessee Music & Printing Company in "New Songs"

298 Jesus Is Calling

Fanny J. Crosby

George C. Stebbins

1. Je - sus is ten - der - ly call - ing thee home, Call - ing to - day,
2. Je - sus is call - ing the wea - ry to rest, Call - ing to - day,
3. Je - sus is wait - ing; O come to Him now, Wait - ing to - day,
4. Je - sus is plead - ing; O list to His voice, Hear Him to - day,

call - ing to - day; Why from the sun - shine of love wilt thou roam
call - ing to - day; Bring Him thy bur - den and thou shalt be blest;
wait - ing to - day; Come with thy sins, at His feet low - ly bow;
hear Him to - day; They who be - lieve on His name shalt re - joice;

REFRAIN

Far - ther and far - ther a - way?
He will not turn thee a - way.
Come and no long - er de - lay.
Quick - ly a - rise and a - way.

Call - - ing to - day,
Call - ing, call-ing to - day, to - day,

Call - - ing to - day,
Call - ing, call - ing to - day, to - day;

Je - - - sus is
Je - sus is ten - der - ly

call - - - ing, Is ten - der - ly call - ing to - day.
call - ing to - day,

Jesus, I Come

William T. Sleeper

George C. Stebbins

1. Out of my bond-age, sor-row, and night, Je-sus, I come,
2. Out of my shame-ful fail-ure and loss, Je-sus, I come,
3. Out of un-rest and ar-ro-gant pride, Je-sus, I come,
4. Out of the fear and dread of the tomb, Je-sus, I come,

Je-sus, I come; In-to Thy free-dom, glad-ness, and light,
Je-sus, I come; In-to the glo-rious gain of Thy cross,
Je-sus, I come; In-to Thy bless-ed will to a-bide,
Je-sus, I come; In-to the joy and light of Thy home,

Je-sus, I come to Thee; Out of my sick-ness
Je-sus, I come to Thee; Out of earth's sor-rows
Je-sus, I come to Thee; Out of my-self to
Je-sus, I come to Thee; Out of the depths of

in-to Thy health, Out of my want and in-to Thy wealth,
in-to Thy balm, Out of life's storms and in-to Thy calm,
dwell in Thy love, Out of de-spair in-to rap-tures a-bove,
ru-in un-told, In-to the peace of Thy shel-ter-ing fold,

Out of my sin and in-to Thy - self, Je - sus, I come to Thee.
Out of dis - tress to ju - bi - lant psalm, Je - sus, I come to Thee.
Up - ward for aye on wings like a dove, Je - sus, I come to Thee.
Ev - er Thy glo - rious face to be - hold, Je - sus, I come to Thee.

300 Just As I Am

Charlotte Elliott

William B. Bradbury

1. Just as I am, with - out one plea, But
2. Just as I am, and wait - ing not To
3. Just as I am, tho' tossed a - bout With
4. Just as I am, poor, wretch - ed, blind; Sight,
5. Just as I am, Thou wilt re - ceive, Wilt

that Thy blood was shed for me, And that Thou bidd'st me
rid my soul of one dark blot, To Thee whose blood can
many a con - flict, many a doubt, Fight-ings with - in and
rich - es, heal - ing of the mind, Yea, all I need in
wel - come, par - don, cleanse, re - lieve, Be - cause Thy prom - ise

come to Thee, O Lamb of God, I come! I come!
cleanse each spot, O Lamb of God, I come! I come!
fears with-out, O Lamb of God, I come! I come!
Thee to find, O Lamb of God, I come! I come!
I be - lieve, O Lamb of God, I come! I come!

Softly And Tenderly

301

Will L. Thompson   Will L. Thompson

1. Soft - ly and ten - der - ly Je - sus is call - ing, Call - ing for
2. Why should we tar - ry when Je - sus is plead - ing, Plead - ing for
3. Time is now fleet - ing, the mo - ments are pass - ing, Pass - ing from
4. Oh! for the won - der - ful love He has prom - ised, Prom - ised for

you and for me;   See, on the por - tals He's wait-ing and watch-ing,
you and for me?   Why should we lin - ger and heed not His mer-cies,
you and from me; Shad-ows are gath - er - ing, death-beds are com-ing,
you and for me;   Tho' we have sinned He has mer - cy and par-don,

REFRAIN

Watch - ing for you and for me.
Mer - cies for you and for me?
Com - ing for you and for me.
Par - don for you and for me.

Come home,   come home,
               Come home,   come home,

Ye who are wea - ry come home;   Ear - nest - ly, ten - der - ly,

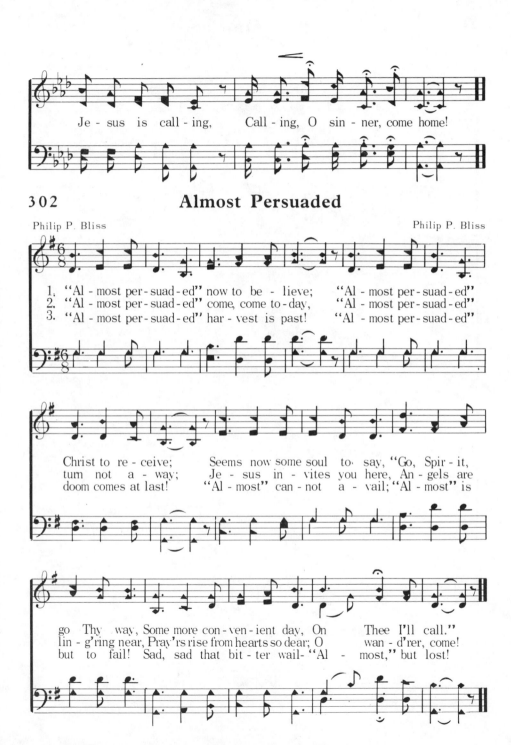

Je - sus is call - ing, Call - ing, O sin - ner, come home!

302 **Almost Persuaded**

Philip P. Bliss

Philip P. Bliss

1. "Al - most per - suad - ed" now to be - lieve; "Al - most per - suad - ed"
2. "Al - most per - suad - ed" come, come to - day, "Al - most per - suad - ed"
3. "Al - most per - suad - ed" har - vest is past! "Al - most per - suad - ed"

Christ to re - ceive; Seems now some soul to say, "Go, Spir - it,
turn not a - way; Je - sus in - vites you here, An - gels are
doom comes at last! "Al - most" can - not a - vail; "Al - most" is

go Thy way, Some more con - ven - ient day, On Thee I'll call."
lin - g'ring near, Pray'rs rise from hearts so dear; O wan - d'rer, come!
but to fail! Sad, sad that bit - ter wail- "Al - most," but lost!

Pass Me Not

Fanny J. Crosby

William H. Doane

1. Pass me not, O gen - tle Sav - iour, Hear my hum - ble cry;
2. Let me at Thy throne of mer - cy Find a sweet re - lief;
3. Trust - ing on - ly in Thy mer - it, Would I seek Thy face;
4. Thou the spring of all my com - fort, More than life to me,

While on oth - ers Thou art call - ing, Do not pass me by.
Kneel - ing there in deep con - tri - tion, Help my un - be - lief.
Heal my wound - ed, bro - ken spir - it, Save me by Thy grace.
Whom have I on earth be - side Thee? Whom in heav'n but Thee?

REFRAIN

Sav - iour, Sav - iour, Hear my hum - ble cry;

While on oth - ers Thou art call - ing, Do not pass me by.

Honey In The Rock

F. A. Graves   F. A. Graves

1. O my broth-er, do you know the Sav-iour, Who is won-drous, kind and true? He's the "Rock of your sal-va-tion!"

2. Have you "tast-ed that the Lord is gra-cious?" Do you walk in the way that's new? Have you drunk from the liv-ing foun-tain?

3. Then go out thro' the streets and by-ways, Preach the word to the man-y or few; Say to ev-'ry fall-en broth-er,

REFRAIN

There's Hon-ey in the Rock for you. Oh, there's Hon-ey in the Rock, my broth-er, my broth-er, There's Hon-ey in the Rock for you, for you; Leave your sins for the blood to cov-er, There's Hon-ey in the Rock for you, for you.

Let Him In

J. B. Atchinson

E. O. Excell

1. There's a stran-ger at the door,
2. O - pen now to Him your heart,
3. Hear you now His lov - ing voice?
4. Now ad - mit the heav'n-ly guest,

Let
Let the Sav-iour in,

Him in;
Let the Sav - iour in;
He has been there oft be -
If you wait He will de -
Now, oh, now make Him your
He will make for you a

fore,
part,
choice,
feast,

Let
Let the Sav - iour in,
Him
Let the Sav - iour in;

in;

Let Him in, ere He is gone, Let Him in
Let Him in, He is your friend, He your soul
He is stand - ing at your door, Joy to you
He will speak your sins for - giv'n, And when earth

the Ho - ly One, Je - sus Christ, the Fa - ther's
will sure de - fend, He will keep you to the
He will re - store, And His name you will a -
ties all are riv'n, He will take you home to

Son,
end, Let Him in.
dore, Let the Sav - iour in, Let the Sav - iour in.
heav'n,

306   Art Thou Weary?

Tr. by John M. Neale   Henry W. Baker

1. Art thou wea - ry, heav - y lad - den, Art thou sore dis - trest?
2. Hath He marks to lead me to Him, If He be my guide?
3. If I still hold close - ly to Him, What hath He at last?
4. If I ask Him to re - ceive me, Will He say me nay?

"Come to Me," saith One, "and, com - ing, Be at rest."
"In His feet and hands are wound-prints, And His side."
"Sor - row van - quished, la - bor end - ed, Jor - dan passed."
"Not till earth and not till heav - en Pass a - way.

There's A Great Day Coming

Will L. Thompson

Will L. Thompson

1. There's a great day com - ing, A great day com - ing, There's a great day
2. There's a bright day com - ing, A bright day com - ing, There's a bright day
3. There's a sad day com - ing, A sad day com - ing, There's a sad day

com - ing by and by; When the saints and the sin - ners shall be
com - ing by and by; But its bright-ness shall on - ly come to
com - ing by and by; When the sin - ner shall hear his doom, "De -

part - ed right and left,
them that love the Lord, Are you read - y for that day to come?
part, I know ye not,"

REFRAIN

Are you read - y? Are you read - y? Are you read - y for the

judg - ment day? Are you read - y? Are you read - y for the judg - ment day?

308   Only Trust Him

John H. Stockton   John H. Stockton

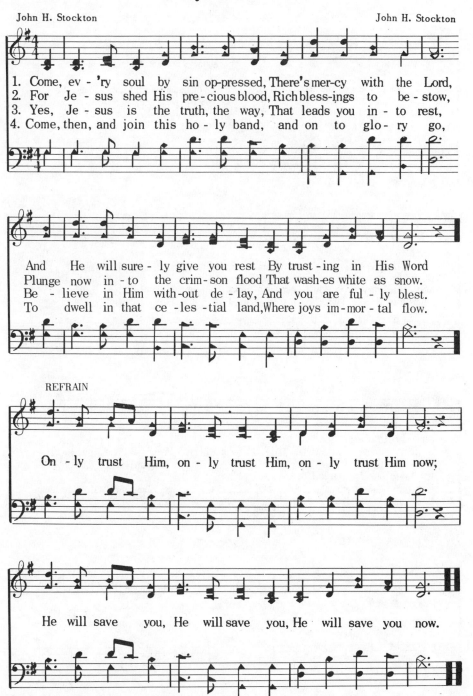

1. Come, ev - 'ry soul by sin op-pressed, There's mer-cy with the Lord,
2. For Je - sus shed His pre - cious blood, Rich bless-ings to be - stow,
3. Yes, Je - sus is the truth, the way, That leads you in - to rest,
4. Come, then, and join this ho - ly band, and on to glo - ry go,

And He will sure - ly give you rest By trust - ing in His Word
Plunge now in - to the crim - son flood That wash-es white as snow.
Be - lieve in Him with-out de - lay, And you are ful - ly blest.
To dwell in that ce - les - tial land, Where joys im - mor - tal flow.

REFRAIN

On - ly trust Him, on - ly trust Him, on - ly trust Him now;

He will save you, He will save you, He will save you now.

Look And Live

W. A. Ogden

W. A. Ogden

1. I've a mes-sage from the Lord, Hal-le-lu-jah! The mes-sage un - to
2. I've a mes-sage full of love, Hal-le-lu-jah! A mes-sage, O my
3. Life is of-fered un - to you, Hal-le-lu-jah! E - ter - nal life thy
4. I will tell you how I came, Hal-le-lu-jah! To Je - sus when He

you I'll give; 'Tis re-cord-ed in His Word, Hal-le-lu-jah! It is
friend, for you; 'Tis a mes-sage from a-bove, Hal-le-lu-jah! Je - sus
soul shall have; If you'll on - ly look to Him, Hal-le-lu-jah! Look to
made me whole: 'Twas be-liev-ing on His name, Hal-le-lu-jah! I

REFRAIN

on - ly that you "look and live."
said it, and I know 'tis true. "Look and live," my broth - er,
Je - sus who a - lone can save. "Look and live," my broth - er,
trust-ed and He saved my soul.

live, Look to Je - sus now and live; 'Tis re - cord - ed
live, "Look and live,"

in His Word, Hal - le - lu - jah! It is on - ly that you "look and live."

310

Why Do You Wait?

George F. Root   George F. Root

1. Why do you wait, dear broth - er, O why do you
2. Do you not feel, dear broth - er, His Spir - it now
3. Why do you wait, dear broth - er? The har - vest is

tar - ry so long? Your Sav - iour is wait - ing to
striv - ing with - in? O why not ac - cept His sal -
pass - ing a - way; Your Sav - iour is long - ing to

give you A place in His sanc - ti - fied throng.
va - tion, And throw off thy bur - den of sin?
bless you, There's dan - ger and death in de - lay.

REFRAIN

1   2

Why not? why not? Why not come to Him now? now?

Are You Washed In The Blood?

Elisha A. Hoffman

Elisha A. Hoffman

1. Have you been to Je - sus for the cleans-ing power? Are you
2. Are you walk - ing dai - ly by the Sav - iour's side? Are you
3. When the Bride-groom com - eth will your robes be white? Are you
4. Lay a - side the gar - ments that are stained with sin, And be

washed in the blood of the Lamb? Are you ful - ly trust - ing in His
washed in the blood of the Lamb? Do you rest each mo - ment in the
washed in the blood of the Lamb? Will your soul be read - y for the
washed in the blood of the Lamb; There's a fountain flow - ing for the

grace this hour? Are you washed in the blood of the Lamb?
Cru - ci - fied? Are you washed in the blood of the Lamb?
man-sions bright, And be washed in the blood of the Lamb?
soul un - clean, O be washed in the blood of the Lamb.

REFRAIN

Are you washed in the blood, In the
Are you washed in the blood,

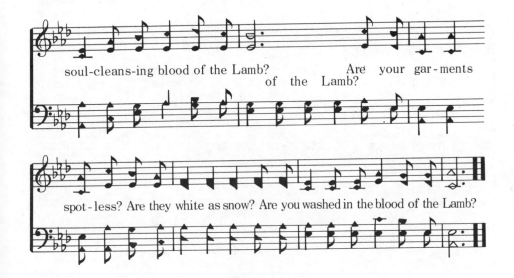

soul-cleans-ing blood of the Lamb? Are your gar-ments
of the Lamb?

spot-less? Are they white as snow? Are you washed in the blood of the Lamb?

312   I Am Coming To The Cross

William McDonald

William G. Fischer

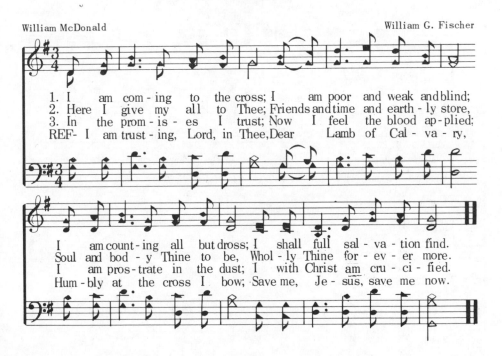

1. I am com-ing to the cross; I am poor and weak and blind;
2. Here I give my all to Thee; Friends and time and earth-ly store,
3. In the prom-is-es I trust; Now I feel the blood ap-plied;
REF- I am trust-ing, Lord, in Thee, Dear Lamb of Cal-va-ry,

I am count-ing all but dross; I shall full sal-va-tion find.
Soul and bod-y Thine to be, Whol-ly Thine for-ev-er more.
I am pros-trate in the dust; I with Christ am cru-ci-fied.
Hum-bly at the cross I bow; Save me, Je-sus, save me now.

Is Thy Heart Right With God?

Elisha A. Hoffman   Elisha A. Hoffman

1. Have thy af - fec - tions been nailed to the cross? Is thy heart
2. Hast thou do - min - ion o'er self and o'er sin? Is thy heart
3. Is there no more com - dem - na - tion for sin? Is thy heart
4. Are all thy pow'rs un - der Je - sus' con - trol? Is thy heart
5. Art thou now walk - ing in heav - en's pure light? Is thy heart

right with God?   Dost thou count all things for Je - sus but loss?
right with God?   O - ver all e - vil with - out and with - in!
right with God?   Does Je - sus rule in the tem - ple with - in?
right with God?   Does He each mo - ment a - bide in thy soul?
right with God?   Is thy soul wear - ing the gar - ment of white?

REFRAIN

Is thy heart right with God?   Is thy heart right with God,

Washed in the crim - son flood,   Cleansed and made ho - ly,

hum - ble and low - ly,   Right in the sight of God, of God?

314 Let Jesus Come Into Your Heart

Mrs. C. H. Morris   Mrs. C. H. Morris

1. If you are tired of the load of your sin, Let Jesus come into your heart; If you desire a new life to begin, Let Jesus come into your heart.

2. If 'tis for purity now that you sigh, Let Jesus come into your heart; Fountains for cleansing are flowing near by, Let Jesus come into your heart.

3. If there's a tempest your voice cannot still, Let Jesus come into your heart; If there's a void this world never can fill, Let Jesus come into your heart.

4. If you would join the glad songs of the blest, Let Jesus come into your heart; If you would enter the mansions of rest, Let Jesus come into your heart.

REFRAIN

Just now, your doubtings give o'er, Just now, reject Him no more; Just now, throw open the door, Let Jesus come into your heart.

His Way With Thee

Cyrus S. Nusbaum   Cyrus S. Nusbaum

1. Would you live for Je - sus, and be al - ways pure and good?
2. Would you have Him make you free, and fol - low at His call?
3. Would you in His king - dom find a place of con - stant rest?

Would you walk with Him with - in the nar - row road? Would you have Him
Would you know the peace that comes by giv - ing all? Would you have Him
Would you prove Him true in prov - i - den - tial test? Would you in His

bear your bur - den, car - ry all your load? Let Him have His
save you so that you can nev - er fall? Let Him have His
serv - ice la - bor al - ways at your best? Let Him have His

REFRAIN

way   with thee.
way   with thee. His pow'r can make you what you ought to be, His
way   with thee.

blood can cleanse your heart and make you free; His love can fill your soul, and

you will see 'Twas best for Him to have His way with thee.

316

Depth Of Mercy

Charles Wesley

Carl M. von Weber

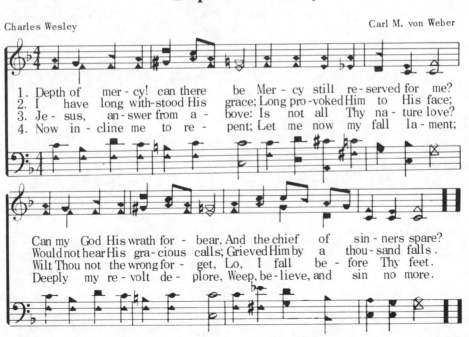

1. Depth of mer - cy! can there be Mer - cy still re - served for me?
2. I have long with-stood His grace; Long pro-voked Him to His face;
3. Je - sus, an - swer from a - bove: Is not all Thy na - ture love?
4. Now in - cline me to re - pent; Let me now my fall la - ment;

Can my God His wrath for - bear, And the chief of sin - ners spare?
Would not hear His gra - cious calls; Grieved Him by a thou-sand falls.
Wilt Thou not the wrong for - get, Lo, I fall be - fore Thy feet.
Deeply my re - volt de - plore, Weep, be-lieve, and sin no more.

In Times Like These

Mrs. Ruth Caye Jones   Mrs. Ruth Caye Jones

1. In times like these you need a Sav-iour, In times like these
2. In times like these you need the Bi - ble, In times like these
3. In times like these I have a Sav-iour, In times like these

you need an an - chor; Be ver - y sure, be ver - y sure,
O be not i - dle; Be ver - y sure, be ver - y sure,
I have an an - chor; I'm ver - y sure, I'm ver - y sure,

Your an - chor holds and grips the sol - id Rock!
Your an - chor holds and grips the sol - id Rock!
My an - chor holds and grips the sol - id Rock!

REFRAIN

This Rock is Je - sus, yes, He's the One, This Rock is Je - sus,

the on - ly One!
Be ver - y sure, be ver - y sure,
Be ver - y sure, be ver - y sure,
I'm ver - y sure, I'm ver - y sure,

Your an - chor holds and grips the sol - id Rock!
Your an - chor holds and grips the sol - id Rock!
My an - chor holds and grips the sol - id Rock!

318   Holy Ghost, With Light Divine

Andrew Reed

Louis M. Gottschalk

1. Ho - ly Ghost, with light di - vine, Shine up-on this heart of mine;
2. Ho - ly Ghost, with pow'r di - vine, Cleanse this guilt-y heart of mine;
3. Ho - ly Spir - it, all di - vine, Dwell with-in this heart of mine;

Chase the shades of night a - way; Turn my dark - ness in - to day.
Long has sin, with-out con - trol, Held do - min - ion o'er my soul.
Cast down ev - 'ry i - dol throne, Reign su - preme, and reign a-lone.

319
Make Me A Blessing

Ira B. Wilson

George S. Schuler

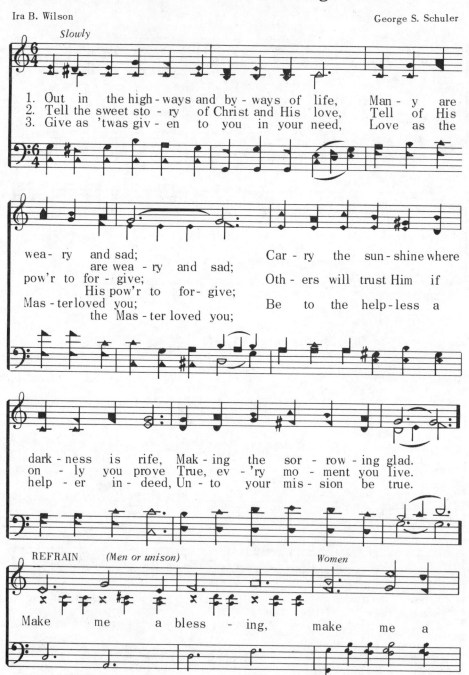

Slowly

1. Out in the high-ways and by-ways of life, Man - y are
2. Tell the sweet sto - ry of Christ and His love, Tell of His
3. Give as 'twas giv - en to you in your need, Love as the

wea - ry and sad;
  are wea - ry and sad; Car - ry the sun - shine where
pow'r to for - give; Oth - ers will trust Him if
  His pow'r to for - give;
Mas - ter loved you; Be to the help - less a
  the Mas - ter loved you;

dark - ness is rife, Mak - ing the sor - row - ing glad.
on - ly you prove True, ev - 'ry mo - ment you live.
help - er in - deed, Un - to your mis - sion be true.

REFRAIN   (Men or unison)   Women

Make   me   a bless - ing,   make   me   a

bless - ing, Out of my life may
Out of my life

Men

rit. *Unison*

Je - sus shine; Make me a

Women

bless - ing, O Sav - iour, I pray,
I pray Thee my Sav - iour,

Tenors

Parts *ad lib.*

Make me a bless - ing to some - one to - day.

All Hail Immanuel

D. R. Van Sickle

Charles H. Gabriel

1. All hail to Thee, Im-man-u-el, we cast our crowns be-fore Thee, Let ev-'ry heart o-bey Thy will, and ev-'ry voice a-dore Thee; In praise to Thee, our Sav-iour King, The vi-brant chords of heav-en ring, And ech-o back the might-y strain:
2. All hail to Thee, Im-man-u-el, the ran-somed hosts sur-round Thee, And earth-ly monarchs clam-or forth their Sov-'reign King to crown Thee; While those redeemed in a-ges gone, As-sembled 'round the great white throne, Break forth into im-mor-tal song:
3. All hail to Thee, Im-man-u-el, our ris-en King and Sav-iour! Thy foes are van-ished, and Thou art Om-nip-o-tent for-ev-er; Death, sin, and hell no long-er reign, And Sa-tan's pow'r is burst in twain, E-ter-nal glo-ry to Thy name:

All hail! all hail! all hail! all hail! Im-man-u-el!
All hail! all hail!

REFRAIN

Hail!
Hail to the King we love so well! Hail! Im-man-u-el, Im-man-u-el!
Hail! Im - man-u-el!
Hail!

Hail!
Hail to the King we love so well! Hail! Im-man-u-el! Im-man-u-el!
Hail! Im - man-u-el!
Hail!

Glo - ry and hon - or and maj - es - ty, Wis - dom and
Glo — ry and maj - es - ty, Wis —

rit . . . .

pow - er   be un - to Thee, Now and ev - er - more!
dom   be un - to Thee,

Hail!   Im - man - u - el! Im - man - u - el!
Hail to the King we love so well! Hail!   Im - man - u - el!
                                   Hail!

Hail!   Im - man - u - el! Im - man - u - el!
Hail to the King we love so well! Hail!   Im - man - u - el!
                                   Hail!

King   of kings and Lord of lords, All hail, Im - man - u - el!

Christ For Me!

Alex Burns

CHORUS

Al x Burns

Christ for me, yes, it's Christ for me! He's my Sav-iour, my Lord and King, I'm so hap-py I shout and sing! Christ for me, yes, it's Christ for me! Ev-'ry day as I go my way, It is Christ for me!

Everybody Ought To Know

CHORUS   Traditional

1. Ev-'ry-bod- y ought to know, ev-'ry-bod- y ought to know,
Ev-'ry-bod- y ought to tell, ev-'ry-bod- y ought to tell,

Ev-'ry-bod- y ought to know, ev-'ry-bod- y ought to know,
Ev-'ry-bod- y ought to tell, ev-'ry-bod- y ought to tell,

Ev-'ry-bod- y ought to know, ev-'ry-bod- y ought to know,
Ev-'ry-bod- y ought to tell, ev-'ry-bod- y ought to tell,

who Je - sus is, who my bless-ed Je - sus is;
who Je - sus ...(Omit)...

is, who my bless-ed Je - sus is.

REFRAIN

He's the Lil - y of the Val
Je - sus is the Lil - y

ley, He's the Bright and Morning Star,
of the Val - ley, He's the shin - ing Star sent

down from heav - en; He's the fair - est of ten

thou sand, Ev - 'ry-
He's the fair - est of the man - y thou-sands,

bod - y ought to know, ev - 'ry - bod - y ought to know.

Yes, I Know

CHORUS

Mrs. Anna W. Waterman   Mrs. Anna W. Waterman

And I know,   yes, I know,   I sure - ly know,
        I sure - ly know,   I sure - ly know,

Je - sus' blood can make the vil - est sin - ner clean,
                              vil - est sin - ner clean,

And I know,   yes, I know,   I sure - ly know,
        I sure - ly know,   I sure - ly know,

Je - sus' blood can make the vil - est sin - ner clean.
                              vil - est sin - ner clean.

Magnify The Lord

A. Tee

CHORUS

A. Tee

Mag - ni - fy the Lord with me, Bless-ed Lamb of Cal - va - ry,

For His grace so rich and free, mag - ni - fy the Lord with me;

Mag - ni - fy the Lord with me, Bless-ed Lamb of Cal - va - ry,

Je - sus gives us lib - er - ty, so mag - ni - fy the Lord with me!

325

Lest I Forget

H. A. Green

CHORUS

H. A. Green

Lest I for - get the stripes for me He suf - fered,

And how for me, the man - y sins He bore;

Lest I for - get His pre - cious blood at Cal - v'ry;

May I be Thine Lord, now and ev - er - more.

Jesus Is The One

CHORUS

Adger M. Pace

Gertie Rast

Je - sus is the One, yes, He's the on - ly One,

Let Him have His way un - til the day is done;

When He speaks you know the clouds will have to go,

Just be - cause He loves you so, loves you so.

327 Come, Ye Thankful People

Henry Alford

George J. Elvey

1. Come, ye thank-ful peo - ple, come, Raise the song of har - vest home!
2. We our - selves are God's own field, Fruit un - to His praise to yield;
3. For the Lord our God shall come, And shall take His har - vest home;

All is safe - ly gath - ered in, Ere the win - ter storms be - gin;
Wheat and tares to - geth - er sown Un - to joy or sor - row grown;
From His field shall purge a - way All that doth of - fend that day;

God, our Mak - er, doth pro - vide For our wants to be sup - plied:
First the blade, and then the ear, Then the full corn shall ap - pear;
Give His an - gels charge at last In the fire the tares to cast;

Come to God's own tem - ple, come, Raise the song of har - vest home.
Lord of har - vest! grant that we Wholesome grain and pure may be.
But the fruit - ful ears to store In His gar - ner ev - er - more.

We Gather Together

Anonymous
Tr. by Theodore Baker

Arr. by Edward Kremser
Netherlands Folk Song

1. We gath - er to - geth - er to ask the Lord's bless - ing,
2. Be - side us to guide us, our God with us join - ing,
3. We all do ex - tol Thee, Thou lea - der in bat - tle,

He chas - tens and has - tens His will to make known;
Or - dain - ing, main - tain - ing His king - dom di - vine;
And pray that Thou still our de - fend - er wilt be.

The wick - ed op - press - ing now cease from dis - tress - ing,
So from the be - gin - ning the fight we were win - ning,
Let Thy con - gre - ga - tion es - cape trib - u - la - tion;

Sing prais - es to His name, He for - gets not His own.
Thou, Lord, wast at our side: the glo - ry be Thine.
Thy name be ev - er praised: O Lord, make us free!

All Men Give Thanks

Delton L. Alford

Delton L. Alford

1. All men give thanks to Christ, the Lord,
2. With hearts of praise re-joice in the Lord,

And make known His deeds in all the earth;
Re - mem - ber the mar - v'lous works He hath done;

Sing un - to Him in psalms of praise,
Oh! sing of His great - ness and His pow'r,

And glo - ry in His ho - ly name.
Give hon - or to Him, He is our God.

Hark! The Herald Angels Sing

Charles Wesley   Felix Mendelssohn Bartholdy

1. Hark! the her - ald an - gels sing, Glo - ry to the new - born King:
2. Hail the heav'n-born Prince of Peace, Hail the Son of right - eous - ness!

Peace on earth, and mer - cy mild, God and sin - ners rec - on - ciled;
Light and life to all He brings, Ris'n with heal - ing in His wings:

Joy - ful, all ye na - tions rise, Join the tri - umph of the skies,
Mild He lays His glo - ry by, Born that man no more may die;

With an - gel - ic hosts pro - claim, Christ is born in Beth - le - hem.
Born to raise the sons of earth, Born to give them sec - ond birth.

Hark! the her - ald an - gels sing, Glo - ry to the new - born King.

331 Joy To The World

From Psalm 98
Issac Watts

Arr. from George F. Handel

1. Joy to the world! the Lord is come; Let earth re-
2. Joy to the earth! the Sav - iour reigns; Let men their
3. No more let sins and sor - rows grow, Nor thorns in -
4. He rules the world with truth and grace, And makes the

ceive her King; Let ev - ery heart pre - pare Him room,
songs em - ploy; While fields and floods, rocks, hills and plains
fest the ground; He comes to make His bless - ings flow
na - tions prove The glo - ries of His right - eous - ness,

And heav'n and na - ture sing, And heav'n and na - ture
Re - peat the sound-ing joy, Re - peat the sound-ing
Far as the curse is found, Far as the curse is
And won - ders of His love, And won - ders of His

1. And heav'n and na - ture sing, And

sing, And heav'n and heav'n and na - ture sing.
joy, Re - peat, re - peat the sound - ing joy.
found, Far as, far as the curse is found.
love, And won - ders and won - ders of His love.

heav'n and na - ture sing.

O Come, All Ye Faithful

Translated by Frederick Oakeley

Wake's Cantus Diversi 1751

1. O come, all ye faith-ful, joy - ful and tri - um-phant, O come ye, O
2. — Sing, choirs of an-gels, sing in ex - ul - ta-tion, O sing, all ye
3. — Yea, Lord, we greet Thee born this hap-py morn-ing, Je - sus, to

come ye to Beth - le - hem; Come and be-hold Him born the King of
bright hosts of heav'n a - bove; Glo - ry to God, all glo - ry in the
Thee be all glo - ry giv'n Word of the Fa -ther, now in flesh ap-

REFRAIN

an - gels:
high - est: O come, let us a - dore Him, O come, let us a-
pear - ing:

dore Him, O come let us a dore Him, Christ, the Lord.

Angels From The Realms Of Glory

James Montgomery

Henry Smart

1. An - gels, from the realms of glo - ry, Wing your flight o'er
2. Shep - herds, in the fields a - bid - ing, Watch - ing o'er your
3. Sag - es, leave your con - tem - pla - tions, Bright - er vi - sions
4. Saints, be - fore the al - tar bend - ing, Watch - ing long in

all the earth; Ye who sang cre - a - tion's sto - ry,
flocks by night, God with man is now re - sid - ing,
beam a - far; Seek the great de - sire of na - tions,
hope and fear, Sud - den - ly the Lord, de - scend - ing,

Now pro - claim Mes - si - ah's birth: Come and wor - ship,
Yon - der shines the in - fant Light: Come and wor - ship,
Ye have seen His na - tal star: Come and wor - ship,
In His tem - ple shall ap - pear: Come and wor - ship,

come and wor - ship, Wor - ship Christ, the new - born King!
come and wor - ship, Wor - ship Christ, the new - born King!
come and wor - ship, Wor - ship Christ, the new - born King!
come and wor - ship, Wor - ship Christ, the new - born King!

Angels We Have Heard On High

Traditional

Old French Carol
Arr. by Warren M. Angell

1. An - gels we have heard on high,   Sweet - ly sing - ing o'er the plains:
2. Shep-herds, why this ju - bi - lee?   Why your joy - ous strains pro-long?
3. Come to Beth - le - hem, and see   Him whose birth the an - gels sing;
4. See Him in a man - ger laid,   Whom the choirs of an - gels praise;

And the moun - tains in re - ply,   Ech - o - ing their joy - ous strains.
What the glad - some ti - dings be   Which in - spire your heav'n-ly song?
Come, a - dore on bend - ed knee   Christ the Lord, the new - born King.
Ma - ry, Jo - seph, lend your aid,   While our hearts in love we raise.

REFRAIN

Glo - - - - ri - a in ex - cel - sis De - o!

Glo - - - - ri - a in ex - cel - sis De - o!

335 Silent Night

Joseph Mohr

Franz Gruber

1. Si - lent night! ho - ly night! All is calm, all is bright 'Round yon
2. Si - lent night! ho - ly night! Shep-herds quake at the sight! Glo - ries
3. Si - lent night! ho - ly night! Son of God, love's pure light Ra - diant

vir - gin moth - er and Child! Ho - ly In - fant, so ten - der and mild,
stream from heav - en a - far, Heav'n-ly hosts sing Al - le - lu - ia;
beams from Thy ho - ly face, With the dawn of re - deem - ing grace,

Sleep in heav - en - ly peace, Sleep in heav - en - ly peace.
Christ, the Sav - iour is born, Christ the Sav - iour is born.
Je - sus, Lord, at Thy birth, Je - sus, Lord, at Thy birth.

336 I Heard The Bells On Christmas Day

Henry W. Longfellow

John Calkin

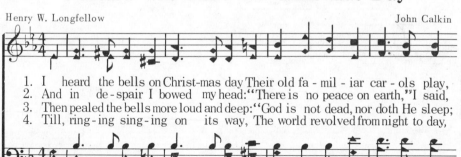

1. I heard the bells on Christ-mas day Their old fa - mil - iar car - ols play,
2. And in de - spair I bowed my head: "There is no peace on earth," I said,
3. Then pealed the bells more loud and deep: "God is not dead, nor doth He sleep;
4. Till, ring - ing sing - ing on its way, The world revolved from night to day,

And wild and sweet the words re-peat Of peace on earth, good will to men.
"For hate is strong, and mocks the song Of peace on earth, good will to men."
The wrong shall fail, the right pre-vail, With peace on earth, good will to men."
A voice, a chime, a chant sub-lime, Of peace on earth, good will to men.

337

Away In A Manger

Martin Luther

Martin Luther

1. A - way in a man-ger, no crib for a bed, The lit - tle Lord
2. The cat - tle are low - ing, the Ba - by a - wakes, But lit - tle Lord
3. Be near me, Lord Je - sus, I ask Thee to stay Close by me for-

Je - sus laid down His sweet head; The stars in the sky looked
Je - sus, no cry - ing He makes; I love Thee, Lord Je - sus! look
ev - er, and love me, I pray; Bless all the dear chil - dren in

down where He lay, The lit - tle Lord Je - sus, a - sleep on the hay.
down from the sky, And stay by my cra - dle till morn - ing is nigh.
Thy ten - der care, Pre - pare us for heav - en to live with Thee there.

338 O Little Town Of Bethlehem

Phillips Brooks

Lewis H. Redner

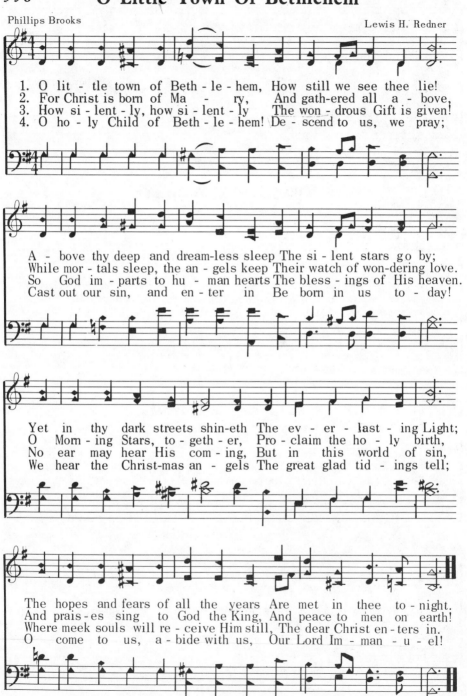

1. O lit - tle town of Beth - le - hem, How still we see thee lie!
2. For Christ is born of Ma - ry, And gath-ered all a - bove,
3. How si - lent - ly, how si - lent - ly The won - drous Gift is given!
4. O ho - ly Child of Beth - le - hem! De - scend to us, we pray;

A - bove thy deep and dream-less sleep The si - lent stars go by;
While mor - tals sleep, the an - gels keep Their watch of won-dering love.
So God im - parts to hu - man hearts The bless - ings of His heaven.
Cast out our sin, and en - ter in Be born in us to - day!

Yet in thy dark streets shin-eth The ev - er - last - ing Light;
O Morn - ing Stars, to - geth - er, Pro - claim the ho - ly birth,
No ear may hear His com - ing, But in this world of sin,
We hear the Christ-mas an - gels The great glad tid - ings tell;

The hopes and fears of all the years Are met in thee to - night.
And prais - es sing to God the King, And peace to men on earth!
Where meek souls will re - ceive Him still, The dear Christ en - ters in.
O come to us, a - bide with us, Our Lord Im - man - u - el!

339 While Shepherds Watched Their Flocks

Nahum Tate

Arr. from George F. Handel

1. While shep - herds watched their flocks by night, All seat - ed on
2. "Fear not!" said he; for might - y dread Had seized their trou -
3. "To you, in Dav - id's town, this day Is born, of Dav -
4. "The heav'n - ly Babe you there shall find To hu - man view
5. "All glo - ry be to God on high, And to the earth

the ground, The an - gel of the Lord came down,
bled mind, "Glad ti - dings of great joy I bring,
id's line, The Sav - iour, who is Christ the Lord;
dis - played, All mean - ly wrapped in swath - ing - bands,
be peace: Good will hence - forth from heav'n to men,

And glo - ry shone a - round, And glo - ry shone a - round.
To you and all man - kind, To you and all man - kind.
And this shall be the sign: And this shall be the sign.
And in a man - ger laid: And in a man - ger laid."
Be - gin and nev - er cease: Be - gin and nev - er cease!"

It Came Upon A Midnight Clear

Edmund H. Sears

Richard S. Willis

1. It came up-on the mid-night clear, That glo-rious song of old,
2. Still thro' the clo-ven skies they come, With peaceful wings un-furled,
3. And ye, be-neath life's crushing load, Whose forms are bend-ing low,
4. For lo, the days are has-t'ning on, By proph-et bards fore-told,

From an-gels bend-ing near the earth To touch their harps of gold:
And still their heav'nly mu-sic floats O'er all the wea-ry world:
Who toil a-long the climb-ing way With pain-ful steps and slow,
When with the ev-er-cir-cling years Comes 'round the age of gold:

"Peace on the earth, good-will to men, From heav'ns all gracious King:"
A-bove its sad and low-ly plains They bend on hov'ring wing:
Look now! for glad and gold-en hours Come swift-ly on the wing;
When peace shall o-ver all the earth Its an-cient splendors fling,

The world in sol-emn still-ness lay To hear the an-gels sing.
And ev-er o'er its Ba-bel sounds The bless-ed an-gels sing.
O rest be-side the wea-ry road, And hear the an-gels sing.
And the whole world give back the song Which now the an-gels sing.

The First Noel

341

Old English Carol

Traditional Melody from
W. Sandy's "Christmas Carols," 1833.

1. The first No - el the an - gel did say, Was to cer - tain poor
2. They look - ed up and saw a star Shin - ing in the
3. And by the light of that same star Three Wise Men
4. Then let us all with one ac - cord Sing prais - es

shep - herds in fields as they lay; In fields where they lay keep - ing their
East be - yond them far, And to the earth it gave great
came from coun - try far; To seek for a king was their in -
to our heav - en - ly Lord Who hath made heav'n and earth of

REFRAIN

sheep, On a cold win - ter's night that was so deep.
light, And so it con - tin - ued both day and night. No - el, No - el,
tent, And to fol - low the star wher - ev - er it went.
naught, And with His blood man - kind hath bought.

No - el, No - el, Born is the King of Is - ra - el.

Sweetest Mother

Gertrude Stoddard Dennstedt

Will M. Ramsey

1. She's a lit - tle old fash - ioned, That sweet moth - er of mine,
2. She's a lit - tle old fash - ioned, That sweet moth - er of mine,
3. She's a lit - tle old fash - ioned, She stays close - ly at home,

There are man - y whose beau - ty Will my moth - er's out - shine;
Tho' e - ven her plain - ness Now my heart - strings en - twine;
So calm and con - tent - ed Al - tho' oth - ers may roam;

She's a lit - tle old fash - ioned As I plain - ly can see
Oth - er hands may be whit - er But none oth - er so dear
And in ten - der young child-hood 'Twas a shel - ter for me

But she is for - ev - er Sweet - est moth - er to me.
For they smoothed my pil - low For man - y a year.
And she who so graced it, Dear - est ev - er shall be.

REFRAIN

She's a lit - tle old fash - ioned, But she's sweet - er each day,

I a - dore her plain fea - tures And her thin locks of gray;

There's a glo - ry a - round her, God a - bides it may be,

And she is for - ev - er Sweet - est moth - er to me.

Tell Mother I'll Be There

Charles M. Fillmore

Charles M. Fillmore

1. When I was but a lit-tle child how well I rec-ol-lect,
2. Tho' I was of-ten way-ward, she was al-ways kind and good,
3. When I be-came a prod-i-gal, and left the old roof-tree,
4. One day a mes-sage came to me, it bade me quick-ly come

How I would grieve my moth-er with my fol-ly and neg-lect;
So pa-tient, gen-tle, lov-ing, when my ways were rough and rude;
She al-most broke her lov-ing heart in mourn-ing af-ter me;
If I would see my moth-er ere the Sav-iour took her home;

And now that she has gone to heav'n I miss her ten-der care,
My child-hood griefs and tri-als she would glad-ly with me share,
And day and night she prayed to God to keep me in His care,
I prom-ised her, be-fore she died, for heav-en to pre-pare,

O Sav-iour, tell my moth-er I'll be there!
I'll be there!

REFRAIN

Tell moth - er I'll be there in an - swer to her prayer;

This mes - sage, bless - ed Sav - iour, to her bear!

Tell moth - er I'll be there, heav'n's joys with her to share;

Yes, tell my dar - ling moth - er I'll be there, I'll be there.

344 If I Could Hear My Mother Pray Again

James Rowe   J. W. Vaughan

Slow with feeling

1. How sweet and hap - py seem those days of which I dream,
2. She used to pray that I on Je - sus would re - ly,
3. With - in the old home - place, her pa - tient, smil - ing face
4. Her work on earth is done, the life - crown has been won,

When mem - o - ry re - calls them now and then!
And al - ways walk the shin - ing gos - pel way;
Was al - ways spread-ing com - fort, hope and cheer;
And she will be at rest with Him a - bove;

And with what rap - ture sweet my wea - ry heart would beat,
So trust - ing still His love I seek that home a - bove,
And when she used to sing to her e - ter - nal King,
And some glad morn - ing she, I know, will wel - come me,

If I could hear my moth - er pray a - gain.
Where I shall meet my moth - er some glad day.
It was the songs the an - gels loved to hear.
To that e - ter - nal home of peace and love.

REFRAIN

If   I   could   hear
If   I   could on - ly   hear   my moth - er pray a - gain,
If   I   could   on - ly hear

If   I   could   hear her ten - der voice   as   then!
If   I   could on - ly

So glad   I'd   be,
So hap - py   I should be,   'twould mean so   much   to me,
So hap - py   I should be

If   I   could hear my moth - er pray a - gain.

The Star-Spangled Banner

Francis Scott Key

Anonymous

1. Oh, say, can you see, by the dawn's ear - ly light,
2. Oh, thus be it ev - er when free men shall stand

What so proud - ly we hailed at the twi - light's last gleam - ing,
Be - tween their loved homes and the war's des - o - la - tion;

Whose broad stripes and bright stars, thro' the per - il - ous fight,
Blest with vic - t'ry and peace, may the heav'n - res - cued land

O'er the ram - parts we watched were so gal - lant - ly stream - ing?
Praise the Pow'r that hath made and pre - served us a na - tion!

And the rock - ets' red glare, the bombs burst - ing in air
Then con - quer we must, when our cause it is just;

Gave proof thro' the night that our flag was still there.
And this be our mot - to: "In God is our trust!"

REFRAIN

Oh, say, does that Star - spang - gled Ban - ner yet wave
And the Star - span - gled Ban - ner in tri - umph shall wave

O'er the land of the free and the home of the brave?
O'er the land of the free and the home of the brave.

Battle Hymn Of The Republic

Julia Ward Howe

American Folk Song

1. Mine eyes have seen the glo-ry of the com-ing of the Lord;
2. I have seen Him in the watch-fires of a hun-dred cir-cling camps;
3. He has sound-ed forth the trum-pet that shall nev-er sound re-treat;
4. In the beau-ty of the lil-ies, Christ was born a-cross the sea,

He is tram-pling out the vin-tage where the grapes of wrath are stored;
They have build-ed Him an al-tar in the eve-ning dews and damps;
He is sift-ing out the hearts of men be-fore His judg-ment seat;
With a glo-ry in His bos-om that trans-fig-ures you and me;

He hath loosed the fate-ful light-ning of His ter-ri-ble swift sword;
I can read His righteous sen-tence by the dim and flar-ing lamps;
O be swift, my soul, to an-swer Him! be jub-i-lant, my feet!
As He died to make men ho-ly, let us die to make men free,

REFRAIN

His truth is march-ing on.
His day is march-ing on.
Our God is march-ing on.
While God is march-ing on.

Glo-ry! glo-ry, hal-le-

lu - jah! Glo - ry! glo - ry, hal - le - lu - jah! Glo - ry!

glo - ry, hal - le - lu - jah! Our God is march - ing on.

347   **America**

Samuel F. Smith   Anonymous

1. My coun - try, 'tis of thee, Sweet land of lib - er - ty,
2. My na - tive coun - try, thee, Land of the no - ble free,
3. Let mu - sic swell the breeze, And ring from all the trees
4. Our fa - thers' God, to Thee, Au - thor of lib - er - ty,

Of thee I sing: Land where my fa - thers died, Land of the
Thy name I love: I love thy rocks and rills, Thy woods and
Sweet free-dom's song: Let mor - tal tongues a - wake; Let all that
To Thee we sing: Long may our land be bright With free - dom's

pil - grims' pride, From ev - ery moun-tain-side Let free - dom ring!
tem - pled hills; My heart with rap - ture thrills Like that a-bove.
breathe par-take; Let rocks their si - lence break, The sound pro-long.
ho - ly light; Pro - tect us by Thy might, Great God, our King!

America, The Beautiful

Katharine Lee Bates

Samuel A. Ward

1. O beau-ti-ful for spa-cious skies, For am-ber waves of grain,
2. O beau-ti-ful for pil-grim feet, Whose stern, im-pas-sioned stress
3. O beau-ti-ful for he-roes proved In lib-er-at-ing strife,
4. O beau-ti-ful for pa-triot dream That sees, be-yond the years,

For pur-ple moun-tain maj-es-ties A-bove the fruit-ed plain!
A thor-ough-fare for free-dom beat A-cross the wil-der-ness!
Who more than self their coun-try loved, And mer-cy more than life!
Thine al-a-bas-ter cit-ies gleam, Un-dimmed by hu-man tears!

A-mer-i-ca! A-mer-i-ca! God shed His grace on thee,
A-mer-i-ca! A-mer-i-ca! God mend thine ev-ery flaw,
A-mer-i-ca! A-mer-i-ca! May God thy gold re-fine,
A-mer-i-ca! A-mer-i-ca! God shed His grace on thee,

And crown thy good with broth-er-hood From sea to shin-ing sea.
Con-firm thy soul in self-con-trol, Thy lib-er-ty in law.
Till all suc-cess be no-ble-ness, And ev-ery gain di-vine.
And crown thy good with broth-er-hood From sea to shin-ing sea.

349 Does Jesus Care?

Frank E. Graeff

J. Lincoln Hall

1. Does Je - sus care when my heart is pained Too deep - ly for mirth or song; As the bur - dens press, And the cares dis - tress, And the way grows wea - ry and long?

2. Does Je - sus care when my way is dark With a name - less dread and fear? As the day - light fades In - to deep night shades, Does He care e - nough to be near?

3. Does Je - sus care when I've said, "good-by" To the dear - est on earth to me; And my sad heart aches Till it near - ly breaks, Is it aught to Him? Does He see?

REFRAIN

O yes, He cares, I know He cares, His heart is touched with my grief; When the days are wea - ry, The long night drear - y, I know my Sav - iour cares, He cares.

Safe In The Arms Of Jesus

Fanny J. Crosby

W. H. Doane

1. Safe in the arms of Je - sus, Safe on His gen - tle breast,
2. Safe in the arms of Je - sus, Safe from cor - rod - ing care,
3. Je - sus, my heart's dear ref - uge, Je - sus has died for me;

There by His love o'er-shad - ed, Sweet - ly my soul shall rest.
Safe from the world's temp-ta - tions, Sin can-not harm me there.
Firm on the Rock of A - ges, Ev - er my trust shall be.

Hark! 'tis the voice of an - gels, Borne in a song to me,
Free from the blight of sor - row, Free from my doubts and fears;
Here let me wait with pa - tience, Wait till the night is o'er;

O - ver the fields of glo - ry, O - ver the jas - per sea.
On - ly a few more tri - als, On - ly a few more tears!
Wait till I see the morn - ing Break on the gold-en shore.

REFRAIN

Safe in the arms of Je - sus, Safe on His gen - tle breast,

There by His love o'er-shad - ed, Sweet - ly my soul shall rest.

351 **Nearer, My God, To Thee**

Sarah F. Adams   Lowell Mason

1. Near - er my God, to Thee, Near - er to Thee! E'en tho it be a cross
2. Tho like the wan - der - er, The sun gone down, Darkness be o - ver me,
3. There let the way ap - pear, Steps un - to heav'n; All that Thou send - est me,
4. Then with my wak - ing tho'ts Bright with Thy praise Out of my ston - y griefs

That rais - eth me; Still all my song shall be, Near - er, my
My rest a stone, Yet in my dreams I'd be Near - er, my
In mer - cy giv'n; An - gels to beck - on me Near - er, my
Beth - el I'll raise; So by my woes to be Near - er, my

God, to Thee! Near - er, my God, to Thee, Near - er to Thee!

Where We'll Never Grow Old

James C. Moore   James C. Moore

1. I have heard of a land on the far a - way strand,'Tis a
2. In that beau - ti - ful home where we'll nev - er - more roam, We shall
3. When our work here is done and our life-crown is won, And our

beau - ti - ful home of the soul; Built by Je - sus on high,
be in the sweet by and by; Hap - py praise to the King,
trou - bles and tri - als are o'er; All our sor - rows will end

there we nev - er shall die, 'Tis a land where we nev - er grow old.
thru e - ter - ni - ty sing, 'Tis a land where we nev - er shall die.
and our voic - es will blend, With the loved ones who've gone on be - fore.

REFRAIN

Nev - er grow old,   nev - er grow old, In a
                    Where we'll

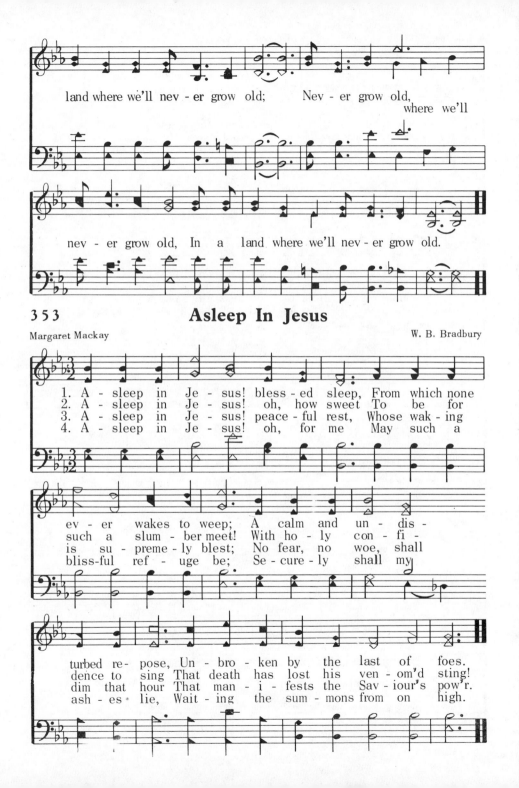

land where we'll nev - er grow old; Nev - er grow old, where we'll

nev - er grow old, In a land where we'll nev - er grow old.

353   Asleep In Jesus

Margaret Mackay

W. B. Bradbury

1. A - sleep in Je - sus! bless - ed sleep, From which none
2. A - sleep in Je - sus! oh, how sweet To be for
3. A - sleep in Je - sus! peace - ful rest, Whose wak - ing
4. A - sleep in Je - sus! oh, for me May such a

ev - er wakes to weep; A calm and un - dis -
such a slum - ber meet! With ho - ly con - fi -
is su - preme - ly blest; No fear, no woe, shall
bliss-ful ref - uge be; Se - cure - ly shall my

turbed re - pose, Un - bro - ken by the last of foes.
dence to sing That death has lost his ven - om'd sting!
dim that hour That man - i - fests the Sav - iour's pow'r.
ash - es lie, Wait - ing the sum - mons from on high.

Farther Along

Rev. W. B. Stevens

Rev. W. B. Stevens
Arr. by J. R. Baxter, Jr.

1. Tempt - ed and tried we're oft made to won - der Why it should be thus
2. When death has come and tak-en our loved ones, It leaves our home so
3. Faith-ful till death said our lov - ing Mas-ter, A few more days to
4. When we see Je - sus com-ing in glo - ry, When He comes from His

all the day long, While there are oth - ers liv - ing a - bout us,
lone - ly and drear; Then do we won - der why oth - ers pros - per,
la - bor and wait; Toils of the road will then seem as noth - ing,
home in the sky; Then we shall meet Him in that bright man - sion,

REFRAIN

Nev - er mo - lest - ed, tho' in the wrong.
Liv - ing so wick - ed year af - ter year. Far - ther a -
As we sweep thru the beau - ti - ful gate.
We'll un - der - stand it all by and by.

long we'll know all a - bout it, Far - ther a - long we'll

un - der - stand why; Cheer up, my broth - er, live in the

sun - shine, We'll un - der - stand it all by and by.

355 Abide With Me

Henry F. Lyte

William H. Monk

1. A - bide with me: fast falls the e - ven - tide; The dark - ness
2. Swift to its close ebbs out life's lit - tle day; Earth's joys grow
3. I need Thy pres - ence ev - 'ry pass - ing hour; What but Thy
4. Hold Thou Thy cross be - fore my clos - ing eyes; Shine thro' the

deep - ens; Lord, with me a - bide: When oth - er help - ers
dim, its glo - ries pass a - way; Change and de - cay in
grace can foil the tempt - er's pow'r? Who like Thy - self my
gloom, and point me to the skies: Heav'n's morn - ing breaks and

fail, and com - forts flee, Help of the help - less, O a - bide with me!
all a - round I see: O Thou who changest not, a - bide with me!
guide and stay can be? Thro' cloud and sun-shine, O a - bide with me!
earth's vain shad-ows flee: In life, in death, O Lord, a - bide with me!

No Tears In Heaven

Robert S. Arnold Robert S. Arnold

1. No tears in heav - en, no sor - rows giv - en, All will be glo - ry
2. Glo - ry is wait - ing, wait - ing up yon - der, Where we shall spend an
3. Some morn-ing yon - der, we'll cease to pon - der O'er things this life has

in that land; There'll be no sad - ness, all will be glad - ness,
end-less day; There with our Sav - iour, we'll be for - ev - er,
bro't to view; All will be clear - er, loved ones be dear - er,

REFRAIN

When we shall join that hap - py band.
Where no more sor - row can dis - may. No tears,
In heav'n where all will be made new. in heav - en fair,

no tears, no tears up there, Sor - row and pain will all have

flown; No tears, in heav-en fair, no tears, no

tears up there, No tears in heav-en will be known.

357   One Sweetly Solemn Thought

Phoebe Cary   R. S. Ambrose?

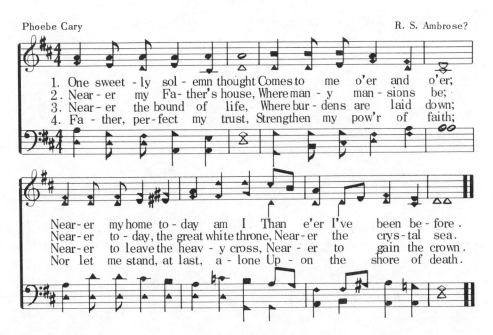

1. One sweet-ly sol-emn thought Comes to me o'er and o'er;
2. Near-er my Fa-ther's house, Where man-y man-sions be;
3. Near-er the bound of life, Where bur-dens are laid down;
4. Fa-ther, per-fect my trust, Strengthen my pow'r of faith;

Near-er my home to-day am I Than e'er I've been be-fore.
Near-er to-day, the great white throne, Near-er the crys-tal sea.
Near-er to leave the heav-y cross, Near-er to gain the crown.
Nor let me stand, at last, a-lone Up-on the shore of death.

358 How Beautiful Heaven Must Be

Mrs. A. S. Bridgewater

A. P. Bland

1. We read of a place that's called heav-en, It's made for the
2. In heav-en no droop-ing nor pin-ing, No wish-ing for
3. Pure wa-ters of life there are flow-ing, And all who will
4. The an-gels so sweet-ly are sing-ing, Up there by the

pure and the free; These truths in God's Word He hath giv - en,
else-where to be; God's light is for - ev - er there shin - ing,
drink may be free; Rare jew - els of splen-dor are glow - ing,
beau - ti - ful sea; Sweet chords from their gold harps are ring - ing,

REFRAIN

How beau - ti - ful heav-en must be. How beau - ti - ful heav-en must

be, must be, Sweet home of the hap - py and free; Fair ha - ven of

rest for the wea - ry, How beau - ti - ful heav - en must be.

Gathering Buds

James Rowe

James D. Vaughan

1. Je - sus has tak - en a beau - ti - ful bud, Out of our
2. Full bloom - ing flow - ers a - lone will not do, Some must be
3. Fa - thers and moth - ers, weep not or be sad, Still on the
4. Bloom - ing in beau - ty in heav - en they are, Bloom - ing for

gar - den of love, Borne it a - way to the cit - y of
young and un - grown; So the frail buds He is gath - er - ing
Sav - iour re - ly; You shall be - hold them a - gain, and be
you and for me; Fol - low the Lord, tho' the cit - y be

REFRAIN

God, Home of the an - gels a - bove.
too, Beau - ti - ful gems for His throne. Gath - er - ing buds,
glad, Beau - ti - ful flow - ers on high.
far, Till our bright blos - soms we see.

gath - er - ing buds, Won - der - ful care will be giv'n; Je - sus is

gath - er - ing, day af - ter day, Buds for the pal - ace of heav'n.

Precious Memories

J. B. F. Wright   J. B. F. Wright

1. Pre - cious mem'ries, un - seen an - gels, Sent from some-where to my soul;
2. Pre - cious fa - ther, lov - ing moth-er, Fly a - cross the lone-ly years;
3. In the still-ness of the mid-night, Ech-oes from the past I hear;
4. As I trav - el on life's path-way, Know not what the years may hold;

How they lin - ger, ev - er near me, And the sa - cred past un - fold.
And old home scenes of my child-hood, In fond mem - o - ry ap - pear.
Old - time sing-ing, glad - ness bring-ing, From that love-ly land some-where.
As I pon - der, hope grows fon - der, Pre-cious mem'ries flood my soul.

REFRAIN

Pre - cious mem'ries, how they lin - ger, How they ev - er flood my soul;

In the still - ness of the mid-night, Pre-cious, sa-cred scenes un-fold.

Will The Circle Be Unbroken?

Ada R. Habershon

Charles H. Gabriel

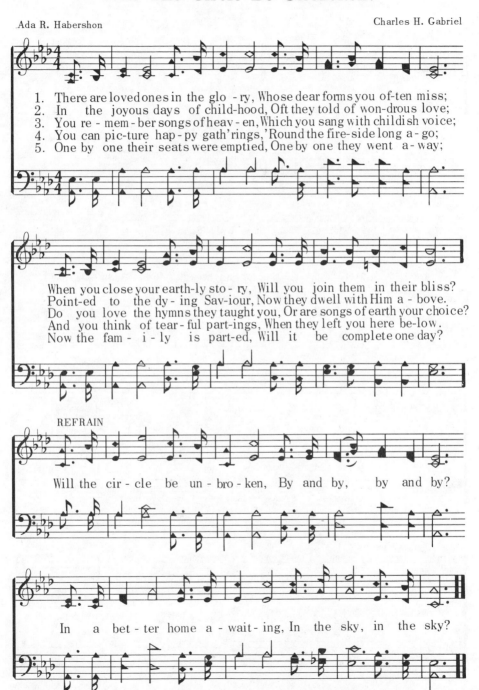

1. There are loved ones in the glo - ry, Whose dear forms you of-ten miss;
2. In the joyous days of child-hood, Oft they told of won-drous love;
3. You re - mem - ber songs of heav - en, Which you sang with childish voice;
4. You can pic-ture hap - py gath'rings, 'Round the fire-side long a - go;
5. One by one their seats were emptied, One by one they went a - way;

When you close your earth-ly sto - ry, Will you join them in their bliss?
Point-ed to the dy - ing Sav-iour, Now they dwell with Him a - bove.
Do you love the hymns they taught you, Or are songs of earth your choice?
And you think of tear - ful part-ings, When they left you here be-low.
Now the fam - i - ly is part-ed, Will it be complete one day?

REFRAIN

Will the cir - cle be un - bro - ken, By and by, by and by?

In a bet - ter home a - wait - ing, In the sky, in the sky?

The Lord Is In His Holy Temple

362

Habakkuk 2:20

George F. Root

The Lord is in His ho-ly tem - ple, The Lord is in His ho-ly tem - ple; Let all the earth keep si-lence, Let all the earth keep si-lence be - fore Him, Keep si-lence, keep si-lence be - fore Him. A - men.

363

Let The Words Of My Mouth

Psalm 19:14

Adolph Baumbach

Let the words of my mouth and the med - i - ta - tion
of my heart be ac - cept - a - ble in Thy sight,
O, Lord, my strength and my Re - deem - er. A - men.

364

We Give Thee But Thine Own

William W. How

Joseph Barnby

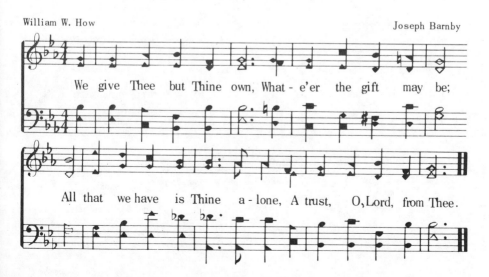

We give Thee but Thine own, What - e'er the gift may be;
All that we have is Thine a - lone, A trust, O, Lord, from Thee.

Glory Be To The Father

(First Setting)

Charles Meineke

Glo - ry be to the Fa - ther, and to the Son, and to the

Ho - ly Ghost; As it was in the be - gin - ning, is

now, and ev - er shall be, world with - out end. A - men, A - men.

Glory Be To The Father

(Second Setting)

From Henry W. Greatorex's "Collection," 1851

Glo - ry be to the Fa - ther, and to the Son, and to the

Ho - ly Ghost; As it was in the be - gin - ning, is now, and

ev - er shall be, world with-out end. A - men, A - men.

367   ## All Things Come Of Thee

Arr. from Ludwig van Beethoven

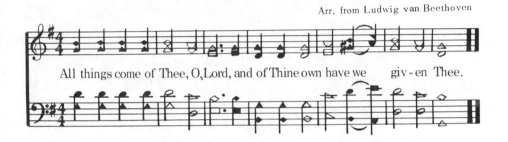

All things come of Thee, O, Lord, and of Thine own have we giv-en Thee.

368   ## Hear Our Prayer, O, Lord

George Whelpton

Hear our prayer, O, Lord, Hear our prayer, O, Lord;

In - cline Thine ear to us, And grant us Thy peace. A - men.

Almighty Father, Hear Our Prayer

Arr. from Felix Mendelssohn

Al - might - y Fa - ther, hear our prayer, and

bless all souls that wait be - fore Thee. A - men.

Sevenfold Amen

John Stainer

A - men, A - - - - - - men,
A - men, A - men, A - - - men, A - - - - - men,
A - - - men, A - - - men,

A - - - men,
A - - - - - - men, A - - - - - men, A - men.
A - - - men,

371 Dresden Amen   372   Threefold Amen

Traditional

John Stainer

A-men, a — men.   A-men, a — men, a — men.

373   **Threefold Amen**

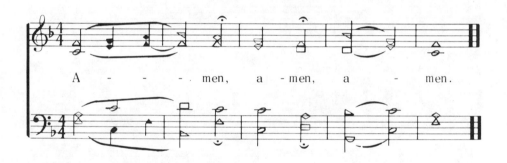

A — — — men, a — men, a — men.

374   **Fourfold Amen**

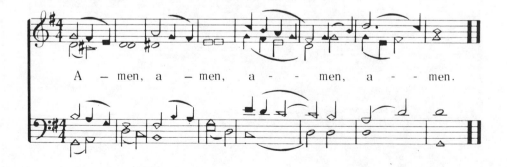

A — men, a — men, a — — men, a — — men.

The Lord Bless You And Keep You

Numbers 6:24-26

Peter C. Lutkin

The Lord bless you and keep you: The Lord lift His coun - te - nance up -

on you,
and give you peace,
and give you peace,
and give you

and give you peace; The Lord make His face to shine up -
peace;
The Lord make His
The Lord

on you, And be gra - cious un - to you, be gra - cious,
And be gra - cious, And be gra - cious,

The Lord be gra - cious, gra - cious un - to you. A - men.

376

God Be With You

Jeremiah F. Rankin

William G. Tomer

1. God be with you till we meet a-gain! By His coun-sels guide, up-
2. God be with you till we meet a-gain! 'Neath His wings se-cure-ly
3. God be with you till we meet a-gain! Keep love's ban-ner float-ing

hold you, With His sheep se-cure-ly fold you; God be with you
hide you, Dai-ly man-na still pro-vide you; God be with you
o'er you, Smite death's threat'ning wave before you; God be with you

REFRAIN

till we meet a-gain! Till we meet! Till we meet!
Till me meet! Till we meet a-gain!

Till we meet at Je - sus' feet; Till we meet!
Till we meet! Till we meet!

Till we meet! God be with you till we meet a-gain!
Till we meet a-gain!

Responsive Readings

1   PRAISE

Psalms 96:1-13; 97:1

O Sing unto the Lord a new song; sing unto the Lord, all the earth.

Sing unto the Lord, bless his name; show forth his salvation from day to day.

Declare his glory among the heathen, his wonders among all people.

For the Lord is great, and greatly to be praised: he is to be feared above all gods.

For all the gods of the nations are idols: but the Lord made the heavens.

Honour and majesty are before him: strength and beauty are in his sanctuary.

Give unto the Lord, O ye kindreds of the people, give unto the Lord glory and strength.

Give unto the Lord the glory due unto his name: bring an offering, and come unto his courts.

O worship the Lord in the beauty of holiness: fear before him, all the earth.

Say among the heathen that the Lord reigneth: the world also shall be established that it shall not be moved: he shall judge the people righteously.

Let the heavens rejoice, and let the earth be glad; let the sea roar, and the fulness thereof.

Let the field be joyful, and all that is therein; then shall all the trees of the wood rejoice.

For he cometh to judge the earth: he shall judge the world with righteousness, and the people with his truth.

The Lord reigneth; let the earth rejoice; let the multitude of isles be glad thereof.

2.   GOD'S WORD

James 1:16-25; John 8:31, 32

Do not err, my beloved brethren.

Every good gift and every perfect gift is from above, and cometh down from the Father of lights, with whom is no variableness, neither shadow of turning.

Of his own will begat he us with the word of truth, that we should be a kind of firstfruits of his creatures.

Wherefore, my beloved brethren, let every man be swift to hear, slow to speak, slow to wrath:

For the wrath if man worketh not the righteousness of God.

Wherefore lay apart all filthiness and superfluity of naughtiness, and receive with meekness the engrafted word, which is able to save your souls.

But be ye doers of the word, and not hearers only, deceiving your own selves.

For if any be a hearer of the word, and not a doer, he is like unto a man beholding his natural face in a glass:

For he beholdeth himself, and goeth his way, and straightway forgetteth what manner of man he was.

But whoso looketh into the perfect law of liberty, and continueth therein, he being not a forgetful hearer, but a doer of the work, this man shall be blessed in his deed.

Then said Jesus to those Jews which believed on him, If ye continue in my word, then are ye my disciples indeed;

And ye shall know the truth, and the truth shall make you free.

3   PROMISE

Psalm 91:1-15

He that dwelleth in the secret place of the most High shall abide under the shadow of the Almighty.

I will say of the Lord, He is my refuge and my fortress: my God; in him will I trust.

Surely he shall deliver thee from the snare of the fowler, and from the noisome pestilence.

He shall cover thee with his feathers, and under his wings shalt thou trust: his truth shall be thy shield and buckler.

Thou shalt not be afraid for the terror by night; nor for the arrow that flieth by day;

Nor for the pestilence that walketh in darkness; nor for the destruction that wasteth at noonday.

A thousand shall fall at thy side, and ten thousand at thy right hand; but it shall not come nigh thee.

Only with thine eyes shalt thou behold and see the reward of the wicked.

Because thou hast made the Lord, which is my refuge, even the most High, thy habitation; There shall no evil befall thee, neither shall any plague come nigh thy dwelling.

For he shall give his angels charge over thee, to keep thee in all thy ways.

They shall bear thee up in their hands, lest thou dash thy foot against a stone.

Thou shalt tread upon the lion and adder: the young lion and the dragon shalt thou trample under feet.

Because he hath set his love upon me, therefore will I deliver him: I will set him on high, because he hath known my name.

He shall call upon me, and I will answer him: I will be with him in trouble; I will deliver him, and honour him.

2 Corinthians 6:1-10; Matthew 5:10-12

We then as workers together with him, beseech you also that ye receive not the grace of God in vain.

(For he saith, I have heard thee in a time accepted, and in the day of salvation have I succored thee:

Behold, now is the accepted time; behold, now is the day of salvation.)

Giving no offense in any thing, that the ministry be not blamed.

But in all things approving ourselves as the ministers of God, in much patience, in afflictions, in necessities, in distresses,

In stripes, in imprisonments, in tumults, in labours, in watchings, in fastings;

By pureness, by knowledge, by longsuffering, by kindness, by the Holy Ghost, by love unfeigned,

By the word of truth, by the power of God, by the armour of righteousness on the right hand and on the left,

By honour and dishonour, by evil report and good report: as deceivers, and yet true;

As unknown, and yet w e l l known; as dying, and, behold, we live; as chastened, and not killed;

As sorrowful, yet alway rejoicing; as poor, yet making many rich; as having nothing, and yet possessing all things.

Blessed are they which are persecuted for righteousness' sake: for their's is the kingdom of heaven.

Blessed are ye, when men shall revile you, an persecute you, and shall say all manner of evil against you falsely, for my sake.

Rejoice, and be exceeding glad: for great is your reward in heaven: for so persecuted they the prophets which were before you.

5　　　THE TEN COMMANDMENTS

Exodus 20:3-17

1. Thou shalt have no other gods before me.

2. **Thou shalt not make unto thee any graven image, or any likeness of any thing that is in heaven above, or that is in the earth beneath, or that is in the water under the earth. Thou shalt not bow down thyself to them, nor serve them: for I the Lord thy God am a jealous God, visiting the iniquity of the fathers upon the children unto the third and fourth generation of them that hate me; And shewing mercy unto thousands of them that love me, and keep my commandments.**

3. Thou shalt not take the name of the Lord thy God in vain; for the Lord will not hold him guiltless that taketh his name in vain.

4. Remember the sabbath day, to keep it holy. Six days shalt thou labour, and do all thy work: But the seventh day is the sabbath of the Lord thy God: in it thou shall not do any work, thou, nor thy son, nor thy daughter, thy manservant, nor thy maidservant, nor thy cattle, nor thy stranger that is within thy gates: For in six days the Lord made heaven and earth, the sea, and all that in them is, and rested the seventh day: wherefore the Lord blessed the sabbath day, and hallowed it.

5. Honour thy father and thy mother: that thy days may be long upon the land which the Lord thy God giveth thee.

6. Thou shalt not kill.

7. Thou shalt not commit adultery.

8. Thou shalt not steal.

9. Thou shalt not bear false witness against thy neighbour.

10. Thou shalt not covet thy neighbour's house, thou shalt not covet thy neighbour's wife, nor his manservant, nor his maidservant, nor his ox, nor his ass, nor any thing that is thy neighbour's.

6   VICTORY

Psalm 40:1-3, 13; 1 Corinthians 15:51-58

I waited patiently for the Lord; and he inclined unto me, and heard my cry.

He brought me up also out of a horrible pit, out of the miry clay, and set my feet upon a rock, and established my goings.

And he hath put a new song in my mouth, even praise unto our God: many shall see it, and fear, and shall trust in the Lord.

Be pleased, O Lord, to deliver me: O Lord, make haste to help me.

Behold, I shew you a mystery; We shall not all sleep, but we shall all be changed,

In a moment, in the twinkling of an eye, at the last trump: for the trumpet shall sound, and the dead shall be raised incorruptible, and we shall be changed.

For this corruptible must put on incorruption, and this mortal must put on immortality.

So when this corruptible shall have put on incorruption, and this mortal shall have put on immortality, then shall be brought to pass the saying that is written, Death is swallowed up in victory.

O death, where is thy sting? O grave, where is thy victory?

The sting of death is sin; and the strength of sin is the law.

But thanks be to God, which giveth us the victory through our Lord Jesus Christ.

Therefore, my beloved brethren, be ye stedfast, unmoveable, always abounding in the work of the Lord, forasmuch as ye know that your labour is not in vain in the Lord.

7   CHRISTIAN LOVE

1 Corinthians 13:1-10, 13

Though I speak with the tongues of men and of angels, and have not charity, I am become as sounding brass, or a tinkling cymbal.

And though I have the gift of prophecy, and understand all mysteries, and all knowledge; and though I have faith, so that I could remove mountains, and have not charity, I am nothing

And though I bestow all my goods to feed the poor, and though I give my body to be burned, and have not charity, it profiteth me nothing.

Charity suffereth long, and is kind; charity envieth not; charity vaunteth not itself, is not puffed up,

Doth not behave itself unseemly, seeketh not her own, is not easily provoked, thinketh no evil;

Rejoiceth not in iniquity, but rejoiceth in the truth;

Beareth all things, believeth all things, hopeth all things, endureth all things.

Charity n e v e r faileth: but whether there be prophecies, they shall fail;

Whether there be tongues, they shall c e a s e; whether there be knowledge, it shall vanish away.

For we know in part, and we prophesy in part.

But when that which is perfect is come, then that which is in part shall be done away.

And now abideth faith, hope, charity, these three; but the greatest of these is charity.

8   HOLINESS

2 Corinthians 7:1; Romans 6:16-18, 21-22;
Hebrews 12:9-14

Having therefore these promises, dearly beloved, let us cleanse ourselves from all filthiness of the flesh and spirit, perfecting holiness in the fear of God.

Know ye not, that to whom ye yield yourselves servants to obey, his servants ye are to whom ye obey; whether of sin unto death, or of obedience unto righteousness?

But God be thanked, that ye were the servants of sin, but ye have obeyed from the heart that form of doctrine which was delivered you.

Being then made free from sin, ye became the servants of righteousness.

What fruit had ye then in those things whereof ye are now ashamed? for the end of those things is death.

But now being made free from sin, and become servants to God, ye have your fruit unto holiness, and the end everlasting life.

Furthermore we have had fathers of our flesh which corrected us, and we gave them reverence: shall we not much rather be in subjection unto the Father of spirits and live?

For they verily for a few days chastened us after their own pleasure; but he for our profit, that we might be partakers of his holiness.

Now no chastening for the present seemeth to be joyous, but grievous: nevertheless afterward it yieldeth the peaceable fruit of righteousness unto them which are exercised thereby.

Wherefore lift up the hands which hang down, and the feeble knees;

And make straight paths for your feet, lest that which is lame be turned out of the way; but let it rather be healed.

Follow peace with all men, and holiness, without which no man shall see the Lord.

9 ASSURANCE

Romans 8:28, 31-39; 2 Timothy 1:12

And we know that all things work together for good to them that love God, to them who are the called according to his purpose.

What shall we then say to these things? If God be for us, who can be against us?

He that spared not his own Son, but delivered him up for us all, how shall he not with him also freely give us all things?

Who shall lay anything to the charge of God's elect? It is God that justifieth.

Who is he that condemneth? It is Christ that died, yea rather, that is risen again, who is even at the right hand of God, who also maketh intercession for us.

Who shall separate us from the love of Christ? shall tribulation, or distress, or persecution, or famine, or nakedness, or peril, or sword?

As it is written, For thy sake we are killed all the day long; we are accounted as sheep for the slaughter.

Nay, in all these things we are more than conquerors through him that loved us.

For I am persuaded, that neither death, nor life, nor angels, nor principalities, nor powers, nor things present, nor things to come

Nor height, nor depth, nor any other creature, shall be able to separate us from the love of God, which is in Christ Jesus our Lord.

For the which cause I also suffer these things: nevertheless I am not ashamed:

For I know whom I have believed, and am persuaded that he is able to keep that which I have committed unto him against that day.

John 3:16; 5:24; 10:10; 11:25, 26;
1 John 5:12, 13; John 10:28; 6:39, 40

For God so loved the world, that he gave his only begotten Son, that whosoever believeth in him should not perish, but have everlasting life.

Verily, verily, I say unto you, He that heareth my word, and believeth on him that sent me, hath everlasting life, and shall not come into condemnation; but is passed from death unto life.

The thief cometh not, but for to steal, and to kill, and to destroy: I am come that they might have life, and that they might have it more abundantly.

I am the resurrection, and the life: he that believeth in me, though he were dead, yet shall he live:

And whosoever liveth and believeth in me shall never die.

He that hath the Son hath life; and he that hath not the Son of God hath not life.

These things have I written unto you that believe on the name of the Son of God; that ye may know that ye have eternal life, and that ye may believe on the name of the Son of God.

And I give unto them eternal life; and they shall never perish, neither shall any man pluck them out of my hand.

And this is the Father's will which hath sent me, that of all which he hath given me I should lose nothing, but should raise it up again at the last day.

And this is the will of him that sent me that everyone which seeth the Son, and believeth on him, may have everlasting life: and I will raise him up at the last day.

11 NEW BIRTH

John 3:1-7, 12-16

There was a man of the Pharisees, named Nicodemus, a ruler of the Jews:

The same came to Jesus by night, and said unto him, Rabbi, we know that thou art a teacher come from God: for no man can do these miracles that thou doest, except God be with him.

Jesus answered and said unto him, Verily, verily, I say unto thee, Except a man be born again, he cannot see the kingdom of God.

Nicodemus saith unto him, How can a man be born when he is old? Can he enter the second time into his mother's womb, and be born?

Jesus answered, Verily, verily, I say unto thee, Except a man be born of water and of the Spirit, he cannot enter into the kingdom of God.

That which is born of the flesh is flesh; and that which is born of the Spirit is spirit.

Marvel not that I said unto thee, Ye must be born again.

If I have told you earthly things, and ye believe not, how shall ye believe, if I tell you of heavenly things?

And no man hath ascended up to heaven, but he that came down from heaven, even the Son of man which is in heaven.

And as Moses lifted up the serpent in the wilderness, even so must the Son of man be lifted up:

That whosoever believeth in him should not perish, but have eternal life.

For God so loved the world, that he gave his only begotten Son, that whosoever believeth in him should not perish, but have everlasting life.

12   SALVATION

Romans 1:16; 10:10, 13; 2 Corinthians 6:2; Philippians 2:12, 13; 1 Thessalonians 5:8, 9; Titus 2:11-14

For I am not ashamed of the gospel of Christ: for it is the power of God unto salvation to every one that believeth; to the Jew first, and also to the Greek.

For with the heart man believeth unto righteousness; and with the mouth confession is made unto salvation.

For whosoever shall call upon the name of the Lord shall be saved.

(For he saith, I have heard thee in a time accepted, and in the day of salvation have I succoured thee: behold, now is the accepted time; behold, now is the day of salvation.)

Wherefore, my beloved, as ye have always obeyed, not as in my presence only, but now much more in my absence, work out your own salvation with fear and trembling.

For it is God which worketh in you both to will and to do of his good pleasure.

But let us, who are of the day, be sober, putting on the breastplate of faith and love; and for an helmet, the hope of salvation.

For God hath not appointed us to wrath, but to obtain salvation by our Lord Jesus Christ.

For the grace of God that bringeth salvation hath appeared to all men,

Teaching us that, denying ungodliness and worldly lusts, we should live soberly, righteously, and godly, in this present world;

Looking for that blessed hope, and the glorious appearing of the great God and our Saviour Jesus Christ;

Who gave himself for us, that he might redeem us from all iniquity, and purify unto himself a peculiar people, zealous of good works.

13 REPENTANCE

Isaiah 55:6, 7; Acts 3:19; Luke 15:18-24; Isaiah 1:18

Seek ye the Lord while he may be found, call ye upon him while he is near:

Let the wicked forsake his way, and the unrighteous man his thoughts: and let him return unto the Lord, and he will have mercy upon him; and to our God, for he will abundantly pardon.

Repent ye therefore, and be converted, that your sins may be blotted out, when the times of refreshing shall come from the presence of the Lord.

I will arise and go to my father, and will say unto him, Father, I have sinned against heaven, and before thee,

And am no more worthy to be called thy son: make me as one of thy hired servants.

And he arose, and came to his father. But when he was yet a great way off, his father saw him and had compassion, and ran, and fell on his neck, and kissed him.

And the son said unto him, Father, I have sinned against heaven, and in thy sight, and am no more worthy to be called thy son.

But the father said to his servants, Bring forth the best robe, and put it on him; and put a ring on his hand, and shoes on his feet:

And bring hither the fatted calf, and kill it; and let us eat, and be merry:

For this my son was dead, and is alive again; he was lost, and is found.

Come now, and let us reason together, saith the Lord: though your sins be as scarlet, they shall be as white as snow;

Though they be red like crimson, they shall be as wool.

14 HOLY GHOST

John 14:16, 17, 26; 16:7, 12-14; Acts 2:1-4

And I will pray the Father, and he shall give you another Comforter, that he may abide with you for ever;

Even the Spirit of truth; whom the world cannot receive, because it seeth him not, neither knoweth him: but ye know him; for he dwelleth with you, and shall be in you.

But the Comforter, which is the Holy Ghost, whom the Father will send in my name, he shall teach you all things, and bring all things to your remembrance, whatsoever I have said unto you.

Nevertheless I tell you the truth; It is expedient for you that I go away: for if I go not away, the Comforter will not come unto you; but if I depart, I will send him unto you.

I have yet many things to say unto you, but ye cannot bear them now.

Howbeit when he, the Spirit of truth, is come, he will guide you into all truth: for he shall not speak of himself; but whatsoever he shall hear, that shall he speak: and he will shew you things to come.

He shall glorify me: for he shall receive of mine, and shall shew it unto you.

And when the day of Pentecost was fully come, they were all with one accord in one place.

And suddenly there came a sound from heaven as of a rushing mighty wind, and it filled all the house where they were sitting.

And there appeared unto them cloven tongues like as of fire, and it sat upon each of them. And they were all filled with the Holy Ghost, and began to speak with other tongues, as the Spirit gave them utterance.

15   SANCTIFICATION

John 17:17, 19; Acts 15:8, 9; Galatians 2:20; Ephesians 4:7, 11-13; 1 Peter 1:15, 16; 1 Thessalonians 5:23, 24

Sanctify them through thy truth: thy word is truth.

And for their sakes I sanctify myself, that they also might be sanctified through the truth.

And God, which knoweth the hearts, bare them witness, giving them the Holy Ghost, even as he did unto us;

And put no difference between us and them, purifying their hearts by faith.

I am crucified with Christ: nevertheless I live; yet not I, but Christ liveth in me: and the life which I now live in the flesh I live by the faith of the Son of God, who loved me, and gave himself for me.

But unto every one of us is given grace according to the measure of the gift of Christ.

And he gave some, apostles; and some, prophets; and some, evangelists; and some, pastors and teachers; For the perfecting of the saints, for the work of the ministry, for the edifying of the body of Christ:

Till we all come in the unity of the faith, and of the knowledge of the Son of God, unto a perfect man, unto the measure of the stature of the fulness of Christ.

But as he which hath called you is holy, so be ye holy in all manner of conversation;

Because it is written, Be ye holy; for I am holy.

And the very God of peace sanctify you wholly; and I pray God your whole spirit and soul and body be preserved blameless unto the coming of our Lord Jesus Christ.

Faithful is he that calleth you, who also will do it.

Proverbs 11:23-25, 30; Psalm 126;
Matthew 28:18-20

The desire of the righteous is only good: but the expectation of the wicked is wrath.

There is that scattereth, and yet increaseth; and there is that withholdeth more than is meet, but it tendeth to poverty.

The liberal soul shall be made fat: and he that watereth shall be watered also himself.

The fruit of the righteous is a tree of life; and he that winneth souls is wise.

Behold, the righteous shall be recompensed in the earth: much more the wicked and the sinner.

When the Lord turned again the captivity of Zion, we were like them that dream.

Then was our mouth filled with laughter, and our tongue with singing: then said they among the heathen, The Lord hath done great things for them.

The Lord hath done great things for us; whereof we are glad.

Turn again our captivity, O Lord, as the streams in the south.

They that sow in tears shall reap in joy.

He that goeth forth and weepeth, bearing precious seed, shall doubtless come again with rejoicing, bringing his sheaves with him.

And Jesus came and spake unto them saying, All power is given unto me in heaven and in earth.

Go ye therefore, and teach all nations, baptizing them in the name of the Father, and of the Son, and of the Holy Ghost:

Teaching them to observe all things whatsoever I have commanded you: and, lo, I am with you alway, even unto the end of the world. Amen.

17   REVIVAL

Psalm 85; 2 Chronicles 7:14

Lord, thou hast been favourable unto thy land: thou hast brought back the captivity of Jacob.

Thou hast forgiven the iniquity of thy people, thou hast covered all their sin. Selah.

Thou has taken away all thy wrath: thou hast turned thyself from the fierceness of thine anger.

Turn us, O God of our salvation, and cause thine anger toward us to cease.

Wilt thou be angry with us for ever? wilt thou draw out thine anger to all generations?

Wilt thou not revive us again: that thy people may rejoice in thee?

Shew us thy mercy, O Lord, and grant us thy salvation.

I will hear what God the Lord will speak: for he will speak peace unto his people, and to his saints: but let them not turn again to folly.

Surely his salvation is nigh them that fear him; that glory may dwell in our land.

Mercy and truth are met together; righteousness and peace have kissed each other.

Truth shall spring out of the earth; and righteousness shall look down from heaven.

Yea, the Lord shall give that which is good; and our land shall yield her increase.

Righteousness shall go before him; and shall set us in the way of his steps.

If my people, which are called by my name, shall humble themselves, and pray, and seek my face, and turn from their wicked ways; then will I hear from heaven, and will forgive their sin, and will heal their land.

18   WATER BAPTISM

Matthew 3:13-17; Romans 6:4-6, 11; Matthew 28:19, 20

Then cometh Jesus from Galilee to Jordan unto John, to be baptized of him. But John forbad him, saying, I have need to be baptized of thee, and comest thou to me?

And Jesus answering said unto him, Suffer it to be so now: for thus it becometh us to fulfill all righteousness. Then he suffered him.

And Jesus, when he was baptized, went up straightway out of the water: and, lo, the heavens were opened unto him, and he saw the Spirit of God descending like a dove, and lighting upon him:

And lo a voice from heaven, saying, This is my beloved Son, in whom I am well pleased.

Therefore we are buried with him by baptism into death: that like as Christ was raised up from the dead by the glory of the Father, even so we also should walk in newness of life.

For if we have been planted together in the likeness of his death, we shall be also in the likeness of his resurrection:

Knowing this, that our old man is crucified with him, that the body of sin might be destroyed, that henceforth we should not serve sin.

Likewise reckon ye also yourselves to be dead indeed unto sin, but alive unto God through Jesus Christ our Lord.

Go ye therefore, and teach all nations, baptizing them in the name of the Father, and of the Son, and of the Holy Ghost:

Teaching them to observe all things whatsoever I have commanded you: and lo, I am with you alway, even unto the end of the world. Amen.

19.   GRACE

Psalm 34:1-9, 17-19; Ephesians 2:1, 4-7

I will bless the Lord at all times: his praise shall continually be in my mouth.

My soul shall make her boast in the Lord: the humble shall hear thereof, and be glad.

O magnify the Lord with me, and let us exalt his name together.

I sought the Lord, and he heard me, and delivered me from all my fears.

They looked unto him, and were lightened: and their faces were not ashamed.

This poor man cried, and the Lord heard him, and saved him out of all his troubles.

The angel of the Lord encampeth round about them that fear him, and delivereth them.

O taste and see that the Lord is good: blessed is the man that trusteth in him.

O fear the Lord, ye his saints: for there is no want to them that fear him.

The righteous cry, and the Lord heareth, and delivereth them out of all their troubles.

The Lord is nigh unto them that are of a broken heart; and saveth such as be of a contrite spirit.

Many are the afflictions of the righteous: but the Lord delivereth him out of them all.

And you hath he quickened, who were dead in trespasses and sins:

But God, who is rich in mercy, for his great love wherewith he loved us, Even when we were dead in sins, hath quickened us together with Christ, (by grace ye are saved;)

And hath raised us up together, and made us sit together in heavenly places in Christ Jesus:

That in the ages to come he might show the exceeding riches of his grace, in his kindness toward us, through Christ Jesus.

20   STEWARDSHIP

Proverbs 3:5, 9, 10; Malachi 3:10;
Luke 6:38; 2 Corinthians 8:9; 9:6-8;
1 Corinthians 4:2

Trust in the Lord with all thine heart; and lean not unto thine own understanding.

Honour the Lord with thy substance, and with the firstfruits of all thine increase:

So shall thy barns be filled with plenty, and thy presses shall burst out with new wine.

Bring ye all the tithes into the storehouse, that there may be meat in mine house, and prove me now herewith, saith the Lord of hosts, if I will not open you the windows of heaven, and pour you out a blessing, that there shall not be room enough to receive it.

Give, and it shall be given unto you; good measure, pressed down, and shaken together, and running over, shall men give into your bosom. For with the same measure that ye mete withal it shall be measured to you again.

For ye know the grace of our Lord Jesus Christ, that, though he was rich, yet for your sakes he became poor, that ye through his poverty might be rich.

But this I say, He which soweth sparingly shall reap also sparingly; and he which soweth bountifully shall reap also bountifully.

Every man according as he purposeth in his heart, so let him give; not grudgingly, or of necessity: for God loveth a cheerful giver.

And God is able to make all grace abound toward you; that ye, always having all sufficiency in all things, may abound to every good work:

Moreover it is required in stewards, that a man be found faithful.

21 CONSECRATION

Colossians 3:1-4; 1 Peter 1:13-16;
2 Corinthians 5:14, 15;
Galatians 2:20; 6:14

If ye then be risen with Christ, seek those things which are above, where Christ sitteth on the right hand of God.

Set your affection on things above, not on things on the earth.

For ye are dead, and your life is hid with Christ in God.

When Christ, who is our life, shall appear, then shall ye also appear with him in glory.

Wherefore gird up the loins of your mind, be sober, and hope to the end for the grace that is to be brought unto you at the revelation of Jesus Christ;

As obedient children, not fashioning yourselves according to the former lusts in your ignorance:

But as he which hath called you is holy, so be ye holy in all manner of conversation;

Because it is written, Be ye holy; for I am holy.

For the love of Christ constraineth us; because we thus judge, that if one died for all, then were all dead:

And that he died for all, that they which live should not henceforth live unto themselves, but unto him which died for them, and rose again.

I am crucified with Christ: nevertheless I live; yet not I, but Christ liveth in me: and the life which I now live in the flesh I live by the faith of the Son of God, who loved me, and gave himself for me.

But God forbid that I should glory, save in the cross of our Lord Jesus Christ, by whom the world is crucified unto me, and I unto the world.

22   MY SHEPHERD

Ezekiel 34:11-15; Psalm 23

For thus saith the Lord God; Behold, I, even I, will both search my sheep, and seek them out.

As a shepherd seeketh out his flock in the day that he is among his sheep that are scattered; so will I seek out my sheep, and will deliver them out of all places where they have been scattered in the cloudy and dark day.

And I will bring them out from the people, and gather them from the countries, and will bring them to their own land, and feed them upon the mountains of Israel by the rivers, and in all the inhabited places of the country.

I will feed them in a good pasture, and upon the high mountains of Israel shall their fold be:

There shall they lie in a good fold, and in a fat pasture shall they feed upon the mountains of Israel.

I will feed my flock, and I will cause them to lie down, saith the Lord God.

The Lord is my shepherd; I shall not want.

He maketh me to lie down in green pastures: he leadeth me beside the still waters.

He restoreth my soul: he leadeth me in the paths of righteousness for his name's sake.

Yea, though I walk through the valley of the shadow of death, I will fear no evil: for thou art with me; thy rod and thy staff they comfort me.

Thou preparest a table before me in the presence of mine enemies: thou anointest my head with oil; my cup runneth over.

Surely goodness and mercy shall follow me all the days of my life: and I will dwell in the house of the Lord forever.

23   HEALING
*Luke 4:38-40; 17:12-17, 19;
James 5:14, 15*

And he arose out of the synagogue, and entered into Simon's house. And Simon's wife's mother was taken with a great fever; and they besought him for her.

And he stood over her, and rebuked the fever; and it left her: and immediately she arose and ministered unto them.

Now when the sun was setting, all they that had any sick with divers diseases brought them unto him; and he laid his hands on every one of them, and healed them.

And as he entered into a certain village, there met him ten men that were lepers, which stood afar off:

And they lifted up their voices, and said, Jesus, Master, have mercy on us.

And when he saw them, he said unto them, Go shew yourselves unto the priests. And it came to pass, that, as they went, they were cleansed.

And one of them, when he saw that he was healed, turned back, and with a loud voice glorified God.

And fell down on his face at his feet, giving him thanks: and he was a Samaritan.

And Jesus answering said, Were there not ten cleansed? but where are the nine?

And he said unto him, Arise, go thy way: thy faith hath made thee whole.

Is any sick among you? let him call for the elders of the church; and let them pray over him, anointing him with oil in the name of the Lord:

And the prayer of faith shall save the sick, and the Lord shall raise him up; and if he have committed sins, they shall be forgiven him.

24   THE BLOOD

Hebrews 9:11-20

But Christ being come an high priest of good things to come, by a greater and more perfect tabernacle, not made with hands, that is to say, not of this building;

Neither by the blood of goats and calves, but by his own blood he entered in once into the holy place, having obtained eternal redemption for us.

For if the blood of bulls and of goats, and the ashes of a heifer sprinkling the unclean sanctifieth to the purifying of the flesh:

How much more shall the blood of Christ, who through the eternal Spirit offered himself without spot to God, purge your conscience from dead works to serve the living God?

And for this cause he is the mediator of the new testament, that by means of death, for the redemption of the transgressions that were under the first testament, they which are called might receive the promise of eternal inheritance.

For where a testament is, there must also of necessity be the death of the testator.

For a testament is of force after men are dead: otherwise it is of no strength at all while the testator liveth.

Whereupon neither the first testament was dedicated without blood.

For when Moses had spoken every precept to all the people according to the law, he took the blood of calves and of goats, with water, and scarlet wool, and hyssop, and sprinkled both the book, and all the people,

Saying, This is the blood of the testament which God hath enjoined unto you.

Psalm 1:1-6; Jeremiah 17:5-8

Blessed is the man that walketh not in the counsel of the ungodly, nor standeth in the way of sinners, nor sitteth in the seat of the scornful.

But his delight is in the law of the Lord; and in his law doth he meditate day and night.

And he shall be like a tree planted by the rivers of water, that bringeth forth his fruit in his season; his leaf also shall not wither; and whatsoever he doeth shall prosper.

The ungodly are not so; but are like the chaff which the wind driveth away.

Therefore the ungodly shall not stand in the judgment, nor sinners in the congregation of the righteous.

For the Lord knoweth the way of the righteous: but the way of the ungodly shall perish.

Thus saith the Lord; Cursed be the man that trusteth in man, and maketh flesh his arm, and whose heart departeth from the Lord.

For he shall be like the heat in the desert, and shall not see when good cometh; but shall inhabit the parched places in the wilderness, in a salt land and not inhabited.

Blessed is the man that trusteth in the Lord, and whose hope the Lord is.

For he shall be as a tree planted by the waters, and that spreadeth out her roots by the river, and shall not see when the heat cometh, but her leaf shall be green; and shall not be careful in the year of drought, neither shall cease from yielding fruit.

26   THE LORD'S DAY

Genesis 2:2, 3; Exodus 20:8-11; Mark 2:23-28; John 20:19

And on the seventh day God ended his work which he had made; and he rested on the seventh day from all his work which he had made.

And God blessed the seventh day, and sanctified it: because that in it he had rested from all his work which God created and made.

Remember the sabbath day, to keep it holy. Six days shalt thou labour, and do all thy work:

But the seventh day is the sabbath of the Lord thy God: in it thou shalt not do any work, thou, nor thy son, nor thy daughter, thy manservant, nor thy maidservant, nor thy cattle, nor thy stranger that is within thy gates:

For in six days the Lord made heaven and earth, the sea, and all that in them is, and rested the seventh day: wherefore the Lord blessed the sabbath day, and hallowed it.

And it came to pass, that he went through the corn fields on the sabbath day; and his disciples began, as they went, to pluck the ears of corn.

And the Pharisees said unto him, Behold, why do they on the sabbath day that which is not lawful?

And he said unto them, Have ye never read what David did, when he had need, and was an hungred, he, and they that were with him?

How he went into the house of God in the days of Abiathar the high priest, and did eat the shewbread, which is not lawful to eat but for the priests, and gave also to them which were with him?

And he said unto them, The sabbath was made for man, and not man for the sabbath:

Therefore the Son of man is Lord also of the sabbath.

Then the same day at evening, being the first day of the week, when the doors were shut where the disciples were assembled for fear of the Jews, came Jesus and stood in the midst, and saith unto them, Peace be unto you.

27   FULNESS OF GOD

John 1:1, 14; Colossians 2:9, 10;
John 1:16; Ephesians 3:14-21

In the beginning was the Word, and the Word was with God, and the Word was God.

And the Word was made flesh, and dwelt among us,

(And we beheld his glory, the glory as of the only begotten of the Father,) full of grace and truth.

For in him dwelleth all the fulness of the Godhead bodily.

And ye are complete in him, which is the head of all principality and power.

And of his fullness have all we received, and grace for grace.

For this cause I bow my knees unto the Father of our Lord Jesus Christ,

Of whom the whole family in heaven and earth is named,

That he would grant you, according to the riches of his glory, to be strengthened with might by his Spirit in the inner man;

That Christ may dwell in your hearts by faith; that ye, being rooted and grounded in love,

May be able to comprehend with all saints what is the breadth, and length, and depth, and height;

And to know the love of Christ, which passeth knowledge, that ye might be filled with all the fulness of God.

Now unto him that is able to do exceeding abundantly above all that we ask or think, according to the power that worketh in us,

Unto him be glory in the church by Christ Jesus throughout all ages, world without end. Amen.

THE CROSS

.Luke 23:26, 32-42

And as they led him away, they laid hold upon one Simon, a Cyrenian, coming out of the country, and on him they laid the cross, that he might bear it after Jesus.

And there were also two other malefactors, led with him to be put to death.

And when they were come to the place, which is called Calvary, there they crucified him, and the malefactors, one on the right hand, and the other on the left.

Then said Jesus, Father, forgive them; for they know not what they do. And they parted his raiment, and cast lots.

And the people stood beholding. And the rulers also with them derided him, saying, He saved others; let him save himself, if he be Christ, the chosen of God.

And the soldiers also mocked him, coming to him, and offering him vinegar,

And saying, If thou be the king of the Jews, save thyself.

And a superscription also was written over him in letters of Greek, and Latin, and Hebrew, THIS IS THE KING OF JEWS.

And one of the malefactors which were hanged railed on him, saying, If thou be Christ, save thyself and us.

But the other answering rebuked him, saying, Dost not thou fear God, seeing thou art in the same condemnation?

And we indeed justly; for we receive the due reward of our deeds: but this man hath done nothing amiss.

And he said unto Jesus, Lord, remember me when thou comest into thy kingdom.

29   COMFORT AND CONSOLATION

John 14:1-4; Isaiah 40:1, 2, 9-11, 29-31

Let not your heart be troubled: ye believe in God, believe also in me.

In my Father's house are many mansions: if it were not so, I would have told you. I go to prepare a place for you.

And if I go and prepare a place for you, I will come again, and receive you unto myself; that where I am, there ye may be also.

And whither I go ye know, and the way ye know.

Comfort ye, comfort ye my people, saith your God.

Speak ye comfortably to Jerusalem, and cry unto her, that her warfare is accomplished, that her iniquity is pardoned: for she hath received of the Lord's hand double for all her sins.

O Zion, that bringest good tidings, get thee up into the high mountain; O Jerusalem, that bringest good tidings, lift up thy voice with strength; lift it up, be not afraid; say unto the cities of Judah, Behold your God!

Behold, the Lord God will come with strong hand, and his arm shall rule for him: behold, his reward is with him, and his work before him.

He shall feed his flock like a shepherd: he shall gather the lambs with his arm, and carry them in his bosom, and shall gently lead those that are with young.

He giveth power to the faint; and to them that have no might he increaseth strength.

Even the youths shall faint and be weary, and the young men shall utterly fall:

But they that wait upon the Lord shall renew their strength; they shall mount up with wings as eagles; they shall run, and not be weary; and they shall walk, and not faint.

30 FAITH

Hebrews 11:1-10

Now faith is the substance of things hoped for, the evidence of things not seen.

For by it the elders obtained a good report.

Through faith we understand that the worlds were framed by the word of God. so that things which are seen were not made of things which do appear.

By faith Abel offered unto God a more excellent sacrifice than Cain, by which he obtained witness that he was righteous, God testifying of his gifts: and by it he being dead yet speaketh.

By faith Enoch was translated that he should not see death; and was not found, because God had translated him: for before his translation he had this testimony, that he pleased God.

But without faith it is impossible to please him: for he that cometh to God must believe that he is, and that he is a rewarder of them that diligently seek him.

By faith Noah, being warned of God of things not seen as yet, moved with fear, prepared an ark to the saving of his house; by the which he condemned the world, and became heir of the righteousness which is by faith.

By faith Abraham, when he was called to go out into a place which he should after receive for an inheritance, obeyed; and he went out, not knowing whither he went.

By faith he sojourned in the land of promise, as in a strange country, dwelling in tabernacles with Isaac and Jacob, the heirs with him of the same promise:

For he looked for a city which hath foundations, whose builder and maker is God.

TRUST

Psalm 27:1-8, 10, 13, 14

The Lord is my light and my salvation; whom shall I fear?

The Lord is the strength of my life; of whom shall I be afraid?

When the wicked, even mine enemies and my foes, came upon me to eat up my flesh, they stumbled and fell.

Though a host should encamp against me, my heart shall not fear: though war should rise against me, in this will I be confident.

One thing have I desired of the Lord, that will I seek after; that I may dwell in the house of the Lord all the days of my life, to behold the beauty of the Lord, and to enquire in his temple.

For in the time of trouble he shall hide me in his pavilion: in the secret of his tabernacle shall he hide me; he shall set me up upon a rock.

And now shall mine head be lifted up above mine enemies round about me: therefore will I offer in his tabernacle sacrifices of joy; I will sing, yea, I will sing praises unto the Lord.

Hear, O Lord, when I cry with my voice: have mercy also upon me, and answer me.

When thou saidst, Seek ye my face; my heart said unto thee, Thy face, Lord, will I seek.

When my father and my mother forsake me, then the Lord will take me up.

I had fainted, unless I had believed to see the goodness of the Lord in the land of the living.

Wait on the Lord: be of good courage, and he shall strengthen thine heart: wait, I say, on the Lord.

32   SECOND COMING

2 Peter 3:9-14; Matthew 24:42-44

The Lord is not slack concerning his promise, as some men count slackness; but is longsuffering to us-ward, not willing that a n y should perish, but that all should come to repentance.

But the day of the Lord will come as a thief in the night;

In the which the heavens shall pass away with a great noise, and the elements shall melt with fervent heat, the earth also and the works that are therein shall be burned up.

Seeing then that all these things shall be dissolved, what manner of persons ought ye to be in all holy conversation and godliness,

Looking for and hasting unto the coming of the day of God, wherein the heavens being on fire shall be dissolved, and the elements shall melt w i t h fervent heat?

Nevertheless we, according to his promise, look for new heavens and a new earth, wherein dwelleth righteousness.

Wherefore, beloved, seeing that ye look for such things, be diligent that ye may be found of him in peace, without spot, and blameless.

Watch therefore: for ye know not what hour your Lord doth come.

But know this, that if the goodman of the house had known in what watch the thief would come, he would have watched, and would not have suffered his house to be broken up.

Therefore be ye also ready: for in such an hour as ye think not the Son of man cometh.

33   DEDICATION

Romans 12:1-11

I beseech you therefore, brethren, by the mercies of God, that ye present your bodies a living sacrifice, holy, acceptable unto God, which is your reasonable service.

And be not conformed to this world: but be ye transformed by the renewing of your mind, that ye may prove what is that good, and acceptable, and perfect will of God.

For I say, through the grace given unto me, to every man that is among you, not to think of himself more highly than he ought to think; but to think soberly, according as God hath dealt to every man the measure of faith.

For as we have many members in one body, and all members have not the same office: So we, being many, are one body in Christ, and every one members one of another.

Having then gifts differing according to the grace that is given to us, whether prophecy, let us prophesy according to the proportion of faith;

Or ministry, let us wait on our ministering; or he that teacheth, on teaching;

Or he that exhorteth, on exhortation: he that giveth, let him do it with simplicity; he that ruleth, with diligence; he that showeth mercy, with cheerfulness.

Let love be without dissimulation. Abhor that which is evil; cleave to that which is good.

Be kindly affectioned one to another with brotherly love; in honour preferring one another;

Not slothful in business; fervent in spirit; serving the Lord.

Romans 5:1; 8:6; Isaiah 26:3; John 14:27;
Galatians 5:22, 23; Philippians 4:6, 7, 9;
Hebrews 13:20, 21; Luke 2:14

Therefore being justified by faith, we have peace with God through our Lord Jesus Christ:

For to be carnally minded is death; but to be spiritually minded is life and peace.

Thou wilt keep him in perfect peace, whose mind is stayed on thee: because he trusteth in thee.

Peace I leave with you, my peace I give unto you: not as the world giveth, give I unto you.

Let not your heart be troubled, neither let it be afraid.

But the fruit of the Spirit is l o v e, joy, peace, longsuffering, gentleness, goodness, faith, meekness, temperance: against s u c h there is no law.

Be careful for nothing; but in every thing by prayer and supplication with thanksgiving let your requests be made unto God.

Those things, which ye have both learned, and received, a n d heard, and seen in me, do: and the God of peace shall be with you.

And the peace of God, which passeth all understanding, s h a l l keep your hearts and minds through Christ Jesus.

Now the God of peace, that brought again from the dead our Lord Jesus, that great shepherd of the sheep, through the blood of the everlasting covenant,

Make you perfect in every good work to do his will, working in you that which is wellpleasing in his sight, through Jesus Christ; to whom be glory for ever and ever.

Glory to God in the highest, and on earth peace, good will toward men.

35 **JESUS CHRIST**

Matthew 1:18-25

Now the birth of Jesus Christ was on this wise: When as his mother Mary was espoused to Joseph, before they came together, she was found with child of the Holy Ghost.

Then Joseph her husband, being a just man, and not willing to make her a public example, was minded to put her away privily.

But while he thought on these things, behold, the angel of the Lord appeared unto him in a dream, saying, Joseph, thou son of David, fear not to take unto thee Mary thy wife: for that which is conceived in her is of the Holy Ghost.

And she shall bring forth a son, and thou shalt call his name JESUS: for he shall save his people from their sins.

Now all this was done, that it might be fulfilled which was spoken of the Lord by the prophet, saying,

Behold, a virgin shall be with child, and shall bring forth a son, and they shall call his name Emmanuel, which being interpreted is, God with us.

Then Joseph being raised from sleep did as the angel of the Lord had bidden him, and took unto him his wife:

And knew her not till she had brought forth her firstborn son: and he called his name JESUS.

36   INVITATION

*Isaiah 55:1-6; Matthew 11:28-30;
Revelation 22:17*

Ho, every one that thirsteth, come ye to the waters, and he that hath no money; come ye, buy, and eat; yea, come, buy wine and milk without money and without price.

Wherefore do ye spend money for that which is not bread? and your labour for that which satisfieth not? hearken diligently unto me, and eat ye that which is good, and let your soul delight itself in fatness.

Incline your ear, and come unto me: hear, and your soul shall live; and I will make an everlasting covenant with you, even the sure mercies of David.

Behold, I have given him for a witness to the people, a leader and commander to the people.

Behold, thou shalt call a nation that thou knowest not, and nations that knew not thee shall run unto thee, because of the Lord thy God, and for the Holy One of Israel; for he hath glorified thee.

Seek ye the Lord while he may be found call ye upon him while he is near:

Come unto me, all ye that labour and are heavy laden, and I will give you rest.

Take my yoke upon you, and learn of me; for I am meek and lowly in heart: and ye shall find rest unto your souls.

For my yoke is easy, and my burden is light.

And the Spirit and the bride say, Come. And let him that heareth say, Come. And let him that is athirst come. And whosoever will, let him take the water of life freely.

Matthew 16:18, 19; Acts 2:41, 42;
1 Corinthians 12:12, 27;
Ephesians 5:24-27

And I say also unto thee, That thou art Peter, and upon this rock I will build my church; and the gates of hell shall not prevail against it.

And I will give unto thee the keys of the kingdom of heaven: and whatsoever thou shalt bind on earth shall be bound in heaven: and whatsoever thou shalt loose on earth shall be loosed in heaven.

Then they that gladly received his word were baptized: and the same day there were added unto them about three thousand souls.

And they continued stedfastly in the apostles' doctrine and fellowship, and in breaking of bread, and in prayers. . . . And the Lord added to the church daily such as should be saved.

For as the body is one, and hath many members, and all the members of that one body, being many, are one body: so also is Christ.

Now ye are the body of Christ, and members in particular.

Therefore as the church is subject unto Christ, so let the wives be to their own husbands in every thing.

Husbands, love your wives, even as Christ also loved the church, and gave himself for it;

That he might sanctify and cleanse it with the washing of water by the word,

That he might present it to himself a glorious church, not having spot, or wrinkle, or any such thing; but that it should be holy and without blemish.

38   MISSIONARIES FOR THE MASTER

Mark 16:15; Romans 10:8-15

And he said unto them, Go ye into all the world, and preach the gospel to every creature.

But what saith it? The word is nigh thee, even in thy mouth, and in thy heart; that is, the word of faith, which we preach;

That if thou shalt confess with thy mouth the Lord Jesus, and shalt believe in thine heart that God hath raised him from the dead, thou shalt be saved.

For with the heart man believeth unto righteousness; and with the mouth confession is made unto salvation.

For the scripture saith, Whosoever believeth on him shall not be ashamed.

For there is no difference between the Jew and the Greek: for the same Lord over all is rich unto all that call upon him.

For whosoever shall call upon the name of the Lord shall be saved.

How then shall they call on him in whom they have not believed? and how shall they believe in him of whom they have not heard? and how shall they hear without a preacher?

And how shall they preach, except they be sent? as it is written,

How beautiful are the feet of them that preach the gospel of peace, and bring glad tidings of good things!

39   HEAVEN

Revelation 21:1-7; Isaiah 35:10

And I saw a new heaven and a new earth: for the first heaven and the first earth were passed away; and there was no more sea.

And I John saw the holy city, new Jerusalem, coming down from God out of heaven, prepared as a bride adorned for her husband.

And I heard a great voice out of heaven saying, Behold, the tabernacle of God is with men, and he will dwell with them, and they shall be his people, and God himself shall be with them, and be their God.

And God shall wipe away all tears from their eyes; and there shall be no more death, neither sorrow, nor crying, neither shall there be any more pain: for the former things are passed away.

And he that sat upon the throne said, Behold, I make all things new. And he said unto me, Write: for these words are true and faithful.

And he said unto me, It is done. I am Alpha and Omega, the beginning and the end. I will give unto him that is athirst of the fountain of the water of life freely.

He that overcometh shall inherit all things; and I will be his God and he shall be my son.

And the ransomed of the Lord shall return, and come to Zion with songs and everlasting joy upon their heads: they shall obtain joy and gladness, and sorrow and sighing shall flee away.

Proverbs 31:10-25

Who can find a virtuous woman? for her price is far above rubies.

The heart of her husband doth safely trust in her, so that he shall have no need of spoil.

She will do him good and not evil all the days of her life.

She seeketh wool, and flax, and worketh willingly with her hands.

She is like the merchants' ships; she bringeth her food from afar.

She riseth also while it is yet night and giveth meat to her household, and a portion to her maidens.

She considereth a field, and buyeth it: with the fruit of her hands she planteth a vineyard.

She girdeth her loins with strength, and strengtheneth her arms.

She perceiveth that her merchandise is good: her candle goeth not out by night.

She layeth her hands to the spindle, and her hands hold the distaff.

She stretcheth out her hand to the poor; yea, she reacheth forth her hands to the needy.

She is not afraid of the snow for her household: for all her household are clothed with scarlet.

She maketh herself coverings of tapestry; her clothing is silk and purple.

Her husband is known in the gates, when he sitteth among the elders of the land.

She maketh fine linen, and selleth it; and delivereth girdles unto the merchant.

Strength and honour are her clothing; and she shall rejoice in time to come.

41   JOY

Psalms 95:1-6; 98:1-9

O come, let us sing unto the Lord: let us make a joyful noise to the rock of our salvation.

Let us come before his presence with thanksgiving, and make a joyful noise unto him with psalms.

For the Lord is a great God, and a great King above all gods.

In his hand are the deep places of the earth: the strength of the hills is his also.

The sea is his, and he made it: and his hands formed the dry land.

O come, let us worship and bow down: let us kneel before the Lord our maker.

O sing unto the Lord a new song; for he hath done marvellous things: his right hand, and his holy arm, hath gotten him the victory.

The Lord hath made known his salvation: his righteousness hath he openly showed in the sight of the heathen.

He hath remembered his mercy and his truth toward the house of Israel: all the ends of the earth have seen the salvation of our God.

Make a joyful noise unto the Lord, all the earth: make a loud noise, and rejoice, and sing praise,

Sing unto the Lord with the harp; with the harp, and the voice of a psalm.

With trumpets and sound of cornet make a joyful noise before the Lord, the King.

Let the sea roar, and the fulness thereof; the world, and they that dwell therein.

Let the floods clap their hands: let the hills be joyful together Before the Lord; for he cometh to judge the earth: with righteousness shall he judge the world, and the people with equity.

42   WORSHIP

Psalm 24:1-10; John 4:22-24

The earth is the Lord's, and the fulness thereof; the world, and they that dwell therein.

For he hath founded it upon the seas, and established it upon the floods.

Who shall ascend into the hill of the Lord? or who shall stand in his holy place?

He that hath clean hands, and a pure heart; who hath not lifted up his soul unto vanity, nor sworn deceitfully.

He shall receive the blessing from the Lord, and righteousness from the God of his salvation.

This is the generation of them that seek him, that seek thy face, O Jacob.

Lift up your heads, O ye gates; and be ye lift up, ye everlasting doors; and the King of glory shall come in.

Who is this King of glory?

The Lord strong and mighty, the Lord mighty in battle.

Lift up your heads, O ye gates; even lift them up, ye everlasting doors; and the King of glory shall come in.

Who is this King of glory? The Lord of hosts, he is the King of glory.

Ye worship ye know not what: we know what we worship: for salvation is of the Jews.

But the hour cometh, and now is, when the true worshippers shall worship the Father in spirit and in truth: for the Father seeketh such to worship him.

God is a Spirit: and they that worship him must worship him in spirit and in truth.

43 THE RESURRECTION

1 Peter 1:3-5; 1 Corinthians 15:51-58

Blessed be the God and Father of our Lord Jesus Christ, which according to his abundant mercy hath begotten us again unto a lively hope by the resurrection of Jesus Christ from the dead.

To an inheritance incorruptible, and undefiled, and that fadeth not away, reserved in heaven for you,

Who are kept by the power of God through faith unto salvation ready to be revealed in the last time.

Behold, I shew you a mystery; We shall not all sleep, but we shall all be changed,

In a moment, in the twinkling of an eye, at the last trump: for the trumpet shall sound, and the dead shall be raised incorruptible, and we shall be changed.

For this corruptible must put on incorruption, and this mortal must put on immortality.

So when this corruptible shall have put on incorruption, and this mortal shall have put on immortality, then shall be brought to pass the saying that is written, Death is swallowed up in victory.

O death, where is thy sting? O grave, where is thy victory?

The sting of death is sin; and the strength of sin is the law.

But thanks be to God, which giveth us the victory through our Lord Jesus Christ.

Therefore, my beloved brethren, be ye stedfast, unmoveable, always abounding in the work of the Lord,

Forasmuch as ye know that your labour is not in vain in the Lord.

44 THANKSGIVING

Psalm 107:1-15

O give thanks unto the Lord, for he is good: for his mercy endureth for ever.

Let the redeemed of the Lord say so, whom he hath redeemed from the hand of the enemy;

And gathered them out of the lands, from the east, and from the west, from the north, and from the south.

They wandered in the wilderness in a solitary way; they found no city to dwell in. Hungry and thirsty, their soul fainted in them.

Then they cried unto the Lord in their trouble, and he delivered them out of their distresses.

And he led them forth by the right way, that they might go to a city of habitation.

Oh that men would praise the Lord for his goodness, and for his wonderful works to the children of men!

For he satisfieth the longing soul, and filleth the hungry soul with goodness.

Such as sit in darkness and in the shadow of death, being bound in affliction and iron;

Because they rebelled against the words of God, and condemned the counsel of the most High:

Therefore he brought down their heart with labour; they fell down, and there was none to help.

Then they cried unto the Lord in their trouble, and he saved them out of their distresses.

He brought them out of darkness and the shadow of death, and brake their bands in sunder.

Oh that men would praise the Lord for his goodness, and for his wonderful works to the children of men!

45   **CHRISTMAS**

Isaiah 7:14; 9:2, 6-7; Luke 2:1, 3-7;
Galatians 4:4, 5

Therefore the Lord himself shall give you a sign; Behold, a virgin shall conceive, and bear a son, and shall call his name Emmanuel.

The people that walked in darkness have seen a great light: they that dwell in the land of the shadow of death, upon them hath the light shined.

For unto us a child is born, unto us a son is given: and the government shall be upon his shoulder: and his name shall be called Wonderful, Counsellor, The mighty God, The everlasting Father, The Prince of Peace.

Of the increase of his government and peace there shall be no end, upon the throne of David, and upon his kingdom, to order it, and to establish it with judgment and with justice from henceforth even for ever.

And it came to pass in those days, that there went out a decree from Caesar Augustus, that all the world should be taxed.

And all went to be taxed, every one into his own city. And Joseph also went up from Galilee, out of the city of Nazareth, into Judaea, unto the city of David, which is called Bethlehem; (because he was of the house and lineage of David:)

To be taxed with Mary his espoused wife, being great with child.

And so it was, that, while they were there, the days were accomplished that she should be delivered.

And she brought forth her firstborn son, and wrapped him in swaddling clothes, and laid him in a manger; because there was no room for them in the inn.

But when the fulness of the time was come, God sent forth his Son, made of a woman, made under the law, To redeem them that were under the law, that we might receive the adoption of sons.

Joel 2:23, 26-29; Acts 2:1-4

Be glad then, ye children of Zion, and rejoice in the Lord your God: for he hath given you the former rain moderately, and he will cause to come down for you the rain, the former rain, and the latter rain in the first month.

And ye shall eat in plenty and be satisfied, and praise the name of the Lord your God, that hath dealt wondrously with you: and my people shall never be ashamed.

And ye shall know that I am in the midst of Israel, and that I am the Lord your God, and none else: and my people shall never be ashamed.

And it shall come to pass afterward, that I will pour out my spirit upon all flesh; and your sons and your daughters shall prophesy, your old men shall dream dreams, your young men shall see visions: and also upon the servants and upon the handmaids in those days will I pour out my spirit.

And when the day of Pentecost was fully come, they were all with one accord in one place.

And suddenly there came a sound from heaven as of a rushing mighty wind, and it filled all the house where they were sitting.

And there appeared unto them cloven tongues like as of fire, and it sat upon each of them.

And they were filled with the Holy Ghost, and began to speak with other tongues, as the Spirit gave them utterance.

47 PRAYER

Hebrews 11:6; John 14:13, 14;
Matthew 7:7-11; Acts 4:31

But without faith it is impossible to please him: for he that cometh to God must believe that he is, and that he is a rewarder of them that diligently seek him.

And whatsoever ye shall ask in my name, that will I do, that the Father may be glorified in the Son.

If ye shall ask any thing in my name, I will do it.

Ask, and it shall be given you; seek, and ye shall find; knock, and it shall be opened unto you:

For every one that asketh receiveth; and he that seeketh findeth; and to him that knocketh it shall be opened.

Or what man is there of you, whom if his son ask bread, will he give him a stone? Or if he ask a fish, will he give him a serpent?

If ye then, being evil, know how to give good gifts unto your children, how much more shall your Father which is in heaven give good things to them that ask him?

And when they had prayed, the place was shaken where they were assembled together; and they were all filled with the Holy Ghost, and they spake the word of God with boldness.

Matthew 5:1-12

And seeing the multitudes, he went up into a mountain: and when he was set, his disciples came unto him:

And he opened his mouth, and taught them, saying,

Blessed are the poor in spirit: for their's is the kingdom of heaven.

Blessed are they that mourn: for they shall be comforted.

Blessed are the meek: for they shall inherit the earth.

Blessed are they which do hunger and thirst after righteousness: for they shall be filled.

Blessed are the merciful: for they shall obtain mercy.

Blessed are the pure in heart: for they shall see God.

Blessed are the peacemakers: for they shall be called the children of God.

Blessed are they which are persecuted for righteousness' sake: for their's is the kingdom of heaven.

Blessed are ye, when men shall revile you, and persecute you, and shall say all manner of evil against you falsely, for my sake.

Rejoice, and be exceeding glad: for great is your reward in heaven: for so persecuted they the prophets which were before you.

PLEDGE TO THE AMERICAN FLAG

I pledge allegiance to the flag of the United States of America and to the republic for which it stands; one nation under God, indivisible, with liberty and justice for all.

50   PLEDGE TO THE CHRISTIAN FLAG

I pledge allegiance to the Christian flag and to the Saviour for whose kingdom it stands; one Saviour, crucified, risen, and coming again, with life and liberty to all who believe.

51   PLEDGE TO THE BIBLE

I pledge allegiance to the Bible, God's Holy Word, and will make it a lamp unto my feet, a light unto my path, and hide its words in my heart that I may not sin against God.

I Corinthians 16:2; II Corinthians 9:7, 8:9; Acts 20:35; Psalm 41:1; Proverbs 19:17, 84:11; Malachi 3:8-10

Upon the first day of the week let everyone of you lay by him in store, as God hath prospered him.

Every man according as he purposeth in his heart, so let him give, not grudgingly, or of necessity: for God loveth a cheerful giver.

It is more blessed to give than to receive.

Blessed is he that considereth the poor; the Lord will deliver him in time of trouble.

He that hath pity upon the poor, lendeth unto the Lord.

For the Lord God is a sun and shield: the Lord will give grace and glory: no good thing will he withhold from them that walk uprightly.

Honor the Lord with thy substance and with the firstfruits of all thine increase.

Will a man rob God? Yet ye have robbed me. But ye say, Wherein have we robbed thee? In tithes and offerings.

Bring ye all the tithes into the storehouse, that there may be meat in mine house, and prove me now herewith, saith the Lord of hosts, if I will not open you the windows of heaven, and pour you out a blessing, that there shall not be room enough to receive it.

For ye know the grace of our Lord Jesus Christ, that, though he was rich, yet for your sakes he became poor, that ye through his poverty might be rich.

COMMUNION

Matt. 26:17-20; 26-29; 1 Cor. 11:25-26

Now the first day of the feast of unleavened bread the disciples came to Jesus, saying unto him, Where wilt thou that we prepare for thee to eat the passover?

And he said, Go into the city to such a man, and say unto him, The Master saith, My time is at hand; I will keep the passover at thy house with my disciples.

And the disciples did as Jesus had appointed them; and they made ready the passover.

Now when the even was come, he sat down with the twelve.

And as they were eating, Jesus took bread, and blessed it, and brake it, and gave it to the disciples, and said,

Take, eat; this is my body.

And he took the cup, and gave thanks, and gave it to them, saying.

Drink ye all of it; For this is my blood of the new testament, which is shed for many for the remission of sins.

This do ye, as oft as ye drink it, in remembrance of me. For as often as ye eat this bread, and drink this cup, ye do show the Lord's death till he come.

But I say unto you, I will not drink henceforth of this fruit of the vine, until that day when I drink it new with you in my Father's kingdom.

491

THE LORD'S PRAYER

Our Father which art in heaven,

Hallowed be thy name.

Thy kingdom come.

Thy will be done in earth, as it is in heaven.

Give us this day our daily bread.

And forgive us our debts, as we forgive our debtors.

And lead us not into temptation, but deliver us from evil:

For thine is the kingdom and the power, and the glory, for ever.

Amen.

INDEX OF RESPONSIVE READINGS

Assurance	9	Lord's Prayer, The	53
Beatitudes	48	Missionaries For The Master	38
Blood, The	24	Mother	40
		My Shepherd	22
Christian Life	7		
Christmas	45	New Birth	11
Church, The	37		
Communion	52	Peace With God	34
Comfort and Consolation	29	Pentecost	46
Consecration	21	Pledge To The American Flag	49
Cross, The	28	Pledge To The Bible	51
		Pledge To Christian Flag	50
Dedication	33	Praise	1
		Prayer	47
Eternal Life	10	Promise	3
Faith	30	Repentence	13
Fellowship	4	Resurrection, The	43
Fullness of God	27	Revival	17
Giving and Tithing	52	Salvation	12
Godly, The	25	Sanctification	15
God's Word	2	Second Coming	32
Grace	19	Soul Winning	16
		Stewardship	20
Healing	23		
Heaven	39	Ten Commandments, The	
Holiness	8	Thanksgiving	44
Holy Ghost	14	Trust	31
Invitation	36	Victory	6
Jesus Christ	35	Water Baptism	18
Joy	41	Worship	42
Lord's Day, The	26		

CALLS TO WORSHIP

O come let us worship and bow down, let us kneel before the Lord our maker. For he is our God, and we are the people of his pasture, and the sheep of his hand.

God is light and the father of lights in whom is no variableness neither shadow that is cast by turning.

O Lord, send out thy light and thy truth, let them lead us to thy holy hill

God is love, and he that dwelleth in love dwelleth in God and God in him.

Praise ye the Lord.

The Lord's name be praised. From the rising of the sun to the going down of the same, the Lord's name is to be praised.

Let our prayers be set forth as incense before him, the lifting up of our hands as the evening sacrifice.

The day goeth away, and the shadows of the evening are stretched out; but it shall come to pass, that at evening time there shall be light.

O that men would praise the Lord for his goodness, and for his wonderful works to the children of men.

The Lord is good to all, and his tender mercies are over all his works.

Blessed be the Lord God, the God of Israel, who only doeth wondrous things;

And blessed be his glorious name forever; and let the whole earth be filled with his glory.

Enter into his gates with thanksgiving, and into his courts with praise.

For the Lord is good; his mercy is everlasting; and his truth endureth to all generations.

Thus saith the high and lofty one, that inhabiteth eternity, whose name is Holy: I dwell in the high and holy place, with him also that is of contrite and humble spirit, to revive the spirit of the humble, and to revive the heart of the contrite ones.

Seek ye the Lord while he may be found; call ye upon him while he is near:

Let the wicked forsake his way, and the unrighteous man his thoughts; and let him return unto the Lord, and he will have mercy upon him;

And to our God, for he will abundantly pardon.

GENERAL INDEX

Titles in CAPITALS; First lines in lower case; First line of refrain in *Italics*.

-A-

A CHARGE TO KEEP, 237
A DEEP, SETTLED PEACE, 126
A friend of Jesus, O what bliss, 146
A GLORIOUS CHURCH, 115
A MIGHTY FORTRESS IS OUR GOD, 31
A SHELTER IN THE TIME OF STORM, 47
A wonderful Saviour is Jesus, my Lord, 142
A WORLD-WIDE REVIVAL, 251
ABIDE WITH ME, 355
Alas! and did my Saviour bleed? 58
ALL CREATURES OF OUR GOD AND KING, 7
ALL HAIL IMMANUEL, 320
ALL HAIL THE POWER OF JESUS' NAME (Ellor), 3
ALL HAIL THE POWER OF JESUS' NAME (Holden), 2
ALL HAIL THE POWER OF JESUS' NAME (Shrubsole), 4
All hail to Thee, Immanuel, 320
ALL I NEED, 138
ALL MEN GIVE THANKS, 329
All that I have, all that I am, 281
ALL THINGS COME OF THEE, 367
All to Jesus I surrender, 275
ALMIGHTY FATHER, HEAR OUR PRAYER, 369
ALMOST PERSUADED, 302
AM I A SOLDIER OF THE CROSS? 171
AMAZING GRACE, 186
AMENS:
    Dresden, 371
    Fourfold, 374
    Sevenfold, 370
    Threefold, 373
    Threefold (Stainer), 372
AMERICA, 347
AMERICA, THE BEAUTIFUL, 348
And He walks with me, 197
And I know, yes, I know, 40
ANGELS FROM THE REALMS OF GLORY, 333
ANGELS WE HAVE HEARD ON HIGH, 334
Are you afflicted in body? 77
Are you living in the shadow, 141
Are you ready? 307
ARE YOU WASHED IN THE BLOOD? 311
ART THOU WEARY? 306
As we journey on t'ward heaven's, 141
As we look around us, 240
ASLEEP IN JESUS, 353
AT THE CROSS, 58
AT THE CROWNING, 224
AWAY IN A MANGER, 337

-B-

BACK OF THE CROSS, 65
BATTLE HYMN OF THE REPUBLIC, 346
Be not dismayed whate'er betide, 36
BEAUTIFUL SAVIOUR, 41
BECAUSE OF CALVARY, 187
BEGIN, MY TONGUE, 201
BENEATH THE CROSS OF JESUS, 63
BLESSED ASSURANCE, 133
BLESSED BE THE NAME, 37
BLESSED REDEEMER, 60
BLEST BE THE TIE, 130
BREAK THOU THE BREAD OF LIFE, 110
BREATHE ON ME, BREATH OF GOD, 100
BRING THEM IN, 245
BRINGING IN THE SHEAVES, 243
By His grace I shall reach heaven, 228
BY MY SPIRIT, 108

-C-

Called unto holiness, Church of our God, 270

496

Calling today, 298
CAST THY BURDEN ON THE LORD, 266
CALVARY COVERS IT ALL, 185
CHRIST AROSE, 80
CHRIST FOR ME, 321
Christ had to go to Calvary, 64
Christ, our Redeemer died on the cross, 73
CHRIST THE LORD IS RISEN TODAY, 82
CHRIST THE LORD SHALL TRIUMPH, 128
CHRIST THE LORD WAS REALLY THERE, 174
CLEANSE ME, 277
COME AND DINE, 144
Come, every soul by sin, 308
Come home, come home, 301
COME, THOU ALMIGHTY KING, 11
COME, THOU FOUNT, 16
Come, we that love the Lord, 160
COME, YE THANKFUL PEOPLE, 327
Coming home, 297
COUNT YOUR BLESSINGS, 147
CROWN HIM WITH MANY CROWNS, 83

-D-

Dear Jesus all my sins forgave, 178
Dear Lord, I'll be a witness, 286
DEEPER, DEEPER, 272
DEPTH OF MERCY, 316
Do you hear them coming, brother? 115
DOES JESUS CARE? 349
Don't you hear the bells now ringing? 207
Down at the cross, 17
DOXOLOGY, 21

-E-

ENOUGH FOR ME, 153
EVERYBODY OUGHT TO KNOW, 322

-F-

FAIREST LORD JESUS, 41
Fairest of ten thousand, 28
FAITH FOR TODAY, 124
FAITH OF OUR FATHERS, 161

FALL FRESH ON ME, 97
Far dearer than all, 185
FARTHER ALONG, 354
FIGHT THE GOOD FIGHT, 163
FILL ME NOW, 92
Foes may betide me, 211
Follow Thee is my desire, 283
FOOTPRINTS OF JESUS, 50
For a world-wide revival, 251
For every bitter tear I shed, 168
FOR ME TO LIVE IS CHRIST, 195
FOR THE BEAUTY OF THE EARTH, 14
For you I am praying, 257
FRIENDSHIP WITH JESUS, 146

-G-

GATHERING BUDS, 359
GIVE ME OIL IN MY LAMP, 105
GIVE OF YOUR BEST TO THE MASTER, 287
Gloria in excelsis deo, 334
Glory and honor be to the King, 172
GLORY BE TO THE FATHER (1st setting), 365
GLORY BE TO THE FATHER (2nd setting), 366
Glory, glory, hallelujah, 346
Glory, I am saved from sin, 274
GLORY TO HIS NAME (Parks), 28
GLORY TO HIS NAME (Stockton), 17
GO TO JESUS, 140
GOD BE WITH YOU, 376
GOD IS LOVE, 168
GOD IS PRESENT EVERYWHERE, 260
GOD MOVES IN A MYSTERIOUS WAY, 184
GOD OF OUR FATHERS, 34
God sent His mighty pow'r, 103
GOD WILL TAKE CARE OF YOU, 36
GOT ANY RIVERS? 264
GUIDE ME, O THOU GREAT JEHOVAH, 33

-H-

Hail the Son of Righteousness, 28
HALLELUJAH FOR THE CROSS, 62
Hallelujah, thine the glory, 247
HALLELUJAH! WE SHALL RISE, 89

HALLELUJAH, WHAT A SAVIOUR! 39
HAPPY DAY, 177
HARK! THE HERALD ANGELS SING, 330
Hark! 'tis the shepherd's voice, 245
HAVE FAITH IN GOD, 129
Have thy affections been nailed, 313
Have you been to Jesus, 311
HAVE YOU COUNTED THE COST? 295
HAVE YOU HEARD ABOUT THAT CITY? 221
HE ABIDES, 106
HE HAD TO GO TO CALVARY, 64
HE HIDETH MY SOUL, 142
HE INCLUDED ME, 148
HE IS ALIVE, 87
HE KEEPS ME SINGING, 145
HE LEADETH ME! 127
He lifted me out of the deep, 179
HE LIVES, 86
HE ROSE TRIUMPHANTLY, 84
He taught me how to watch and pray, 169
HE WAS NAILED TO THE CROSS FOR ME, 66
He will not grieve me, 211

HEAD OF THE CHURCH TRIUMPHANT, 117
HEAR OUR PRAYER, O LORD, 368
Hear the Lord of harvest, 238
HEAVEN WILL SURELY BE WORTH IT ALL, 218
HEAVENLY SUNLIGHT, 198
HE'LL KEEP ME, 135
He's precious to me, 200
He's the Lily of the Valley, 53
HIDDEN PEACE, 126
HIGHER GROUND, 269
HIS BLOOD IS ON MY SOUL, 178
His pow'r can make you, 315
HIS WAY WITH THEE, 315
HOLINESS UNTO THE LORD, 270
HOLY BIBLE, BOOK DIVINE, 113
HOLY GHOST, WITH LIGHT DIVINE, 318
HOLY, HOLY, HOLY, 12
HOLY SPIRIT, USE ME, 109
HONEY IN THE ROCK, 304
Hover o'er me, Holy Spirit, 92
HOW ABOUT YOUR HEART? 296

HOW BEAUTIFUL HEAVEN MUST BE, 358
HOW FIRM A FOUNDATION, 121
How marvelous, how wonderful, 25
How precious is the name, 200
How sweet and happy seem, 344

-I-

I am all on the altar, 85
I AM COMING TO THE CROSS, 312
I am drinking today, 193
I am facing home at last, 137
I AM PRAYING FOR YOU, 257
I AM RESOLVED, 289
I am so glad that Jesus loves me, 43
I am so glad that our Father in heaven, 43
I am so happy in Christ, 148
I am trusting, Lord, in Thee, 312
I am watching for the coming, 88
I am weak, but Thou art strong, 288
I can hear my Saviour calling, 282
I CAN, I WILL, I DO BELIEVE, 132
I cannot tell thee whence it came, 126
I come to the garden alone, 197
I fell upon my knees one day, 226
I have a Saviour, 257
I have a song I love to sing, 188
I have found a friend in Jesus, 53
I have heard of a land, 352
I hear the Saviour say, 59
I heard a story, 221
I heard an old, old story, 182
I HEARD THE BELLS ON CHRISTMAS DAY, 336
I know not why God's wondrous grace, 122
I KNOW WHOM I HAVE BELIEVED, 122
I love that grand old story, 44
I LOVE THY KINGDOM, LORD, 189
I LOVE TO TELL THE STORY, 152
I must needs go home, 154
I MUST TELL JESUS, 265
I NEED THE PRAYERS, 268
I NEED THEE EVERY HOUR, 292
I NEVER LIVED UNTIL I LIVED FOR JESUS, 181
I remember how my Saviour, 233
I SEE JESUS, 222
I serve a risen Saviour, 86

I SHALL BE CHANGED, 90
I SHALL KNOW HIM, 208
I SHALL REACH HOME, 211
I SING BECAUSE I'M HAPPY, 190
I stand amazed, 25
I SURRENDER ALL, 275
I SURRENDER TO THEE, 281
I wandered alone down sin's, 199
I wandered along the downward road, 180
I want my friends to pray for me, 268
I was on my knees in prayer, 174
I was sin stained within, 75
I was sinking deep in sin, 166
I WILL FOLLOW THEE, 283
I will hasten to Him, 289
I will meet you in the morning, 212
I WILL PRAISE HIM, 176
I WILL SING OF MY REDEEMER, 38
I WILL SING THE WONDROUS
    STORY, 40
I would like to be at the crowning, 224
I would serve thee, Jesus, 109
I WOULDN'T MISS IT FOR THE
    WORLD, 228
I'D TELL THE WORLD, 203
If God could speak and bring the world,
    262
If I could count my blessings, 203
IF I COULD HEAR MY MOTHER PRAY
    AGAIN, 344
IF I KNEW OF A LAND, 229
If the Lord could speak this world, 90
If the road before you offers, 255
If you are tired of the load, 314
I'LL BE AT HOME, 226
I'LL GO WHERE YOU WANT ME TO
    GO, 279
I'LL LIVE FOR HIM, 285
I'LL MEET YOU IN THE MORNING,
    212
I'll never be lonely, 231
I'll never forget that day, 179
I'LL THANK HIM, I'LL PRAISE HIM,
    223
I'm completely trusting Jesus, 137
I'M GLAD HE LIFTED ME OUT, 179
I'm kneeling at the mercy seat, 132
I'm looking away beyond the dark, 232
I'M MOVING UP SOME DAY, 227

I'm pressing on the upward way, 269
I'm rejoicing night and day, 106
I'M WALKING WITH JESUS, 196
In the Book of God so precious, 95
In the cross, 291
IN THE GARDEN, 197
In the resurrection morning, 89
IN THE SHADOW OF THE CROSS, 141
In this world I've tried most everything,
    181
IN TIMES LIKE THESE, 317
Is there a mountain in your way? 108
IS THY HEART RIGHT WITH GOD?
    313
IS YOUR ALL ON THE ALTAR? 293
ISN'T HE WONDERFUL! 67
IT CAME UPON THE MIDNIGHT
    CLEAR, 340
IT IS WELL WITH MY SOUL, 131
It may not be on the mountain's height,
    279
It will be a grand tomorrow, 215
IT'S REAL, 183
I've a message from the Lord, 309
I've anchored my soul, 165
I've been on Mount Pisgah's lofty height,
    104
I've been singing and rejoicing, 219
I've found a friend who is all, 175
I've started on a journey, 227
I've started out to win a place, 228
I've wandered far away from God, 297

-J-

Jesus, a wonderful friend to me, 65
JESUS BREAKS EVERY FETTER, 85
JESUS CALLS US, 294
Jesus Christ is made to me, 138
Jesus has a table spread, 144
Jesus has taken a beautiful bud, 359
JESUS, I COME, 299
Jesus included me, 148
JESUS IS ALL THE WORLD TO ME, 46
JESUS IS CALLING, 298
JESUS IS PRECIOUS TO ME, 200
Jesus is tenderly calling thee home, 298
JESUS IS THE ONE, 326
JESUS IS THE SWEETEST NAME I
    KNOW, 134

Jesus, Jesus, how I trust Him, 54
Jesus, Jesus, Jesus, sweetest name, 145
Jesus, keep me near the cross, 291
JESUS KEEPS ME PURE WITHIN, 274
JESUS, LOVER OF MY SOUL, 51
JESUS LOVES EVEN ME, 43
JESUS LOVES ME, 42
JESUS LOVES THE LITTLE CHILDREN, 151
JESUS NEVER FAILS, 136
JESUS PAID IT ALL, 59
JESUS PASSED BY, 172
JESUS SAVES, 235
JESUS SHALL REIGN, 244
JESUS, THE VERY THOUGHT OF THEE, 173
JESUS, USE ME, 286
JESUS WILL HEAR ME WHEN I PRAY, 267
JOY TO THE WORLD, 331
JUST A CLOSER WALK WITH THEE, 288
JUST AS I AM, 300
Just now your doubtings give o'er, 314

-L-

LEAD ON, O KING ETERNAL, 13
LEANING ON THE EVERLASTING ARMS, 22
LEST I FORGET, 325
LET HIM IN, 305
LET JESUS COME INTO YOUR HEART, 314
Let me live, blessed Lord, 280
Let me tell you how the Lord, 174
LET ME TOUCH HIM, 284
LET MY LIFE BE A LIGHT, 280
LET THE FIRE FALL, 98
LET THE HOLY GHOST COME IN, 271
LET THE WORDS OF MY MOUTH, 363
LET US SING, 29
Life is so designed, 135
Lift your voice in song, 29
LIKE A MIGHTY ARMY, 120
LIVING IN CHRIST, 194
LOOK AND LIVE, 309
LOOK FOR ME, 210
Lord, as of old at Pentecost, 96
Lord, begin Thy work in me, 278

Lord, I come to Thee, 278
Lord, I give my life to Thee, 276
LORD, I'M COMING HOME, 297
Lord, lift me up and let me stand, 269
LORD, SEND A REVIVAL (McKinney), 249
LORD, SEND A REVIVAL (Triplett), 252
Lord, send the old-time power, 96
LORD, SPEAK TO ME, 239
LORD, TO BE MORE LIKE THEE, 278
LOVE DIVINE, 24
LOVE LIFTED ME, 166
Low in the grave He lay, 80

-M-

MAGNIFY THE LORD, 324
MAKE ME A BLESSING, 319
"Man of Sorrows," what a name, 39
Many are the heartaches, 255
MARCH ON, O CHURCH OF GOD, 159
Mine eyes have seen the glory, 346
MORE ABOUT JESUS, 45
MUST JESUS BEAR THE CROSS ALONE? 61
My country, 'tis of thee, 347
MY FAITH LOOKS UP TO THEE, 8
MY GOD CAN DO ANYTHING, 81
MY HOPE IS BUILT, 125
MY JESUS, I LOVE THEE, 52
MY SAVIOUR FIRST OF ALL, 208
MY SAVIOUR'S LOVE, 25
My soul in sad exile, 165

-N-

NATURALIZED FOR HEAVEN, 219
NEAR THE CROSS, 291
NEAR TO THE HEART OF GOD, 23
NEARER, MY GOD, TO THEE, 351
NO TEARS IN HEAVEN, 356
No tongue can ever tell, 187
Noel, noel, 341
Not by might, not by pow'r, 108
NOTHING BUT THE BLOOD, 69

-O-

O beautiful for spacious skies, 348
O BLESSED HOLY SPIRIT, 102

O COME, ALL YE FAITHFUL, 332
O come, let us adore Him, 332
O FOR A THOUSAND TONGUES TO
   SING, 19
O for a thousand tongues to sing, 37
O GOD, OUR HELP IN AGES PAST, 32
O HAPPY DAY (arr. Harris), 169
O happy day that fixed my choice, 177
O Jesus, blest Redeemer, 23
O JESUS, I HAVE PROMISED, 290
O land of rest for thee I sigh, 242
O LITTLE TOWN OF BETHLEHEM, 338
O Lord, send the pow'r, 91
O love of God, 35
O love surpassing knowledge, 153
O LOVE THAT WILT NOT LET ME GO,
   5
O MASTER, LET ME WALK WITH
   THEE, 155
O my brother, do you know the Saviour,
   304
O precious is the flow, 69
O SAY, BUT I'M GLAD, 191
O what a Saviour, 49
O WORD OF GOD INCARNATE, 111
O WORSHIP THE KING, 6
Often I'm hindered on my way, 218
Oh, deeper yet I pray, 272
OH, HOW I LOVE JESUS, 143
Oh, how well do I remember, 183
Oh, Jesus is a Rock, 47
Oh, our Lord is coming back, 88
Oh, say, can you see, 345
Oh, spread the tidings round, 93
Oh, the fire is burning, 104
Oh, the joy of sins forgiv'n, 78
Oh, to be His hand extended, 284
Oh, what joy 'twill be, 224
Oh, yes, He cares, 349
OLD-TIME POWER, 91
On a hill far away, 57
On Christ, the solid Rock I stand, 125
Once a man named Stephen, 222
Once I was in bondage, 170
Once I was in bondage, 274
Once I was straying, 49
ONE SWEETLY SOLEMN THOUGHT,
   357
ONLY BELIEVE, 79

ONLY TRUST HIM, 308
ONWARD, CHRISTIAN SOLDIERS, 158
Our blessed Lord was slain, 84
OUR LORD'S RETURN TO EARTH, 88
Out in the highways and byways, 319
Out of my bondage, 299
OVER YONDER, 230

-P-

PASS ME NOT, 303
PENTECOSTAL FIRE IS FALLING, 95
PENTECOSTAL POWER, 96
People often see you, 296
Praise God, from whom all blessings, 21
PRAISE HIM! PRAISE HIM! 18
Praise the Lord, praise the Lord, 20
PRAISE THE SAVIOUR, 209
Praise to the Father, 26
PRAISE TO THE LORD, THE
   ALMIGHTY, 1
Praise ye the Father! 10
PRAISE YE THE TRIUNE GOD! 10
Praises to the Prince of Peace, 27
PRAY TILL YOUR PRAYERS GO
   THROUGH, 263
PRECIOUS MEMORIES, 360
Precious name, oh, how sweet, 156

-R-

REMEMBER, 233
RESCUE THE PERISHING, 246
REST BEYOND, 216
REVIVE THY WORK, 248
REVIVE US AGAIN, 247
RISE UP, O MEN OF GOD, 118
ROCK OF AGES, 9

-S-

SAFE IN THE ARMS OF JESUS, 350
SAVED BY THE BLOOD, 70
SAVED, SAVED! 175
Saviour, Saviour, hear my humble, 303
Search me, O God, 277
Send a revival in me, Lord, 252
Send a revival, O Christ, my Lord, 249
SEND THE FIRE, 101
SEND THE LIGHT, 236

Send the pow'r, O Lord, 251
She's a little old fashioned, 342
Showers of blessing, 253
SILENT NIGHT, 335
SINCE I HAVE BEEN REDEEMED, 188
Since Jesus saved my soul, 202
Sing, O sing, of my Redeemer, 38
Sing the wondrous love of Jesus, 205
Sing them over again to me, 112
SING UNTO THE LORD, 30
So, I'll cherish the old rugged, 57
Soft as the voice of an angel, 139
SOFTLY AND TENDERLY, 301
Some men live for wealth, 195
SOMEWHERE IN HEAVEN, 204
Soon I'll come to cross the mighty, 230
Souls are crying, men are dying, 240
Sowing in the morning, 243
SPEAK, MY LORD, 238
SPIRIT OF GOD DESCEND, 94
SPIRIT OF THE LIVING GOD, 97
STAND UP FOR JESUS, 157
STANDING ON THE PROMISES, 114
SWEET HOUR OF PRAYER, 254
Sweetly, Lord, have we heard, 50
Sweetest note in seraph song, 55
SWEETEST MOTHER, 342

-T-

TAKE IT TO THE LORD IN PRAYER, 255
TAKE MY LIFE AND LET IT BE, 276
TAKE THE NAME OF JESUS WITH YOU, 156
TAKE TIME TO BE HOLY, 273
TELL ME MORE ABOUT JESUS, 44
TELL ME THE OLD, OLD STORY, 150
TELL MOTHER I'LL BE THERE, 343
Tempted and tried, 354
THANK YOU, LORD, 71
THAT GLAD REUNION DAY, 213
THAT HEAVENLY HOME, 232
THE BEAUTIFUL GARDEN OF PRAYER, 259
THE CHURCH OF GOD SHALL EVER STAND, 119
THE CHURCH'S ONE FOUNDATION, 116

THE COMFORTER HAS COME, 93
The cross it standeth fast, 62
THE FIRE IS BURNING, 104
THE FIRST NOEL, 341
THE FOUNTAIN THAT WILL NEVER RUN DRY, 193
THE GREAT PHYSICIAN (Grogan), 77
THE GREAT PHYSICIAN (Stockton), 55
THE HAVEN OF REST, 165
THE HEALING WATERS, 78
THE HOMECOMING WEEK, 220
THE LILY OF THE VALLEY, 53
THE LORD BLESS YOU AND KEEP YOU, 375
THE LORD IS IN HIS HOLY TEMPLE, 362
The Lord is my fortress strong, 128
THE LORD IS MY SHEPHERD, 199
The Lord shall overcome, 128
THE LORD WILL COME, 225
The Lord's our rock, 47
THE LOVE OF GOD (Ellis), 167
THE LOVE OF GOD (Lehman), 35
THE MESSAGE OF THE CROSS, 170
THE OLD RUGGED CROSS, 57
The power, the power! 99
THE SPIRIT OF THE LORD IS UPON ME, 202
THE STAR-SPANGLED BANNER, 345
THE WAY OF THE CROSS LEADS HOME, 154
There are loved ones in the glory, 361
There are some people who hold, 261
THERE IS A FOUNTAIN, 76
There is a highway of faith, 124
There is a place of quiet rest, 23
There is a song in my heart today, 191
There is a story of long ago, 172
There is a story of the sweet Son, 87
THERE IS POWER IN THE BLOOD, 68
There is wonder-working pow'r, 72
THERE SHALL BE SHOWERS OF BLESSING, 253
There will be a happy meeting, 213
THERE WILL DAWN A BRIGHTER DAY, 231
There's a call comes ringing, 236
There's a deep, settled peace, 126
There's a garden where Jesus is, 259

THERE'S A GREAT DAY COMING, 307
There's a land beyond the river, 207
There's a line that is drawn, 295
There's a name above all others, 56
There's a stranger at the door, 305
THERE'S A WIDENESS IN GOD'S MERCY, 149
There's within my heart a melody, 145
They were gathered in an upper, 98
They were in an upper chamber, 91
They who seek the throne of grace, 260
THIS IS MY FATHER'S WORLD, 15
This is my story, this is my song, 133
This rock is Jesus, 317
This world is not my home, 196
Thou Christ of burning, cleansing, 101
Through the message of the cross, 170
THROW OUT THE LIFE-LINE, 241
Till we meet, 376
'Tis a glorious church, 115
'TIS BURNING IN MY SOUL, 103
'TIS SO SWEET TO TRUST IN JESUS, 54
TO BE LIKE JESUS, 258
TO GOD BE THE GLORY, 20
TRUST AND OBEY, 123
TRUSTING JESUS, 137

-U-

Up Calv'ry's mountain one dreadful, 60
Up from the grave He arose, 80
Upon our journey here below, 220

-V-

VICTORY AHEAD, 162
VICTORY IN JESUS, 182

-W-

WAITING ON THE LORD, 99
Walking in sunlight, 198
We are often bowed with a load, 215
WE GATHER AT THY TABLE, LORD, 234
WE GATHER TOGETHER, 328
WE GIVE THEE BUT THINE OWN, 364
We have heard the joyful sound, 235
We praise Thee, O God, 247

We read of a place that's called, 358
We shall rise, hallelujah! 89
Well, I know of a land, 229
We'll sing of His redeeming grace, 30
WE'LL WORK TILL JESUS COMES, 242
WE'RE MARCHING TO ZION, 160
WHAT A CHANGE IN MY LIFE, 180
What a fellowship, what a joy, 22
WHAT A FRIEND WE HAVE IN JESUS, 48
WHAT A LOVELY NAME, 56
WHAT A SAVIOUR, 49
What a wonderful, wonderful Saviour, 66
What can wash away my sin? 69
What He has done for others, 140
WHAT THE WORLD NEEDS IS JESUS, 250
WHEN I CAN READ MY TITLE CLEAR, 217
When I get to heaven, 223
When I get to heaven some sweet, 231
WHEN I SEE THE BLOOD, 73
When I was but a little child, 343
When I was sinking in despair, 192
When I'm tried on every hand, 267
When my life-work is ended, 208
When peace, like a river, 131
When the cares of life get heavy, 140
When the hosts of Israel, 162
WHEN THE ROLL IS CALLED UP YONDER, 206
When the trumpet of the Lord shall, 206
WHEN THEY RING THE GOLDEN BELLS, 207
When upon life's billows, 147
WHEN WE ALL GET TO HEAVEN, 205
When we walk with the Lord, 123
When we're inside the gates, 220
When you get to heaven, 210
When your life is dreary, 263
WHERE HE LEADS ME, 282
Where the healing waters flow, 78
WHERE THE SHADES OF LOVE LIE DEEP, 215
WHERE WE'LL NEVER GROW OLD, 352
WHILE SHEPHERDS WATCHED THEIR FLOCKS, 339
WHISPER A PRAYER, 256

WHISPER THE NAME OF JESUS, 261
WHISPERING HOPE, 139
WHITER THAN SNOW, 75
WHO IS ON THE LORD'S SIDE? 164
WHY DO YOU WAIT? 310
WILL THE CIRCLE BE UNBROKEN?
 361
WILL YOU MEET ME IN HEAVEN? 214
WIN THE LOST AT ANY COST, 240
Wisdom, righteousness, and pow'r, 138
WITHOUT HIM, 107
WONDERFUL, 74
WONDERFUL JOY, 192
WONDERFUL POWER IN THE BLOOD,
 72
Wonderful, wonderful, Jesus is to me, 74

WONDERFUL WORDS OF LIFE, 112
WORSHIP THE KING, 27
WORSHIP THE TRIUNE GOD, 26
Worthy is the Lamb that's slain, 27
Would you be free, 68
Would you live for Jesus, 315

-Y-

YES, GOD IS ABLE, 262
YES, I KNOW, 323
Yes, I know He hears my prayer, 267
Yes, I'll sing the wondrous story, 40
Yes, Jesus loves me, 42
You have longed for sweet peace, 293
You may look for me, 210

TOPICAL INDEX

ADORATION

All Creatures Of Our God And
 King, 7
All Hail Immanuel, 320
All Men Give Thanks, 329
Come Thou Almighty King, 11
Crown Him With Many
 Crowns, 83
Doxology, 21
For The Beauty Of The Earth,
 14
Glory To His Name (Parks), 28
Hallelujah, What A Saviour, 39
Holy, Holy, Holy, 12
I Will Praise Him, 176
Love Divine, 24
Magnify The Lord, 324
O Worship The King, 6
Praise Him! Praise Him! 18
Praise To The Lord, The
 Almighty, 1
Praise Ye The Triune God, 10
Sing Unto The Lord, 30
Worship The Triune God, 26

AFFLICTION

Have Faith In God, 129
O Love That Wilt Not Let Me
 Go, 5

Take The Name Of Jesus With
 You, 156
The Great Physician, 77
The Healing Waters, 78
What A Friend We Have In
 Jesus, 48

ASPIRATION

A Charge To Keep, 237
Breathe On Me, Breath Of God,
 100
Come, Thou Fount, 16
Heavenly Sunlight, 198
Higher Ground, 269
I Shall Reach Home, 211
I'll Live For Him, 285
Let My Life Be A Light, 280
Lord, To Be More Like Thee,
 278
More About Jesus, 45
Near The Cross, 291
Nearer, My God, To Thee, 351
O Master, Let Me Walk With
 Thee, 155
Spirit Of God, Descend, 94
Victory Ahead, 162

ASSURANCE

A Deep, Settled Peace, 126
Blessed Assurance, 133

Christ The Lord Was Really
 There, 174
Does Jesus Care? 349
Enough For Me, 153
God Will Take Care Of You, 36
Hallelujah! We Shall Rise, 89
He Hideth My Soul, 142
He Lives, 86
How Firm A Foundation, 121
I Know Whom I Have Believed,
 122
It Is Well With My Soul, 131
Jesus Will Hear Me When I
 Pray, 267
Safe In The Arms Of Jesus, 350
Standing On The Promises, 114
The Lord Is My Shepherd, 199
There Is Power In The Blood,
 68
There Shall Be Showers Of
 Blessing, 253
There Will Dawn A Brighter
 Day, 231
When The Roll Is Called Up
 Yonder, 206
Yes, God Is Able, 262

ATONEMENT

At The Cross, 58
Back Of The Cross, 65

Blessed Redeemer, 60
Calvary Covers It All, 185
I Will Sing Of My Redeemer, 38
I Will Sing The Wondrous Story, 40
Jesus Paid It All, 59
My Saviour's Love, 25
Rock Of Ages, 9
The Old Rugged Cross, 57
There Is A Fountain, 76
There Is Power In The Blood, 68

BAPTISM

My Faith Looks Up To Thee, 8
Take My Life And Let It Be, 276
Where He Leads Me, 282

BENEDICTION

Amens:
  Dresden, 371
  Fourfold, 374
  Sevenfold, 370
  Threefold, 373
  Threefold (Stainer), 372
God Be With You, 376
Let The Words Of My Mouth, 363
Take The Name Of Jesus, 156
The Lord Bless You And Keep You, 375

BIBLE (See Word of God)

BLOOD (See Christ, Blood of)

CALL OF CHRIST

Come And Dine, 144
Jesus Calls Us, 294
Jesus Is Calling, 298
Only Trust Him, 308
Softly And Tenderly, 301
Standing On The Promises, 114
Wonderful Words Of Life, 112

CALL TO WORSHIP

Breathe On Me, Breath Of God, 100
Doxology, 21
Glory Be To The Father
  (1st setting), 365
  (2nd setting), 366
Hear Our Prayer, O Lord, 368
Spirit Of God, Descend, 94
Spirit Of The Living God, 97
The Lord Is In His Holy Temple, 362
Worship The Triune God, 26

CALVARY (See Christ)

CHILDREN'S HYMNS

Away In A Manger, 337
Bring Them In, 245
Bringing In The Sheaves, 243
Fairest Lord Jesus, 41
For The Beauty Of The Earth, 14
Give Me Oil In My Lamp, 105
God Be With You, 376
His Way With Thee, 315
Jesus Loves Even Me, 43
Jesus Loves Me, 42
Jesus Loves The Little Children, 151
This Is My Father's World, 15

CHOIR SELECTIONS

A Mighty Fortress, 31
All Hail The Power (Ellor), 3
All Hail The Power (Holden), 2
All Hail The Power (Shrubsole), 4
Blessed Redeemer, 60
Christ Arose, 80
Christ The Lord Is Risen Today, 82
Hallelujah! We Shall Rise, 89
I'll Thank Him, I'll Praise Him, 223
In Times Like These, 317
It Is Well With My Soul, 131
Jesus, Lover Of My Soul, 51
Make Me A Blessing, 319
O Word Of God Incarnate, 111
Praise To The Lord, The Almighty, 1
To God Be The Glory, 20

CHORUSES

By My Spirit, 108
Christ For Me, 321
Count Your Blessings, 147
Everybody Ought To Know, 322
Fill Me Now, 92
Give Me Oil In My Lamp, 105
Got Any Rivers, 264
I Must Tell Jesus, 365
I Surrender To Thee, 281
I Will Follow Thee, 283
Isn't He Wonderful! 67
Jesus Breaks Every Fetter, 85
Jesus Is The One, 326
Jesus Is the Sweetest Name I Know, 134
Jesus Never Fails, 136
Just A Closer Walk, 288
Let The Fire Fall, 98
Let The Holy Ghost Come In, 271
Magnify The Lord, 324
My God Can Do Anything, 81

O Blessed Holy Spirit, 102
Oh, How I Love Jesus, 143
Old-Time Power, 91
Only Believe, 79
Thank You, Lord, 71
To Be Like Jesus, 258
What The World Needs, 250
Whisper A Prayer, 256
Without Him, 107
Wonderful, 74

CHRIST, Birth of

Angels From The Realms Of Glory, 333
Angels We Have Heard On High, 334
Away In A Manger, 337
Hark! The Herald Angels Sing, 330
I Heard The Bells On Christmas Day, 336
It Came Upon The Midnight Clear, 340
Joy To The World, 331
O Come, All Ye Faithful, 332
O Little Town Of Bethlehem, 338
Silent Night, 335
The First Noel, 341
While Shepherds Watched Their Flocks, 339

CHRIST, Blood of

Are You Washed In The Blood? 311
At The Cross, 58
Blessed Redeemer, 60
Calvary Covers It All, 185
Glory To His Name, 17
His Blood Is On My Soul, 178
Jesus Paid It All, 59
My Hope Is Built, 125
Nothing But The Blood, 69
O For A Thousand Tongues To Sing, 19
Saved By The Blood, 70
The Old Rugged Cross, 57
There Is A Fountain, 76
There Is Power In The Blood, 68
Victory Ahead, 162
When I See The Blood, 73
Whiter Than Snow, 75
Wonderful Power In The Blood, 72
Yes, I Know, 323

CHRIST, Cross of

At The Cross, 58
Back Of The Cross, 65
Because Of Calvary, 187

Beneath The Cross Of Jesus, 63
Calvary Covers It All, 185
Hallelujah For The Cross, 62
He Had To Go To Calvary, 64
He Was Nailed To The Cross
For Me, 66
In The Shadow Of The Cross,
141
Lest I Forget, 325
Near The Cross, 291
Remember, 233
Rock Of Ages, 9
The Message Of The Cross, 170
The Old Rugged Cross, 57
The Way Of The Cross Leads
Home, 154
We Gather At Thy Table, Lord,
234

CHRIST—Friend

All I Need, 138
Friendship With Jesus, 146
He Hideth My Soul, 142
He'll Keep Me, 135
I Must Tell Jesus, 265
Jesus Is All The World To Me,
46
Saved, Saved! 175
Take It To The Lord In Prayer,
255
The Lily Of The Valley, 53
The Lord Is My Shepherd, 199
What A Friend We Have In
Jesus, 48

CHRIST—King

All Hail The Power (Ellor), 3
All Hail The Power (Holden), 2
All Hail The Power (Shrubsole),
4
Christ The Lord Shall Triumph,
128
Come, Thou Almighty King, 11
Crown Him With Many
Crowns, 83
Head Of The Church
Triumphant, 117
Lead On, O King Eternal, 13
O Worship The King, 6

CHRIST—Likeness to

Footprints Of Jesus, 50
I'm Walking With Jesus, 196
Jesus Keeps Me Pure Within,
274
Living In Christ, 194
Lord, To Be More Like Thee,
278
More About Jesus, 45
Near To The Heart Of God, 23
Rock Of Ages, 9

Take Time To Be Holy, 273
The Haven Of Rest, 165
The Lily Of The Valley, 53
To Be Like Jesus, 258

CHRIST, Love of

Blessed Redeemer, 60
Beneath The Cross Of Jesus, 63
Does Jesus Care? 349
Jesus Is Precious To Me, 200
Jesus, Lover Of My Soul, 51
Love Divine, 24
Love Lifted Me, 166
My Saviour's Love, 25
Praise Him! Praise Him! 18
Tell Me The Old, Old Story,
150
Tell Me More About Jesus, 44
The Fountain That Will Never
Run Dry, 193

CHRIST, Name of

All Hail The Power (Ellor), 3
All Hail The Power (Holden), 2
All Hail The Power (Shrubsole),
4
Blessed Be The Name, 37
Glory To His Name, 17
Glory To His Name (Parks), 28
Jesus Breaks Every Fetter, 85
Jesus Is All The World To Me,
46
Jesus Is The Sweetest Name I
Know, 134
More About Jesus, 45
O For A Thousand Tongues, 19
Take The Name Of Jesus With
You, 156
The Lily Of The Valley, 53
What A Lovely Name, 56
Whisper The Name Of Jesus,
261

CHRIST, Praise of

All Hail The Power (Ellor), 3
All Hail The Power (Holden), 2
All Hail The Power (Shrubsole),
4
All I Need, 138
Blessed Assurance, 133
Blessed Redeemer, 60
Christ The Lord Is Risen Today,
82
Come, Thou Almighty King, 11
Crown Him With Many Crowns,
83
Depth Of Mercy, 316
Doxology, 21
Fairest Lord Jesus, 41
For The Beauty Of The Earth,
14

Hallelujah! What A Saviour, 39
I Love To Tell The Story, 152
I Will Praise Him, 176
Jesus Is All The World To Me,
46
Jesus, Lover Of My Soul, 51
More About Jesus, 45
My Jesus, I Love Thee, 52
My Saviour's Love, 25
O For A Thousand Tongues, 19
O Word Of God Incarnate, 111
Praise Him! Praise Him! 18
Praise The Saviour, 209
The Lily Of The Valley, 53
To God Be The Glory, 20

CHRIST, Reign of

All Hail The Power (Ellor), 3
All Hail The Power (Holden), 2
All Hail The Power (Shrubsole),
4
Blessed Be The Name, 37
Crown Him With Many Crowns,
83
Jesus Shall Reign, 244
Praise Him! Praise Him! 18

CHRIST—Resurrection,
(See Easter)

CHRIST—Return of

I Shall Be Changed, 90
Our Lord's Return To Earth, 88
The Lord Will Come, 225
We'll Work Till Jesus Comes,
242

CHRIST, Saviour

Christ The Lord Is Risen, 82
Glory To His Name, 17
Hallelujah! What A Saviour, 39
Happy Day, 177
I Will Sing Of My Redeemer,
38
In Times Like These, 317
Jesus, Lover Of My Soul, 51
Jesus Paid It All, 59
Jesus Saves, 235
O For A Thousand Tongues To
Sing, 19
O Happy Day (arr. Harris), 169
Praise Him! Praise Him! 18
What A Saviour, 49
CHRIST, Suffering of
He Was Nailed To The Cross
For Me, 66
My Saviour's Love, 25
Remember, 233
The Old Rugged Cross, 57

CHRISTIAN LIFE—Songs
of Testimony

A Mighty Fortress, 31

Because Of Calvary, 187
Begin, My Tongue, 201
Christ For Me, 321
For Me To Live Is Christ, 195
Glory To His Name (Parks), 28
He Included Me, 148
He Keeps Me Singing, 145
I Love To Tell The Story, 152
I Never Lived Until I Lived
    For Jesus, 181
I Will Sing The Wondrous
    Story, 40
I'd Tell The World, 203
Jesus Is All The World To Me,
    46
Jesus Is Precious To Me, 200
O Happy Day (arr. Harris), 169
O Say, But I'm Glad, 191
Since I Have Been Redeemed,
    188
Take The Name Of Jesus With
    You, 156
When The Roll Is Called Up
    Yonder, 206

CHRISTIAN LIFE—Healing

The Great Physician, 55
The Great Physician (Grogan),
    77
The Healing Waters, 78
CHRISTIAN LIFE—Songs of
    Reward
Hallelujah! We Shall Rise, 89
Honey In The Rock, 304
How Beautiful Heaven Must
    Be, 358
I See Jesus, 222
I Shall Be Changed, 90
I Wouldn't Miss It For The
    World, 228
I'll Be At Home, 226
No Tears In Heaven, 356
Victory Ahead, 162
We're Marching To Zion, 160
When They Ring The Golden
    Bells, 207

CHRISTIAN LIFE—Spirit-filled
filled (See Holy Spirit)

CHRISTIAN CITIZENSHIP

Christ The Lord Shall Triumph,
    128
Make Me A Blessing, 319
Naturalized For Heaven, 219
Rise Up, O Men Of God, 118

CHRISTIAN WARFARE

A Mighty Fortress, 31
Am I A Soldier Of The Cross?
    171
Fight The Good Fight, 163

Lead On, O King Eternal, 13
Like A Mighty Army, 120
March On, O Church Of God,
    159
Onward, Christian Soldiers, 158
Stand Up For Jesus, 157
Victory Ahead, 162
We're Marching To Zion, 160
Who Is On The Lord's Side?
    164

CHRISTMAS (See Christ, Birth of)

CHURCH

A Glorious Church, 115
Head Of The Church
    Triumphant, 117
Like A Mighty Army, 120
March On, O Church Of God,
    159
O Word Of God Incarnate, 111
Rise Up, O Men Of God, 118
The Church Of God Shall Ever
    Stand, 119
The Church's One Foundation,
    116

COMFORT

A Deep, Settled Peace, 126
A Shelter In The Time Of
    Storm, 47
Abide With Me, 355
Cast Thy Burden On The Lord,
    266
Count Your Blessings, 147
Go To Jesus, 140
God Will Take Care Of You, 36
He Abides, 106
I Must Tell Jesus, 265
Jesus Never Fails, 136
Jesus, The Very Thought Of
    Thee, 173
Near To The Heart Of God, 23
Nearer, My God, To Thee, 351
No Tears In Heaven, 356
O Love That Wilt Not Let Me
    Go, 15
Safe In The Arms Of Jesus, 350
The Haven Of Rest, 165

CONFESSION (Invitation)

Cleanse Me, 277
I Surrender All, 275
Jesus, I Come, 299
Jesus Is Calling, 298
Just As I Am, 300
Pass Me Not, 303

CONSECRATION

Beneath The Cross Of Jesus, 63

Breathe On Me, Breath Of God,
    100
Deeper, Deeper, 272
Footprints of Jesus, 50
Give Of Your Best To The
    Master, 287
I Surrender All, 275
I Will Follow Thee, 283
I'll Go Where You Want Me
    To Go, 279
I'll Live For Him, 285
Is Your All On The Altar? 293
Jesus Calls Us, 294
Jesus, Use Me, 286
Just A Closer Walk With Thee,
    288
Just As I Am, 300
Make Me A Blessing, 319
Near The Cross, 291
O Jesus, I Have Promised, 290
O Master, Let Me Walk With
    Thee, 155

CONVERSION— (See Invitation)

COURAGE

A Mighty Fortress Is Our God,
    31
Farther Along, 354
Have Faith In God, 129
Rise Up, O Men Of God, 118
Stand Up For Jesus, 157
Victory In Jesus, 182

CROSS—(See Christ, Cross of)

DEVOTION

Almighty Father, Hear Our
    Prayer, 369
Beneath The Cross Of Jesus, 63
Breathe On Me, Breath Of God,
    100
Cleanse Me, 277
I Can, I Will, I Do Believe, 132
I Need Thee Every Hour, 292
I Will Follow Thee, 283
Jesus Is All The World To Me,
    46
Jesus Use Me, 286
My Faith Looks Up To Thee, 8
My Jesus, I Love Thee, 52
Nearer, My God, To Thee, 351
Take My Life And Let It Be,
    276

DISCIPLESHIP

A Charge To Keep, 237
Footprints Of Jesus, 50
For Me To Live Is Christ, 195
Give Of Your Best To The
    Master, 287

His Way With Thee, 315
I Am Resolved, 289
I Will Follow Thee, 283
I'll Go Where You Want Me
  To Go, 279
I'm Walking With Jesus, 196
In The Shadow Of The Cross,
  141
Jesus Calls Us, 294
Let Me Touch Him, 284
Let My Life Be A Light, 280
Must Jesus Bear The Cross
  Alone? 61
My Jesus, I Love Thee, 52
O Jesus, I Have Promised, 290
Rescue The Perishing, 246
Rise Up, O Men Of God, 118
Speak, My Lord, 238
Stand Up For Jesus, 157
We'll Work Till Jesus Comes,
  242
Where He Leads Me, 282
Win The Lost At Any Cost, 240

EASTER—Resurrection of Christ

Christ Arose, 80
Hallelujah, We Shall Rise, 89
He Is Alive, 87
He Lives, 86
He Rose Triumphantly, 84

FAITH

Faith For Today, 124
Faith Of Our Fathers, 161
Hallelujah For The Cross, 62
Have Faith In God, 129
I Can, I Will, I Do Believe, 132
I Know Whom I Have Believed,
  122
My Faith Looks Up To Thee, 8
O God, Our Help In Ages Past,
  32
Only Believe, 79
Pass Me Not, 303
Standing On The Promises, 114
Trust And Obey, 123
Trusting Jesus, 137

FELLOWSHIP

Blest Be The Tie That Binds,
  130
Come And Dine, 144
Friendship With Jesus, 146
God Be With You, 376
Leaning On The Everlasting
  Arms, 22
Let Us Sing, 29
Rise Up, O Men Of God, 118
Take Time To Be Holy, 273
We Gather Together, 328

FUNERAL

Abide With Me, 355
Asleep In Jesus, 353
Gathering Buds, 359
God Will Take Care Of You, 36
I'll Meet You In The Morning,
  212
It Is Well With My Soul, 131
Nearer, My God, To Thee, 351
O Love That Wilt Not Let Me
  Go, 5!
Precious Memories, 360
Rock Of Ages, 9
Safe In The Arms Of Jesus, 350
That Glad Reunion Day, 213
Where We'll Never Grow Old,
  352
Will The Circle Be Unbroken,
  361

GOD, Creator

All Creatures Of Our God And
  King, 7
For The Beauty Of The Earth,
  14
Praise To The Lord, The
  Almighty, 1
This Is My Father's World, 15

GOD—Faithfulness of (See Discipleship)

GOD—Love
Calvary Covers It All, 185
God Is Love, 168
I Love To Tell The Story, 152
Love Divine, 24
Love Lifted Me, 166
Tell Me The Old, Old Story, 150
The Love Of God (Ellis), 167
The Love Of God (Lehman), 35

GOD—Majesty and Power

A Mighty Fortress, 31
Christ The Lord Shall Triumph,
  128
Come, Thou Almighty King, 11
Head Of The Church
  Triumphant, 117
Holy, Holy, Holy, 12
O God, Our Help In Ages Past,
  32
O Worship The King, 6
Praise To The Lord, The
  Almighty, 1
Praise Ye The Triune God, 10
To God Be The Glory, 20
Worship The King, 27

GOD—Presence of

Christ The Lord Was Really
  There, 174

God Is Present Everywhere, 260
Guide Me, O Thou Great
  Jehovah, 33
He Abides, 106
He Leadeth Me, 127

GOD—Providence

All Things Come Of Thee, 367
Christ The Lord Shall Triumph,
  128
God Moves In A Mysterious
  Way, 184
God Of Our Fathers, 34
God Will Take Care Of You, 36
How Firm A Foundation, 121
O God, Our Help In Ages Past,
  32
O Worship The King, 6
Praise To The Lord, The
  Almighty, 1
Yes, God Is Able, 262

GOD—Refuge

A Mighty Fortress, 31
A Shelter In The Time Of
  Storm, 47
Guide Me, O Thou Great
  Jehovah, 33
Jesus, Lover Of My Soul, 51
The Haven Of Rest, 165
There's A Wideness In God's
  Mercy, 149

GOD—Word of

Break Thou The Bread Of Life,
  110
Holy Bible, Book Divine, 113
In Times Like These, 317
O Word Of God Incarnate, 111
Standing On The Promises, 114
Wonderful Words Of Life, 112

GOSPEL

Because Of Calvary, 187
For Me To Live Is Christ, 195
Glory To His Name (Parks), 28
God Is Love, 168
Happy Day, 177
Hallelujah! We Shall Rise, 89
Have You Heard About That
  City? 221
Holy Bible, Book Divine, 113
Honey In The Rock, 304
I Love To Tell The Story, 152
I Never Lived Until I Lived
  For Jesus, 181
If I Knew Of A Land, 229
I'll Thank Him, I'll Praise Him,
  223
I'm Glad He Lifted Me Out, 179
Jesus Passed By, 172

Jesus Will Hear Me When I Pray, 267
O Happy Day (arr. Harris), 169
Saved By The Blood, 70
Wonderful Joy, 192

GRACE

Amazing Grace, 186
Come, Thou Fount, 16
Depth Of Mercy, 316
He Included Me, 148
Jesus Saves, 235
Nothing But The Blood, 69
Rescue The Perishing, 246
Revive Us Again, 247
Rock Of Ages, 9
Since I Have Been Redeemed, 188
The Way Of The Cross Leads Home, 154

GRATITUDE
(See Thankfulness)

HEAVEN

At The Crowning, 224
Angels From The Realms Of Glory, 333
Have You Heard About That City? 221
Heaven Will Surely Be Worth It All, 218
How Beautiful Heaven Must Be, 358
I Shall Reach Home, 211
I'll Be At Home, 226
Look For Me, 210
My Saviour First Of All, 208
No Tears In Heaven, 356
One Sweetly Solemn Thought, 357
Over Yonder, 230
Rest Beyond, 216
That Glad Reunion Day, 213
That Heavenly Home, 232
The Homecoming Week, 220
The Way Of The Cross Leads Home, 154
There Will Dawn A Brighter Day, 231
Victory Ahead, 162
We're Marching To Zion, 160
When I Can Read My Title Clear, 217
When The Roll Is Called Up Yonder, 206
When They Ring The Golden Bells, 207
When We All Get To Heaven, 205
Where We'll Never Grow Old, 352

Will You Meet Me In Heaven? 214

HOLINESS

A Glorious Church, 115
All I Need, 138
Breathe On Me, Breath Of God, 100
Come, Thou Almighty King, 11
Fill Me Now, 92
Holiness Unto The Lord, 270
I Surrender All, 275
I Surrender To Thee, 281
In The Shadow Of The Cross, 141
Lord, To Be More Like Thee, 278
Love Divine, 24
My Hope Is Built, 125
O Blessed Holy Spirit, 102
Old-Time Power, 91
Pentecostal Power, 96
Send The Fire, 101
Spirit Of God, Descend, 94
Spirit Of The Living God, 97
Take Time To Be Holy, 273
The Fire Is Burning, 104
To Be Like Jesus, 258

HOLY SPIRIT

Breathe On Me, Breath Of God, 100
By My Spirit, 108
Fill Me Now, 92
He Abides, 106
Holy Ghost, With Light Divine, 318
Holy Spirit, Use Me, 109
Let The Fire Fall, 98
Let The Holy Ghost Come In, 271
O Blessed Holy Spirit, 102
Old-Time Power, 91
Pentecostal Fire Is Falling, 95
Pentecostal Power, 96
Send The Fire, 101
Spirit Of God, Descend, 94
Spirit Of The Living God, 97
The Comforter Has Come, 93
The Fire Is Burning, 104
The Fountain That Will Never Run Dry, 193
The Spirit Of The Lord Is Upon Me, 202
'Tis Burning In My Soul, 103
Waiting On The Lord, 99

HOPE

Farther Along, 354
I'm Moving Up Some Day, 227
Look And Live, 309
My Hope Is Built, 125

Nearer, My God, To Thee, 351
O God, Our Help In Ages Past, 32
There's A Great Day Coming, 307
Waiting On The Lord, 99
We'll Work Till Jesus Comes, 242
When I Can Read My Title Clear, 217
Whispering Hope, 139

INVITATION—Conversion

Almost Persuaded, 302
Art Thou Weary? 306
Have You Counted The Cost? 295
His Way With Thee, 315
How About Your Heart? 296
I Am Coming To The Cross, 312
I Am Resolved, 289
In Times Like These, 317
Is Your Heart Right With God? 313
Jesus, I Come, 299
Jesus Is Calling, 298
Just As I Am, 300
Let Him In, 305
Let Jesus Come Into Your Heart, 314
Lord, I'm Coming Home, 297
Pass Me Not, 303
Softly And Tenderly, 301
Why Do You Wait? 310
Will The Circle Be Unbroken? 361

INVITATION—Consecration

At The Cross, 58
Beneath The Cross Of Jesus, 63
Breathe On Me, Breath Of God, 100
Cleanse Me, 277
Give Of Your Best To The Master, 287
Higher Ground, 269
I Surrender All, 275
I Surrender To Thee, 281
I'll Go Where You Want Me To Go, 279
Is Your All On The Altar, 293
Jesus Calls Us, 294
Jesus, I Come, 299
Just As I Am, 300
Nearer, My God, To Thee, 351
Pass Me Not, 303
Take My Life And Let It Be, 276
Who Is On The Lord's Side? 164

JESUS (See Christ)

509

JOY

A Shelter In The Time Of Storm, 47
Blessed Assurance, 133
Christ Arose, 80
Christ The Lord Is Risen Today, 82
Happy Day, 177
He Included Me, 148
He Keeps Me Singing, 145
I Sing Because I'm Happy, 190
I'm Glad He Lifted Me Out, 179
In The Garden, 197
Jesus Is All The World To Me, 46
Joy To The World, 331
Let Us Sing, 29
Naturalized For Heaven, 219
No Tears In Heaven, 356
O Happy Day (Harris), 169
Wonderful Joy, 192

KINGDOM

Heaven Will Surely Be Worth It All, 218
How Beautiful Heaven Must Be, 358
I Love Thy Kingdom, Lord, 189
Lead On, O King Eternal, 13
No Tears In Heaven, 356
O Worship The King, 6
LOVE—God's love for man
God Is Love, 168
I Sing Because I'm Happy, 190
Jesus Loves Even Me, 43
Love Divine, 24
Love Lifted Me, 166
My Saviour's Love, 25
O Love That Wilt Not Let Me Go, 5
Remember, 233
The Love Of God (Ellis) 167
The Love Of God (Lehman) 35
To God Be The Glory, 20
What The World Needs Is Jesus, 250
Where The Shades Of Love Lie Deep, 215

LOVE—Man's love for God

Doxology, 21
For Me To Live Is Christ, 195
Give Of Your Best To The Master, 287
He Keeps Me Singing, 145
I Love To Tell The Story, 152
I Will Sing Of My Redeemer, 38
Jesus Is All The World To Me, 46
Jesus Is The Sweetest Name I Know, 134
My Jesus, I Love Thee, 52
Oh, How I Love Jesus, 143

MISSIONS

Bring Them In, 245
Bringing In The Sheaves, 243
I Love To Tell The Story, 152
I'll Go Where You Want Me To Go, 279
Jesus Shall Reign, 244
Jesus, Use Me, 286
Let My Life Be A Light, 280
Rescue The Perishing, 246
Send The Light, 236
Throw Out The Life-Line, 241
Win The Lost At Any Cost, 240

MOTHER

If I Could Hear My Mother Pray Again, 344
Sweetest Mother, 342
Tell Mother I'll Be There, 343

PATRIOTISM

America, 347
America, The Beautiful, 348
Battle Hymn Of The Republic, 346
Faith Of Our Fathers, 161
God Of Our Fathers, 34
The Star-Spangled Banner, 345

PEACE

A Deep, Settled Peace, 126
A Shelter In The Time Of Storm, 47
He Keeps Me Singing, 145
It Is Well With My Soul, 131
Near To The Heart Of God, 23
Safe In The Arms Of Jesus, 350
The Haven Of Rest, 165
What The World Needs Is Jesus, 250

PENTECOST

Let The Fire Fall, 98
O Blessed Holy Spirit, 102
Old-Time Power, 91
Pentecostal Fire Is Falling, 95
Pentecostal Power, 96
Send The Fire, 101
The Fire Is Burning, 104

PRAISE

All Hail Immanuel 320
All Hail The Power (Ellor), 3
All Hail The Power (Holden), 2
All Hail The Power (Shrubsole), 4
All Creatures Of Our God And King, 7

All Men Give Thanks, 329
Blessed Be The Name, 37
Come, Thou Almighty King, 7
Doxology, 21
For The Beauty Of The Earth, 14
Glory To His Name, 17
God Of Our Fathers, 34
Hallelujah For The Cross, 62
Hallelujah! What A Saviour, 39
Holy, Holy, Holy, 12
I Will Praise Him, 176
I Will Sing Of My Redeemer, 38
I Will Sing The Wondrous Story, 40
I'll Thank Him, I'll Praise Him, 223
Isn't He Wonderful! 67
O Worship The King, 6
Praise Him! Praise Him! 18
Praise To The Lord, The Almighty, 1
Praise Ye The Triune God, 10
Sing Unto The Lord, 30
To God Be The Glory, 20

PRAYER

Abide With Me, 355
Almighty Father, Hear Our Prayer, 369
Cast Thy Burdens On The Lord, 266
Cleanse Me, 277
Hear Our Prayer, O Lord, 368
I Am Praying For You, 257
I Must Tell Jesus, 265
I Need The Prayers, 268
If I Could Hear My Mother Pray Again, 344
In The Garden, 197
Jesus Will Hear Me When I Pray, 267
Pray Till Your Prayers Go Through, 263
Sweet Hour Of Prayer, 254
Take It To The Lord In Prayer, 255
The Beautiful Garden Of Prayer, 259
What A Friend We Have In Jesus, 48
Whisper A Prayer, 256
Yes, God Is Able, 262

REPENTANCE

Cleanse Me, 277
Have You Counted The Cost? 295
I Am Resolved, 289
Jesus, I Come, 299
Jesus Paid It All, 59
Lord, I'm Coming Home, 297
Pass Me Not, 303

510

RESPONSES

All Things Come Of Thee, 366
Amens, 370-374
Glory Be To The Father, 365-366
Hear Our Prayer, O Lord, 368
Let The Words Of My Mouth, 363
We Give Thee But Thine Own, 364

RESURRECTION (See Easter)

REVIVAL

A World-Wide Revival, 251
Let The Fire Fall, 98
Lord, Send A Revival (McKinney), 249
Lord, Send A Revival (Triplett), 252
Pentecostal Power, 96
Revive Thy Work, 248
Revive Us Again, 247
Send The Fire, 101
There Shall Be Showers Of Blessing, 253

SALVATION

All I Need, 138
Amazing Grace, 186
Are You Washed In The Blood? 311
At The Cross, 58
Calvary Covers It All, 185
Glory To His Name, 17
Happy Day, 177
He Had To Go To Calvary, 64
He Was Nailed To The Cross For Me, 66
I'll Thank Him, I'll Praise Him, 223
It's Real, 183
Jesus Paid It All, 59
Jesus Saves, 235
Look And Live, 309
My Faith Looks Up To Thee, 8
My Hope Is Built, 125
Nothing But The Blood, 69
O Say, But I'm Glad, 191
Only Trust Him, 308
Saved By The Blood, 70
Saved, Saved, 175
What A Change In My Life, 180

SECURITY

A Shelter In The Time Of Storm, 47
God Of Our Fathers, 34
God Will Take Care Of You, 36
Have Faith In God, 129
He Hideth My Soul, 142
He'll Keep Me, 135
How Firm A Foundation, 121
I Know Whom I Have Believed, 122
I Need Thee Every Hour, 292
It Is Well With My Soul, 131
Jesus Never Fails, 136
Leaning On The Everlasting Arms, 22
My Faith Looks Up To Thee, 8
My Hope Is Built, 125
Rock Of Ages, 9
Safe In The Arms Of Jesus, 350
Standing On The Promises, 114
The Haven Of Rest, 165
'Tis So Sweet To Trust In Jesus, 54

SERVICE

A Charge To Keep, 237
Give Of Your Best To The Master, 287
I Will Follow Thee, 283
I'll Go Where You Want Me To Go, 279
Jesus Use Me, 286
Let My Life Be A Light, 280
Lord, Speak To Me, 239
Make Me A Blessing, 319
Must Jesus Bear The Cross Alone, 61
Rescue The Perishing 246
Send The Light, 236
Take My Life And Let It Be, 276
Win The Lost At Any Cost, 240

SOUL-WINNING

A World-Wide Revival, 251
Bring Them In, 245
Bringing In The Sheaves, 243
I Love To Tell The Story, 152
Let My Life Be A Light, 280
Lord, Send A Revival (McKinney), 249

Lord, Send A Revival (Triplett), 252
Make Me A Blessing, 319
Rescue The Perishing, 246
Send The Light, 236
Throw Out The Life-Line, 241
What The World Needs Is Jesus, 250
Win The Lost At Any Cost, 240

STEWARDSHIP (See Discipleship)

THANKFULNESS

All Men Give Thanks, 329
Come, Ye Thankful People, 327
Count Your Blessings, 147
For The Beauty Of The Earth, 14
I'll Thank Him, I'll Praise Him, 223
O Worship The King, 6
We Gather Together, 328

TRUST

Faith For Today, 124
Faith Of Our Fathers, 161
Have Faith In God, 129
I Can, I Will, I Do Believe, 132
My Faith Looks Up To Thee, 8
Standing On The Promises, 114
'Tis So Sweet To Trust in Jesus, 54
Only Believe, 79
Only Trust Him, 308
Trust And Obey, 123
Trusting Jesus, 137

YOUTH

Christ For Me, 321
Give Of Your Best To The Master, 287
Got Any Rivers? 264
He Keeps Me Singing, 145
He Lives, 86
Isn't He Wonderful, 67
Make Me A Blessing, 319
Onward, Christian Soldiers, 158
Praise Him! Praise Him! 18
Rise Up, O Men Of God, 118
Saved, Saved! 175
To God Be The Glory, 20
Who Is On The Lord's Side? 164

BENEDICTIONS

Now the God of peace, that brought again from the dead our Lord Jesus, that great shepherd of the sheep, through the blood of the everlasting covenant, Make you perfect in every good work to do his will, working in you that which is wellpleasing in his sight, through Jesus Christ; to whom be glory for ever and ever. Amen.

HEBREWS 13:20, 21

Now our Lord Jesus Christ himself, and God, even our Father, which hath loved us, and hath given us everlasting consolation and good hope through grace, Comfort your hearts, and stablish you in every good word and work.

2 THESSALONIANS 2:16, 17

The Lord bless thee, and keep thee: The Lord make his face shine upon thee, and be gracious unto thee: The Lord lift up his countenance upon thee, and give thee peace. Amen.

NUMBERS 6:24, 26

Now unto him that is able to keep you from falling, and to present you faultless before the presence of his glory with exceeding joy, To the only wise God our Saviour, be glory and majesty, dominion and power, both now and ever. Amen.

JUDE 24, 25

The grace of our Lord Jesus Christ be with your spirit. Amen.

PHILEMON 25